Enclosure

ENCOUNTERS

Series Editors

Robert J. Nelson, UNIVERSITY OF ILLINOIS
Gerald Weales, UNIVERSITY OF PENNSYLVANIA

A series of collections of plays in which the selection is based on the relationship the plays have to one another in theme or structure. The works chosen are each of intrinsic value, but their "encounter" with one another in the same volume enhances the interest of each.

Enclosure

A Collection of Plays

Edited by Robert J. Nelson
and Gerald Weales

DAVID McKAY COMPANY, INC., NEW YORK

ENCLOSURE

A Collection of Plays

International Standard Book Number: 0–679–30073–2 (paper)
0–679–50531–8 (cloth)

LIBRARY OF CONGRESS CATALOG CARD NUMBER: 74–23084
MANUFACTURED IN THE UNITED STATES OF AMERICA
Designed by Angela Foote

Contents

Introduction

In a superficial sense, every play is an "enclosure play": the action takes place either within or against the obvious "frame" of the physical stage. This external approach to our concept encompasses even those attempts that, throughout the history of the theater, have seemed to deny the stage-as-enclosure: processional plays, staging-in-the round, happenings, etc. Such attempts depend, at least in part, on their very break with the idea of the enclosed stage as the physical setting of the action, however loose or unstructured in time and place that action may be.

Yet, within this all-encompassing notion of stage action as enclosed action, there are equally obvious common-sense distinctions to be made. The most obvious deals with the physical setting of the action: there are plays that take place wholly or largely "inside," with the containing space as large as a house (Ibsen's *A Doll's House*) or as small as a funeral urn (Beckett's *Play*, in which the stage directions indicate that the director should strive to create the impression that the urns in which the characters are to be found are smaller than human-size). The place is a thing with which to catch a conscience, a setting in which characters define themselves. In classic examples of enclosure plays (*A Doll's House*, for example) the enclosure is oppressive and constricting, a barrier to purposeful action and a denial of human freedom. Characters are shut-up and shut-in and the idea of character as idiosyncratic and particular is itself defined by the norms of the atmosphere prevailing in the enclosure.

In our selection we begin with such a "pure" or classic expression of the motif: Lorca's *The House of Bernarda Alba*. Here, the characters are all contained and constrained by the House that is run wholly by Bernarda. Various aspects of the setting, action, and language of the play reinforce this central motif: the windows at which the young girls stand to look out upon the world of men (whom one hears but does not see) seem like the bars of a prison (the prison of Spanish culture, for courtship at the window is a hallmark of that culture's tradition). Alternatively, the walls of white, reminders of Bernarda's fanatical insistence on purity, express still another constricting enclosure: that of the convent. Again, taken together, the walls and the windows remind one of a cage within which the restive young women, denied sexual satisfaction, pace like young beasts yearning to respond to the call of the men outside. Ironically, when Bernarda is called "old leopard-face," we see that Bernarda herself is not only keeper in this metaphor but also caged beast herself. (She may, it will occur to readers of the English translation, also ironically be the keeper, however unwittingly, of a "house of ill-repute": her daughters finally reveal themselves as ready to give themselves as the denizens of such a house. However, "house" in this sense would more readily suggest itself to speakers of English than *"casa"* in the same sense would suggest itself to speakers of Spanish.) A prison, a convent, a cage, (and, finally, for Adela, a coffin), the "House" of Bernarda is the principal character of the play, an enclosure assimilating all human activity into its virginal sterility. Wishing to enshrine her daughters as in a temple, Bernarda has lived in a constant space, denying time, within which she and her daughters are finally entombed.

The Temple in Racine's *Athaliah*, on the other hand, is, paradoxically enough, a progressively narrowing space that becomes a final resting place for one character—the tomb of Athaliah, so to speak—and a jumping-off place for her adversaries—the womb, so to speak, of the boy-king whose power she covets. The Temple is a trap for Athaliah, a setting in which her freedom of action is gradually restricted and in which she herself literally disappears. But the Temple is also the occasion for a series of ever more significant epiphanies (Greek: revelatory appearances) revealing the young Eliacin to be the king saved from Athaliah's butchery in order to lead his people out of the Temple. The enclosure is thus both oppressive and liberating, a paradox rendered not only in the setting and action of the play but in its language as well. As Athaliah seeks and succeeds in penetrating deeper and deeper into the sacred temple with her defiling presence, the playwright orchestrates his paradoxical theme of entrapment-*cum*-liberation with shrewd plays on the false *éclat* of the worldly, sacrilegious queen and the more subtle, true *éclat* of the unrevealed redeemer, Joas. The same paradox is heard in the now elegiac and hopeful, now repentant and fearful choral interventions. The hopeful and the true, liberation and fulfillment thus triumph in the time and place of this enclosure play. However, as Athaliah's final menace shows, Racine resolves the paradox only seemingly, for Joas will himself fall into the *trap* of sin that is the lot of all those *enclosed* in the tragedy of the human condition.

Racine's play shows that the enclosure motif is susceptible to the most subtle variations on the classic or pure expression of it we encounter in Lorca. Our next selection shows a perhaps even greater paradoxical use of the motif. At first glance, *Awake and Sing!* seems, in both setting and language, almost literal-minded in its presentation of the apartment-enclosure. The Bergers' mid-Depression Bronx apartment is as much a prison as the House of Bernarda, as much a trap as Racine's Temple. In setting, action, and language, Odets's "realistic" dramatization of this lower middle-class Jewish milieu is as poetic, symbolic, and theatrical as any of our selections. Moe and Hennie are conventions of the stage: the cynical lovers who begin by repeating their hatred of one another only to end, as we know they will, in each other's arms. Moe comes to the Bergers' home to bury himself in its tomblike atmosphere, to rehearse his bitter war experiences, but also to be near Hennie, his first and really last love. Sensitive and romantic beneath his gruff exterior, he penetrates to the dangers of the enclosure: "Make a break or spend the rest of your life in a coffin" he tells Hennie (III). The enclosure of the Bergers' apartment is thus like the Temple in *Athaliah*: a tomb for some (Bessie, Myron), a womb for others (Moe, Hennie, Ralph). One flees, paradoxically, not only by leaping—or flying—from the rooftop of this apartment building (Jacob) but also by remaining within it to learn more about ways to emerge from it: thus Ralph who will cut open old Jacob's books—"I saw he was dead and I was born" says the youth of his grandfather. Is this rebirth perhaps ironic, like the final epiphany of Eliacin-Joas in Racine's play? The very theatricality, the sophisticated dramatic sensibility of actor-playwright Odets suggests that just as we have recall to a functionally "upbeat" convention in the lovers of the play, so we may have a reminder of a less optimistic coupling in the Ralph-Jacob relationship. In occupying his grandfather's room, will Ralph now enclose himself ineffectually in a world of ideas and operatic romance? Does the structure of action work against the lyrical texture of the final scenes, to leave us with a double-edged view of the play's dominant enclosure motif?

Lorca's House, Racine's Temple, Odets' apartment—all offer enclosures into which both actors and spectators penetrate as relatively constant spaces. Though Lorca's is, as we have said, the "purest" example of the genre, Racine and Odets are still close to the Spanish example, for the very idea of "breaking out" depends first on breaking in (*Athaliah*) or remaining within (Ralph in *Awake*).

In Wycherley's *The Country Wife* the enclosure motif works conversely: enclosed space is treated as tangential and precarious from the outset. Pinchwife's lodgings are indeed as fixed a space as that of any other play, and in its very fixity this space functions as the dominant dramatic and symbolic motif of the play. But this fixity is denied not implicitly or paradoxically, but overtly and literally. Lodgings (Pinchwife's or anyone else's) are futile attempts to enclose the unenclosable: human desire in its most impassioned expression, sexual energy. The enclosure of this play is not an impenetrable space (Lorca) or one that can be broken only after being narrowed still more (Racine and Odets). In *The Country Wife* the seemingly open is the really closed (the women and country) and the seemingly closed, the open (the supposedly impotent Horner and the town in general). Wycherley assaults the whole idea of enclosure in the very rapidity of his action, the fantastic wit of his language, the shifting of scene (various settings at Horner's Lodging, different rooms in Pinchwife's House, the Exchange, etc.).

In its attack on the concept of enclosure Wycherley's play (based in part on a more patently "classic" example of enclosure plays in Molière) is strikingly relevant to our own time with its attacks on bourgeois marriage and its call for a frank, tough-minded concern with such questions as women's rights (especially sexual rights), sexual impotence, etc. This is not to say that Wycherley is "modern" in his views on these questions; some readers may see him as pure male chauvinist or a witty dramatic illustrator of "games people play."

The modernity of Wycherley goes beyond these particular variations on the enclosure motif, of course—even as the richness of his play can be grasped through other approaches than our use of the enclosure motif. Each of our selections, in fact, offers other patterns of dramatic and symbolic interest. In each, for example, a strong and mature woman plays a central role, a motif of the action that can be treated quite independently of the enclosure motif. Nevertheless, the possible connections with our central motif are interesting, as we have implied in our variations on the tomb-womb extension of the idea of enclosure, particularly in the case of Bernarda and Athaliah. Other connections between our selections will occur to the reader, whom we now invite to open this volume of plays without foreclosing on any possible "encounters" among them, especially those elaborating on the motif that so clearly links them: enclosure.

Robert J. Nelson

The House of
Bernarda Alba   (1936)*

Federico Garcia Lorca   (*1898-1936*)

In July 1936 Lorca was shot and killed by the Falangists, the conservative political party that supported Francisco Franco in the Spanish Civil War of 1936–39. He thus had no chance to see *Bernarda Alba* produced nor would it be produced in his native country until more than a quarter of a century later. Even now, say colleagues who have seen a production of the play in Madrid in the early 1970s, the playwright's grim depiction of the House of Bernarda and thus of Spain itself is discomfiting to his fellow-countrymen. It is still, in Lorca's own terms in setting the action, "a photographic document." Indeed, more photographically realistic than the other two plays making up Lorca's principal contribution to the modern theater (*Blood Wedding*, 1933, and *Yerma*, 1934), *Bernarda Alba* is no less poetic as it continues to explore the themes of repression and claustration common to the three tragedies (and to such minor comedies as *The Love of Don Perlimplin*, 1933). As Eric Bentley has shown in an essay on his own staging of the play at Dublin's Abbey Theater (1950), much of the poetry lies in the purely theatrical, paraverbal elements of the play: its silences, its suggestions of unrelieved heat, and, of course, the enclosed setting itself. Perhaps even more than

* We gratefully acknowledge the permission to use the translation in Federico Garcia Lorca, *Three Tragedies*, translated by James Graham-Lujan and Richard O'Connell. Copyright 1946 by James Graham-Lujan and Richard O'Connell. Reprinted by permission of New Directions Publishing Corporation.

Lorca's spare, yet poetically brooding dialogue, these "theatrical" elements will convey to non-Spanish audiences that culture's perduring preoccupation with "honor." As Bentley says, "no playwright using the 'closed' form of drama with an indoor setting ever managed better than Lorca to give an impression of a whole village, a whole civilization." * In effect, the dialogue gains much of its poetic and revolutionary force precisely because it resounds against the enclosing House of Bernarda Alba.

This translation of the play was the text of the 1951 production by ANTA (American National Theater and Academy, Cheryl Crawford and Robert Breen, general directors) in which Katina Paxinou played Bernarda and Kim Stanley, Adela, under the direction of Boris Tumarin. The play is a favorite of university and regional theaters; for example, it was produced at the Actors' Workshop (San Francisco) in September 1963, with Beatrice Manley as Bernarda and Eileen Earle as Maria Josefa, under the direction of Lee Breuer. "Playhouse of the Week" also offered the play over TV in the 1960s (co-producers for National Telefilm Associates: Worthington Miner and Lewis Freedman), with Anne Revere as Bernarda, Kathleen Nesbitt as Maria Josefa, Eileen Heckart as Poncia, Susanne Pleshette as Adela, and Lee Grant as Martirio, under the direction of Boris Sagal.

---

other rights not mentioned, should be made to New Directions, 333 Sixth Avenue, New York, N.Y. 10014. Any inquiries about the translation of these plays, or any other works by Federico Garcia Lorca, into any language whatever, should also be made to New Directions, New York, who act as agents for the Garcia Lorca Estate.
    * "The Poet in Dublin" in *In Search of Theater* (New York: Alfred Knopf, 1953), p. 224.

THE HOUSE OF BERNARDA ALBA

A Drama about Women in the Villages of Spain
(La Casa de Bernarda Alba: Drama de mujeres
en los pueblos de España)

Federico Garcia Lorca
TRANSLATED FROM THE SPANISH
BY JAMES GRAHAM-LUJAN AND RICHARD O'CONNELL

CHARACTERS

BERNARDA *(age: 60)*

MARIA JOSEFA, *Bernarda's Mother*
(age: 80)

ANGUSTIAS, *Bernarda's Daughter*
(age: 39)

MAGDALENA, *Bernarda's Daughter*
(age: 30)

AMELIA, *Bernarda's Daughter (age: 27)*

MARTIRIO, *Bernarda's Daughter*
(age: 24)

ADELA, *Bernarda's Daughter (age: 20)*

A MAID *(age: 50)*

LA PONCIA, *A Maid (age: 60)*

PRUDENCIA *(age: 50)*

Women in Mourning

The writer states that these Three Acts are intended as a photographic document.

ACT ONE

A very white room in Bernarda Alba's house. The walls are white. There are arched doorways with jute curtains tied back with tassels and ruffles. Wicker chairs. On the walls, pictures of unlikely landscapes full of nymphs or legendary kings.

It is summer. A great brooding silence fills the stage. It is empty when the curtain rises. Bells can be heard tolling outside.

FIRST SERVANT *(entering)* The tolling of those bells hits me right between the eyes.

PONCIA *(she enters, eating bread and sausage)* More than two hours of mumbo jumbo. Priests are here from all the towns. The church looks beautiful. At the first responsory for the dead, Magdalena fainted.

FIRST SERVANT   She's the one who's left most alone.

PONCIA   She's the only one who loved her father. Ay! Thank God we're alone for a little. I came over to eat.

FIRST SERVANT   If Bernarda sees you . . . !

PONCIA   She's not eating today so she'd just as soon we'd all die of hunger! Domineering old tyrant! But she'll be fooled! I opened the sausage crock.

FIRST SERVANT (*with an anxious sadness*)   Couldn't you give me some for my little girl, Poncia?

PONCIA   Go ahead! And take a fistful of peas too. She won't know the difference today.

VOICE (*within*)   Bernarda!

PONCIA   There's the grandmother! Isn't she locked up tight?

FIRST SERVANT   Two turns of the key.

PONCIA   You'd better put the cross-bar up too. She's got the fingers of a lock-picker!

VOICE (*within*)   Bernarda!

PONCIA (*shouting*)   She's coming!

To The Servant.

Clean everything up good. If Bernarda doesn't find things shining, she'll pull out the few hairs I have left.

SERVANT   What a woman!

PONCIA   Tyrant over everyone around her. She's perfectly capable of sitting on your heart and watching you die for a whole year without turning off that cold little smile she wears on her wicked face. Scrub, scrub those dishes!

SERVANT   I've got blood on my hands from so much polishing of everything.

PONCIA   She's the cleanest, she's the decentest, she's the highest everything! A good rest her poor husband's earned!

The bells stop.

SERVANT   Did all the relatives come?

PONCIA   Just hers. His people hate her. They came to see him dead and make the sign of the cross over him; that's all.

SERVANT   Are there enough chairs?

PONCIA   More than enough. Let them sit on the floor. When Bernarda's father died people stopped coming under this roof. She doesn't want them to see her in her "domain." Curse her!

SERVANT She's been good to you.

PONCIA Thirty years washing her sheets. Thirty years eating her leftovers. Nights of watching when she had a cough. Whole days peeking through a crack in the shutters to spy on the neighbors and carry her the tale. Life without secrets one from the other. But in spite of that—curse her! May the "pain of the piercing nail" strike her in the eyes.

SERVANT Poncia!

PONCIA But I'm a good watchdog! I bark when I'm told and bite beggars' heels when she sics me on 'em. My sons work in her fields—both of them already married, but one of these days I'll have enough.

SERVANT And then . . . ?

PONCIA Then I'll lock myself up in a room with her and spit in her face—a whole year. "Bernarda, here's for this, that and the other!" Till I leave her—just like a lizard the boys have squashed. For that's what she is—she and her whole family! Not that I envy her her life. Five girls are left her, five ugly daughters—not counting Angustias the eldest, by her first husband, who has money—the rest of them, plenty of eyelets to embroider, plenty of linen petticoats, but bread and grapes when it comes to inheritance.

SERVANT Well, *I'd* like to have what they've got!

PONCIA All we have is our hands and a hole in God's earth.

SERVANT And that's the only earth they'll ever leave to us—to us who have nothing!

PONCIA (*at the cupboard*) This glass has some specks.

SERVANT Neither soap nor rag will take them off.

The bells toll.

PONCIA The last prayer! I'm going over and listen. I certainly like the way our priest sings. In the Pater Noster his voice went up, and up—like a pitcher filling with water little by little. Of course, at the end his voice cracked, but it's glorious to hear it. No, there never was anybody like the old Sacristan—Tronchapinos. At my mother's Mass, may she rest in peace, he sang. The walls shook—and when he said "Amen," it was as if a wolf had come into the church.

Imitating him.

A-a-a-a-men!

She starts coughing.

SERVANT   Watch out—you'll strain your windpipe!

PONCIA   I'd rather strain something else!

Goes out laughing.

The Servant scrubs. The bells toll.

SERVANT (*imitating the bells*)   Dong, dong, dong. Dong, dong, dong. May God forgive him!

BEGGAR WOMAN (*at the door, with a little girl*)   Blesséd be God!

SERVANT   Dong, dong, dong. I hope he waits many years for us! Dong, dong, dong.

BEGGAR (*loudly, a little annoyed*)   Blesséd be God!

SERVANT (*annoyed*)   Forever and ever!

BEGGAR   I came for the scraps.

The bells stop tolling.

SERVANT   You can go right out the way you came in. Today's scraps are for me.

BEGGAR   But you have somebody to take care of you—and my little girl and I are all alone!

SERVANT   Dogs are alone too, and they live.

BEGGAR   They always give them to me.

SERVANT   Get out of here! Who let you in anyway? You've already tracked up the place.

The Beggar Woman and Little Girl leave. The Servant goes on scrubbing.

Floors finished with oil, cupboards, pedestals, iron beds—but us servants, we can suffer in silence—and live in mud huts with a plate and a spoon. I hope someday not a one will be left to tell it.

The bells sound again.

Yes, yes—ring away. Let them put you in a coffin with gold inlay and brocade to carry it on—you're no less dead than I'll be, so take what's coming to you, Antonio Maria Benavides—stiff in your broadcloth suit and your high boots—take what's coming to you! You'll never again lift my skirts behind the corral door!

From the rear door, two by two, women in mourning with large shawls and black skirts and fans, begin to enter. They come in slowly until the stage is full.

SERVANT (*breaking into a wail*) Oh, Antonio Maria Benavides, now you'll never see these walls, nor break bread in this house again! I'm the one who loved you most of all your servants.

Pulling her hair.

Must I live on after you've gone? Must I go on living?

The two hundred women finish coming in, and Bernarda and her five daughters enter. Bernarda leans on a cane.

BERNARDA (*to The Servant*) Silence!

SERVANT (*weeping*) Bernarda!

BERNARDA Less shrieking and more work. You should have had all this cleaner for the wake. Get out. This isn't your place.

The Servant goes off crying.

The poor are like animals—they seem to be made of different stuff.

FIRST WOMAN The poor feel their sorrows too.

BERNARDA But they forget them in front of a plateful of peas.

FIRST GIRL (*timidly*) Eating is necessary for living.

BERNARDA At your age one doesn't talk in front of older people.

WOMAN Be quiet, child.

BERNARDA I've never taken lessons from anyone. Sit down.

They sit down. Pause. Loudly:

Magdalena, don't cry. If you want to cry, get under your bed. Do you hear me?

SECOND WOMAN (*to Bernarda*) Have you started to work the fields?

BERNARDA Yesterday.

THIRD WOMAN The sun comes down like lead.

FIRST WOMAN I haven't known heat like this for years.

Pause. They all fan themselves.

BERNARDA Is the lemonade ready?

PONCIA Yes, Bernarda.

She brings in a large tray full of little white jars which she distributes.

BERNARDA Give the men some.

PONCIA They're already drinking in the patio.

BERNARDA Let them get out the way they came in. I don't want them walking through here.

A GIRL (*to Angustias*) Pepe el Romano was with the men during the service.

ANGUSTIAS There he was.

BERNARDA His mother was there. She saw his mother. Neither she nor I saw Pepe . . .

GIRL I thought . . .

BERNARDA The one who *was* there was Darajalí, the widower. Very close to your Aunt. We all of us saw him.

SECOND WOMAN (*aside, in a low voice*) Wicked, worse than wicked woman!

THIRD WOMAN A tongue like a knife!

BERNARDA Women in church shouldn't look at any man but the priest—and him only because he wears skirts. To turn your head is to be looking for the warmth of corduroy.

FIRST WOMAN Sanctimonious old snake!

PONCIA (*between her teeth*) Itching for a man's warmth.

BERNARDA (*beating with her cane on the floor*) Blesséd be God!

ALL (*crossing themselves*) Forever blesséd and praised.

BERNARDA Rest in peace with holy company at your head.

ALL Rest in peace!

BERNARDA With the Angel Saint Michael, and his sword of justice.

ALL Rest in peace!

BERNARDA With the key that opens, and the hand that locks.

ALL Rest in peace!

BERNARDA With the most blesséd, and the little lights of the field.

ALL Rest in peace!

BERNARDA With our holy charity, and all souls on land and sea.

ALL Rest in peace!

BERNARDA Grant rest to your servant, Antonio Maria Benavides, and give him the crown of your blesséd glory.

ALL   Amen.

BERNARDA (*she rises and chants*)   Requiem aeternam donat eis domine.

ALL (*standing and chanting in the Gregorian fashion*)   Et lux perpetua luce ab eis.

They cross themselves.

FIRST WOMAN   May you have health to pray for his soul.

They start filing out.

THIRD WOMAN   You won't lack loaves of hot bread.

SECOND WOMAN   Nor a roof for your daughters.

They are all filing in front of Bernarda and going out. Angustias leaves by the door to the patio.

FOURTH WOMAN   May you go on enjoying your wedding wheat.

PONCIA (*she enters, carrying a money bag*)   From the men—this bag of money for Masses.

BERNARDA   Thank them—and let them have a glass of brandy.

GIRL (*to Magdalena*)   Magdalena . . .

BERNARDA (*to Magdalena, who is starting to cry*)   Sh-h-h-h!

She beats with her cane on the floor.

All the women have gone out.

BERNARDA (*to the women who have just left*)   Go back to your houses and criticize everything you've seen! I hope it'll be many years before you pass under the archway of my door again.

PONCIA   You've nothing to complain about. The whole town came.

BERNARDA   Yes, to fill my house with the sweat from their wraps and the poison of their tongues.

AMELIA   Mother, don't talk like that.

BERNARDA   What other way is there to talk about this curséd village with no river—this village full of wells where you drink water always fearful it's been poisoned?

PONCIA   Look what they've done to the floor!

BERNARDA   As though a herd of goats had passed through.

Poncia cleans the floor.

Adela, give me a fan.

ADELA Take this one.

She gives her a round fan with green and red flowers.

BERNARDA (*throwing the fan on the floor*) Is that the fan to give to a widow? Give me a black one and learn to respect your father's memory.

MARTIRIO Take mine.

BERNARDA And you?

MARTIRIO I'm not hot.

BERNARDA Well, look for another, because you'll need it. For the eight years of mourning, not a breath of air will get in this house from the street. We'll act as if we'd sealed up doors and windows with bricks. That's what happened in my father's house—and in my grandfather's house. Meantime, you can all start embroidering your hope-chest linens. I have twenty bolts of linen in the chest from which to cut sheets and coverlets. Magdalena can embroider them.

MAGDALENA It's all the same to me.

ADELA (*sourly*) If you don't want to embroider them—they can go without. That way yours will look better.

MAGDALENA Neither mine nor yours. I know I'm not going to marry. I'd rather carry sacks to the mill. Anything except sit here day after day in this dark room.

BERNARDA That's what a woman is for.

MAGDALENA Cursed be all women.

BERNARDA In this house you'll do what I order. You can't run with the story to your father any more. Needle and thread for women. Whiplash and mules for men. That's the way it has to be for people who have certain obligations.

Adela goes out.

VOICE Bernarda! Let me out!

BERNARDA (*calling*) Let her out now!

The First Servant enters.

FIRST SERVANT I had a hard time holding her. In spite of her eighty years, your mother's strong as an oak.

BERNARDA   It runs in the family. My grandfather was the same way.

SERVANT   Several times during the wake I had to cover her mouth with an empty sack because she wanted to shout out to you to give her dishwater to drink at least, and some dogmeat, which is what she says you feed her.

MARTIRIO   She's mean!

BERNARDA (*to Servant*)   Let her get some fresh air in the patio.

SERVANT   She took her rings and the amethyst earrings out of the box, put them on, and told me she wants to get married.

The daughters laugh.

BERNARDA   Go with her and be careful she doesn't get near the well.

SERVANT   You don't need to be afraid she'll jump in.

BERNARDA   It's not that—but the neighbors can see her there from their windows.

The Servant leaves.

MARTIRIO   We'll go change our clothes.

BERNARDA   Yes, but don't take the 'kerchiefs from your heads.

Adela enters.

And Angustias?

ADELA (*meaningfully*)   I saw her looking out through the cracks of the back door. The men had just gone.

BERNARDA   And you, what were *you* doing at the door?

ADELA   I went there to see if the hens had laid.

BERNARDA   But the men had already gone!

ADELA (*meaningfully*)   A group of them were still standing outside.

BERNARDA (*furiously*)   Angustias! Angustias!

ANGUSTIAS (*entering*)   Did you want something?

BERNARDA   For what—and at whom—were you looking?

ANGUSTIAS   Nobody.

BERNARDA   Is it decent for a woman of your class to be running after a man the day of her father's funeral? Answer me! Whom were you looking at?

Pause.

ANGUSTIAS   I . . .

BERNARDA   Yes, you!

ANGUSTIAS   Nobody.

BERNARDA   Soft! Honeytongue!

She strikes her.

PONCIA (*running to her*)   Bernarda, calm down!

She holds her. Angustias weeps.

BERNARDA   Get out of here, all of you!

They all go out.

PONCIA   She did it not realizing what she was doing—although it's bad, of course. It really disgusted me to see her sneak along to the patio. Then she stood at the window listening to the men's talk which, as usual, was not the sort one should listen to.

BERNARDA   That's what they come to funerals for.

With curiosity.

What were they talking about?

PONCIA   They were talking about Paca la Roseta. Last night they tied her husband up in a stall, stuck her on a horse behind the saddle, and carried her away to the depths of the olive grove.

BERNARDA   And what did she do?

PONCIA   She? She was just as happy—they say her breasts were exposed and Maximiliano held on to her as if he were playing a guitar. Terrible!

BERNARDA   And what happened?

PONCIA   What had to happen. They came back almost at daybreak. Paca la Roseta with her hair loose and a wreath of flowers on her head.

BERNARDA   She's the only bad woman we have in the village.

PONCIA   Because she's not from here. She's from far away. And those who went with her are the sons of outsiders too. The men from here aren't up to a thing like that.

BERNARDA   No, but they like to see it, and talk about it, and suck their fingers over it.

PONCIA   They were saying a lot more things.

BERNARDA (*looking from side to side with a certain fear*) What things?

PONCIA I'm ashamed to talk about them.

BERNARDA And my daughter heard them?

PONCIA Of course!

BERNARDA That one takes after her aunts: white and mealy-mouthed and casting sheep's eyes at any little barber's compliment. Oh, what one has to go through and put up with so people will be decent and not too wild!

PONCIA It's just that your daughters are of an age when they ought to have husbands. Mighty little trouble they give you. Angustias must be much more than thirty now.

BERNARDA Exactly thirty-nine.

PONCIA Imagine. And she's never had a beau . . .

BERNARDA (*furiously*) None of them has ever had a beau and they've never needed one! They get along very well.

PONCIA I didn't mean to offend you.

BERNARDA For a hundred miles around there's no one good enough to come near them. The men in this town are not of their class. Do you want me to turn them over to the first shepherd?

PONCIA You should have moved to another town.

BERNARDA That's it. To sell them!

PONCIA No, Bernarda, to change. . . . Of course, any place else, they'd be the poor ones.

BERNARDA Hold your tormenting tongue!

PONCIA One can't even talk to you. Do we, or do we not share secrets?

BERNARDA We do not. You're a servant and I pay you. Nothing more.

PONCIA But . . .

FIRST SERVANT (*entering*) Don Arturo's here. He's come to see about dividing the inheritance.

BERNARDA Let's go.

To The Servant.

You start whitewashing the patio.

To La Poncia.

And you start putting all the dead man's clothes away in the chest.

PONCIA   We could give away some of the things.

BERNARDA   Nothing—not a button even! Not even the cloth we covered his face with.

She goes out slowly, leaning on her cane. At the door she turns to look at the two servants. They go out. She leaves.

Amelia and Martirio enter.

AMELIA   Did you take the medicine?

MARTIRIO   For all the good it'll do me.

AMELIA   But you took it?

MARTIRIO   I do things without any faith, but like clockwork.

AMELIA   Since the new doctor came you look livelier.

MARTIRIO   I feel the same.

AMELIA   Did you notice? Adelaida wasn't at the funeral.

MARTIRIO   I know. Her sweetheart doesn't let her go out even to the front doorstep. Before, she was gay. Now, not even powder on her face.

AMELIA   These days a girl doesn't know whether to have a beau or not.

MARTIRIO   It's all the same.

AMELIA   The whole trouble is all these wagging tongues that won't let us live. Adelaida has probably had a bad time.

MARTIRIO   She's afraid of our mother. Mother is the only one who knows the story of Adelaida's father and where he got his lands. Everytime she comes here, Mother twists the knife in the wound. Her father killed his first wife's husband in Cuba so he could marry her himself. Then he left her there and went off with another woman who already had one daughter, and then he took up with this other girl, Adelaida's mother, and married her after his second wife died insane.

AMELIA   But why isn't a man like that put in jail?

MARTIRIO   Because men help each other cover up things like that and no one's able to tell on them.

AMELIA   But Adelaida's not to blame for any of that.

MARTIRIO   No. But history repeats itself. I can see that everything is a terrible repetition. And she'll have the same fate as her mother and grandmother—both of them wife to the man who fathered her.

AMELIA   What an awful thing!

MARTIRIO It's better never to look at a man. I've been afraid
of them since I was a little girl. I'd see them in the yard,
yoking the oxen and lifting grain sacks, shouting and
stamping, and I was always afraid to grow up for fear one of
them would suddenly take me in his arms. God has made
me weak and ugly and has definitely put such things away
from me.

AMELIA Don't say that! Enrique Humanas was after you and
he liked you.

MARTIRIO That was just people's ideas! One time I stood in
my nightgown at the window until daybreak because he let
me know through his shepherd's little girl that he was going
to come, and he didn't. It was all just talk. Then he married
someone else who had more money than I.

AMELIA And ugly as the devil.

MARTIRIO What do men care about ugliness? All they care
about is lands, yokes of oxen, and a submissive bitch who'll
feed them.

AMELIA Ay!

Magdalena enters.

MAGDALENA What are you doing?

MARTIRIO Just here.

AMELIA And you?

MAGDALENA I've been going through all the rooms. Just to
walk a little, and look at Grandmother's needlepoint
pictures—the little woolen dog, and the black man wrestling
with the lion—which we liked so much when we were
children. Those were happier times. A wedding lasted ten
days and evil tongues weren't in style. Today people are
more refined. Brides wear white veils, just as in the cities,
and we drink bottled wine, but we rot inside because of
what people might say.

MARTIRIO Lord knows what went on then!

AMELIA (*to Magdalena*) One of your shoelaces has come
untied.

MAGDALENA What of it?

AMELIA You'll step on it and fall.

MAGDALENA One less!

MARTIRIO And Adela?

MAGDALENA Ah! She put on the green dress she made to wear

for her birthday, went out to the yard, and began shouting: "Chickens! Chickens, look at me!" I had to laugh.

AMELIA   If Mother had only seen her!

MAGDALENA   Poor little thing! She's the youngest one of us and still has her illusions. I'd give something to see her happy.

Pause. Angustias crosses the stage, carrying some towels.

ANGUSTIAS   What time is it?

MAGDALENA   It must be twelve.

ANGUSTIAS   So late?

AMELIA   It's about to strike.

Angustias goes out.

MAGDALENA (*meaningfully*)   Do you know what?

Pointing after Angustias.

AMELIA   No.

MAGDALENA   Come on!

MARTIRIO   I don't know what you're talking about!

MAGDALENA   Both of you know it better than I do, always with your heads together, like two little sheep, but not letting anybody else in on it. I mean about Pepe el Romano!

MARTIRIO   Ah!

MAGDALENA (*mocking her*)   Ah! The whole town's talking about it. Pepe el Romano is coming to marry Angustias. Last night he was walking around the house and I think he's going to send a declaration soon.

MARTIRIO   I'm glad. He's a good man.

AMELIA   Me too. Angustias is well off.

MAGDALENA   Neither one of you is glad.

MARTIRIO   Magdalena! What do you mean?

MAGDALENA   If he were coming because of Angustias' looks, for Angustias as a woman, I'd be glad too, but he's coming for her money. Even though Angustias is our sister, we're her family here and we know she's old and sickly, and always has been the least attractive one of us! Because if she looked like a dressed-up stick at twenty, what can she look like now, now that she's forty?

MARTIRIO   Don't talk like that. Luck comes to the one who least expects it.

AMELIA   But Magdalena's right after all! Angustias has all her father's money; she's the only rich one in the house and that's why, now that Father's dead and the money will be divided, they're coming for her.

MAGDALENA   Pepe el Romano is twenty-five years old and the best looking man around here. The natural thing would be for him to be after you, Amelia, or our Adela, who's twenty—not looking for the least likely one in this house, a woman who, like her father, talks through her nose.

MARTIRIO   Maybe he likes that!

MAGDALENA   I've never been able to bear your hypocrisy.

MARTIRIO   Heavens!

Adela enters.

MAGDALENA   Did the chickens see you?

ADELA   What did you want me to do?

AMELIA   If Mother sees you, she'll drag you by your hair!

ADELA   I had a lot of illusions about this dress. I'd planned to put it on the day we were going to eat watermelons at the well. There wouldn't have been another like it.

MARTIRIO   It's a lovely dress.

ADELA   And one that looks very good on me. It's the best thing Magdalena's ever cut.

MAGDALENA   And the chickens, what did they say to you?

ADELA   They presented me with a few fleas that riddled my legs.

They laugh.

MARTIRIO   What you can do is dye it black.

MAGDALENA   The best thing you can do is give it to Angustias for her wedding with Pepe el Romano.

ADELA (*with hidden emotion*)   But Pepe el Romano . . .

AMELIA   Haven't you heard about it?

ADELA   No.

MAGDALENA   Well, now you know!

ADELA   But it can't be!

MAGDALENA   Money can do anything.

ADELA   Is that why she went out after the funeral and stood looking through the door?

Pause.

And that man would . . .

MAGDALENA   Would do anything.

Pause.

MARTIRIO   What are you thinking, Adela?

ADELA   I'm thinking that this mourning has caught me at the worst moment of my life for me to bear it.

MAGDALENA   You'll get used to it.

ADELA (*bursting out, crying with rage*)   I will not get used to it! I can't be locked up. I don't want my skin to look like yours. I don't want my skin's whiteness lost in these rooms. Tomorrow I'm going to put on my green dress and go walking in the streets. I want to go out!

The First Servant enters.

MAGDALENA (*in a tone of authority*)   Adela!

SERVANT   The poor thing! How she misses her father. . . .

She goes out.

MARTIRIO   Hush!

AMELIA   What happens to one will happen to all of us.

Adela grows calm.

MAGDALENA   The servant almost heard you.

SERVANT (*entering*)   Pepe el Romano is coming along at the end of the street.

Amelia, Martirio and Magdalena run hurriedly.

MAGDALENA   Let's go see him!

They leave rapidly.

SERVANT (*to Adela*)   Aren't you going?

ADELA   It's nothing to me.

SERVANT   Since he has to turn the corner, you'll see him better from the window of your room.

The Servant goes out. Adela is left on the stage, standing doubtfully; after a moment, she also leaves rapidly, going toward her room. Bernarda and La Poncia come in.

BERNARDA Damned portions and shares.

PONCIA What a lot of money is left to Angustias!

BERNARDA Yes.

PONCIA And for the others, considerably less.

BERNARDA You've told me that three times now, when you know I don't want it mentioned! Considerably less; a lot less! Don't remind me any more.

Angustias comes in, her face heavily made up.

Angustias!

ANGUSTIAS Mother.

BERNARDA Have you dared to powder your face? Have you dared to wash your face on the day of your father's death?

ANGUSTIAS He wasn't my father. Mine died a long time ago. Have you forgotten that already?

BERNARDA You owe more to this man, father of your sisters, than to your own. Thanks to him, your fortune is intact.

ANGUSTIAS We'll have to see about that first!

BERNARDA Even out of decency! Out of respect!

ANGUSTIAS Let me go out, Mother!

BERNARDA Let you go out? After I've taken that powder off your face, I will. Spineless! Painted hussy! Just like your aunts!

She removes the powder violently with her handkerchief.

Now get out!

PONCIA Bernarda, don't be so hateful!

BERNARDA Even though my mother is crazy, I still have my five senses and I know what I'm doing.

They all enter.

MAGDALENA What's going on here?

BERNARDA Nothing's 'going on here'!

MAGDALENA (*to Angustias*) If you're fighting over the inherit- ance, you're the richest one and can hang on to it all.

ANGUSTIAS Keep your tongue in your pocketbook!

BERNARDA (*beating on the floor*) Don't fool yourselves into thinking you'll sway me. Until I go out of this house feet first I'll give the orders for myself and for you!

Voices are heard and Maria Josefa, Bernarda's mother, enters. She is very old and has decked out her head and breast with flowers.

MARIA JOSEFA   Bernarda, where is my mantilla? Nothing, nothing of what I own will be for any of you. Not my rings nor my black moiré dress. Because not a one of you is going to marry—not a one. Bernarda, give me my necklace of pearls.

BERNARDA (*to The Servant*)   Why did you let her get in here?

SERVANT (*trembling*)   She got away from me!

MARIA JOSEFA   I ran away because I want to marry—I want to get married to a beautiful manly man from the shore of the sea. Because here the men run from women.

BERNARDA   Hush, hush, Mother!

MARIA JOSEFA   No, no—I won't hush. I don't want to see these single women, longing for marriage, turning their hearts to dust; and I want to go to my home town. Bernarda, I want a man to get married to and be happy with!

BERNARDA   Lock her up!

MARIA JOSEFA   Let me go out, Bernarda!

The Servant seizes Maria Josefa.

BERNARDA   Help her, all of you!

They all grab the old woman.

MARIA JOSEFA   I want to get away from here! Bernarda! To get married by the shore of the sea—by the shore of the sea!

QUICK CURTAIN

ACT TWO

A white room in Bernarda's house. The doors on the left lead to the bedrooms.

Bernarda's Daughters are seated on low chairs, sewing. Magdalena is embroidering. La Poncia is with them.

ANGUSTIAS   I've cut the third sheet.

MARTIRIO   That one goes to Amelia.

MAGDALENA   Angustias, shall I put Pepe's initials here too?

ANGUSTIAS (*dryly*)   No.

MAGDALENA (*calling, from off stage to Adela*)   Adela, aren't you coming?

AMELIA   She's probably stretched out on the bed.

PONCIA   Something's wrong with that one. I find her restless, trembling, frightened—as if a lizard were between her breasts.

MARTIRIO   There's nothing, more or less, wrong with her than there is with all of us.

MAGDALENA   All of us except Angustias.

ANGUSTIAS   I feel fine, and anybody who doesn't like it can pop.

MAGDALENA   We all have to admit the nicest things about you are your figure and your tact.

ANGUSTIAS   Fortunately, I'll soon be out of this hell.

MAGDALENA   Maybe you won't get out!

MARTIRIO   Stop this talk!

ANGUSTIAS   Besides, a good dowry is better than dark eyes in one's face!

MAGDALENA   All you say just goes in one ear and out the other.

AMELIA (*to La Poncia*)   Open the patio door and see if we can get a bit of a breeze.

La Poncia opens the door.

MARTIRIO   Last night I couldn't sleep because of the heat.

AMELIA   Neither could I.

MAGDALENA   I got up for a bit of air. There was a black storm cloud and a few drops even fell.

PONCIA   It was one in the morning and the earth seemed to give off fire. I got up too. Angustias was still at the window with Pepe.

MAGDALENA (*with irony*)   That late? What time did he leave?

ANGUSTIAS   Why do you ask, if you saw him?

AMELIA   He must have left about one-thirty.

ANGUSTIAS   Yes. How did you know?

AMELIA   I heard him cough and heard his mare's hoofbeats.

PONCIA   But I heard him leave around four.

ANGUSTIAS   It must have been someone else!

PONCIA   No, I'm sure of it!

AMELIA   That's what it seemed to me, too.

MAGDALENA   That's very strange!

Pause.

PONCIA   Listen, Angustias, what did he say to you the first time he came by your window?

ANGUSTIAS   Nothing. What should he say? Just talked.

MARTIRIO   It's certainly strange that two people who never knew each other should suddenly meet at a window and be engaged.

ANGUSTIAS   Well, I didn't mind.

AMELIA   I'd have felt very strange about it.

ANGUSTIAS   No, because when a man comes to a window he knows, from all the busybodies who come and go and fetch and carry, that he's going to be told "yes."

MARTIRIO   All right, but he'd have to ask you.

ANGUSTIAS   Of course!

AMELIA (*inquisitively*)   And how did he ask you?

ANGUSTIAS   Why, no way:—"You know I'm after you. I need a good, well brought up woman, and that's you—if it's agreeable."

AMELIA   These things embarrass me!

ANGUSTIAS   They embarrass me too, but one has to go through it!

PONCIA   And did he say anything more?

ANGUSTIAS   Yes, he did all the talking.

MARTIRIO   And you?

ANGUSTIAS   I couldn't have said a word. My heart was almost coming out of my mouth. It was the first time I'd ever been alone at night with a man.

MAGDALENA   And such a handsome man.

ANGUSTIAS   He's not bad looking!

PONCIA   Those things happen among people who have an idea how to do things, who talk and say and move their hand. The first time my husband, Evaristo the Short-tailed, came to my window . . . Ha! Ha! Ha!

AMELIA   What happened?

PONCIA   It was very dark. I saw him coming along and as he went by he said, "Good evening." "Good evening," I said. Then we were both silent for more than half an hour. The sweat poured down my body. Then Evaristo got nearer and nearer as if he wanted to squeeze in through the bars and said in a very low voice—"Come here and let me feel you!"

They all laugh. Amelia gets up, runs, and looks through the door.

AMELIA   Ay, I thought mother was coming!

MAGDALENA   What she'd have done to us!

They go on laughing.

AMELIA   Sh-h-h! She'll hear us.

PONCIA   Then he acted very decently. Instead of getting some other idea, he went to raising birds, until he died. You aren't married but it's good for you to know, anyway, that two weeks after the wedding a man gives up the bed for the table, then the table for the tavern, and the woman who doesn't like it can just rot, weeping in a corner.

AMELIA   You liked it.

PONCIA   I learned how to handle him!

MARTIRIO   Is it true that you sometimes hit him?

PONCIA   Yes, and once I almost poked out one of his eyes!

MAGDALENA   All women ought to be like that!

PONCIA   I'm one of your mother's school. One time I don't know what he said to me, and then I killed all his birds—with the pestle!

They laugh.

MAGDALENA   Adela, child! Don't miss this.

AMELIA   Adela!

Pause.

MAGDALENA   I'll go see!

She goes out.

PONCIA   That child is sick!

MARTIRIO   Of course. She hardly sleeps!

PONCIA   What *does* she do, then?

MARTIRIO   How do I know what she does?

PONCIA   You probably know better than we do, since you sleep with just a wall between you.

ANGUSTIAS   Envy gnaws on people.

AMELIA   Don't exaggerate.

ANGUSTIAS   I can tell it in her eyes. She's getting the look of a crazy woman.

MARTIRIO   Don't talk about crazy women. This is one place you're not allowed to say that word.

Magdalena and Adela enter.

MAGDALENA   Didn't you say she was asleep?

ADELA   My body aches.

MARTIRIO (*with a hidden meaning*)   Didn't you sleep well last night?

ADELA   Yes.

MARTIRIO   Then?

ADELA (*loudly*)   Leave me alone. Awake or asleep, it's no affair of yours. I'll do whatever I want to with my body.

MARTIRIO   I was just concerned about you!

ADELA   Concerned?—curious! Weren't you sewing? Well, continue! I wish I were invisible so I could pass through a room without being asked where I was going!

SERVANT (*entering*)   Bernarda is calling you. The man with the laces is here.

All but Adela and La Poncia go out, and as Martirio leaves, she looks fixedly at Adela.

ADELA   Don't look at me like that! If you want, I'll give you my eyes, for they're younger, and my back to improve that hump you have, but look the other way when I go by.

PONCIA   Adela, she's your sister, and the one who most loves you besides!

ADELA   She follows me everywhere. Sometimes she looks in my room to see if I'm sleeping. She won't let me breathe, and always, "Too bad about that face!" "Too bad about that body! It's going to waste!" But I won't let that happen. My body will be for whomever I choose.

PONCIA (*insinuatingly, in a low voice*)   For Pepe el Romano, no?

ADELA (*frightened*)   What do you mean?

PONCIA   What I said, Adela!

ADELA   Shut up!

PONCIA (*loudly*)   Don't you think I've noticed?

ADELA   Lower your voice!

PONCIA   Then forget what you're thinking about!

ADELA   What do you know?

PONCIA   We old ones can see through walls. Where do you go when you get up at night?

ADELA   I wish you were blind!

PONCIA   But my head and hands are full of eyes, where

something like this is concerned. I couldn't possibly guess your intentions. Why did you sit almost naked at your window, and with the light on and the window open, when Pepe passed by the second night he came to talk with your sister?

ADELA   That's not true!

PONCIA   Don't be a child! Leave your sister alone. And if you like Pepe el Romano, keep it to yourself.

Adela weeps.

Besides, who says you can't marry him? Your sister Angustias is sickly. She'll die with her first child. Narrow waisted, old—and out of my experience I can tell you she'll die. Then Pepe will do what all widowers do in these parts: he'll marry the youngest and most beautiful, and that's you. Live on that hope, forget him, anything; but don't go against God's law.

ADELA   Hush!

PONCIA   I won't hush!

ADELA   Mind your own business. Snooper, traitor!

PONCIA   I'm going to stick to you like a shadow!

ADELA   Instead of cleaning the house and then going to bed and praying for the dead, you root around like an old sow about goings on between men and women—so you can drool over them.

PONCIA   I keep watch; so people won't spit when they pass our door.

ADELA   What a tremendous affection you've suddenly conceived for my sister.

PONCIA   I don't have any affection for any of you. I want to live in a decent house. I don't want to be dirtied in my old age!

ADELA   Save your advice. It's already too late. For I'd leap not over you, just a servant, but over my mother to put out this fire I feel in my legs and my mouth. What can you possibly say about me? That I lock myself in my room and will not open the door? That I don't sleep? I'm smarter than you! See if you can catch the hare with your hands.

PONCIA   Don't defy me, Adela, don't defy me! Because I can shout, light lamps, and make bells ring.

ADELA   Bring four thousand yellow flares and set them about the walls of the yard. No one can stop what has to happen.

PONCIA You like him that much?

ADELA That much! Looking in his eyes I seem to drink his blood in slowly.

PONCIA I won't listen to you.

ADELA Well, you'll have to! I've been afraid of you. But now I'm stronger than you!

Angustias enters.

ANGUSTIAS Always arguing!

PONCIA Certainly. She insists that in all this heat I have to go bring her I don't know what from the store.

ANGUSTIAS Did you buy me the bottle of perfume?

PONCIA The most expensive one. And the face powder. I put them on the table in your room.

Angustias goes out.

ADELA And be quiet!

PONCIA We'll see!

Martirio and Amelia enter.

MARTIRIO (*to Adela*) Did you see the laces?

AMELIA Angustias', for her wedding sheets, are beautiful.

ADELA (*to Martirio, who is carrying some lace*) And these?

MARTIRIO They're for me. For a nightgown.

ADELA (*with sarcasm*) One needs a sense of humor around here!

MARTIRIO (*meaningfully*) But only for me to look at. I don't have to exhibit myself before anybody.

PONCIA No one ever sees us in our nightgowns.

MARTIRIO (*meaningfully, looking at Adela*) Sometimes they don't! But I love nice underwear. If I were rich, I'd have it made of Holland Cloth. It's one of the few tastes I've left.

PONCIA These laces are beautiful for babies' caps and christening gowns. I could never afford them for my own. Now let's see if Angustias will use them for hers. Once she starts having children, they'll keep her running night and day.

MAGDALENA I don't intend to sew a stitch on them.

AMELIA And much less bring up some stranger's children. Look how our neighbors across the road are—making sacrifices for four brats.

PONCIA   They're better off than you. There at least they laugh and you can hear them fight.

MARTIRIO   Well, you go work for them, then.

PONCIA   No, fate has sent me to this nunnery!

Tiny bells are heard distantly as though through several thicknesses of wall.

MAGDALENA   It's the men going back to work.

PONCIA   It was three o'clock a minute ago.

MARTIRIO   With this sun!

ADELA (*sitting down*)   Ay! If only we could go out in the fields too!

MAGDALENA (*sitting down*)   Each class does what it has to!

MARTIRIO (*sitting down*)   That's it!

AMELIA (*sitting down*)   Ay!

PONCIA   There's no happiness like that in the fields right at this time of year. Yesterday morning the reapers arrived. Forty or fifty handsome young men.

MAGDALENA   Where are they from this year?

PONCIA   From far, far away. They came from the mountains! Happy! Like weathered trees! Shouting and throwing stones! Last night a woman who dresses in sequins and dances, with an accordion, arrived, and fifteen of them made a deal with her to take her to the olive grove. I saw them from far away. The one who talked with her was a boy with green eyes—tight knit as a sheaf of wheat.

AMELIA   Really?

ADELA   Are you sure?

PONCIA   Years ago another one of those women came here, and I myself gave my eldest son some money so he could go. Men need things like that.

ADELA   Everything's forgiven *them*.

AMELIA   To be born a woman's the worst possible punishment.

MAGDALENA   Even our eyes aren't our own.

A distant song is heard, coming nearer.

PONCIA   There they are. They have a beautiful song.

AMELIA   They're going out to reap now.

CHORUS

> The reapers have set out
> Looking for ripe wheat;
> They'll carry off the hearts
> Of any girls they meet.

Tambourines and carrañacas are heard. Pause. They all listen in the silence cut by the sun.

AMELIA   And they don't mind the sun!

MARTIRIO   They reap through flames.

ADELA   How I'd like to be a reaper so I could come and go as I pleased. Then we could forget what's eating us all.

MARTIRIO   What do you have to forget?

ADELA   Each one of us has something.

MARTIRIO (*intensely*)   Each one!

PONCIA   Quiet! Quiet!

CHORUS (*very distantly*)

> Throw wide your doors and windows,
> You girls who live in the town
> The reaper asks you for roses
> With which to deck his crown.

PONCIA   What a song!

MARTIRIO (*with nostalgia*)

> Throw wide your doors and windows,
> You girls who live in the town.

ADELA (*passionately*)

> The reaper asks you for roses
> With which to deck his crown.

The song grows more distant.

PONCIA   Now they're turning the corner.

ADELA   Let's watch them from the window of my room.

PONCIA   Be careful not to open the shutters too much because they're likely to give them a push to see who's looking.

The three leave. Martirio is left sitting on the low chair with her head between her hands.

AMELIA (*drawing near her*)   What's wrong with you?

MARTIRIO   The heat makes me feel ill.

AMELIA   And it's no more than that?

MARTIRIO   I was wishing it were November, the rainy days, the frost—anything except this unending summertime.

AMELIA   It'll pass and come again.

MARTIRIO   Naturally.

Pause.

What time did you go to sleep last night?

AMELIA   I don't know. I sleep like a log. Why?

MARTIRIO   Nothing. Only I thought I heard someone in the yard.

AMELIA   Yes?

MARTIRIO   Very late.

AMELIA   And weren't you afraid?

MARTIRIO   No. I've heard it other nights.

AMELIA   We'd better watch out! Couldn't it have been the shepherds?

MARTIRIO   The shepherds come at six.

AMELIA   Maybe a young, unbroken mule?

MARTIRIO (*to herself, with double meaning*)   That's it! That's it. An unbroken little mule.

AMELIA   We'll have to set a watch.

MARTIRIO   No. No. Don't say anything. It may be I've just imagined it.

AMELIA   Maybe.

Pause. Amelia starts to go.

MARTIRIO   Amelia!

AMELIA (*at the door*)   What?

Pause.

MARTIRIO   Nothing.

Pause.

AMELIA   Why did you call me?

Pause.

MARTIRIO   It just came out. I didn't mean to.

Pause.

AMELIA   Lie down for a little.

ANGUSTIAS (*she bursts in furiously, in a manner that makes a great contrast with previous silence*)   Where's that picture of Pepe I had under my pillow? Which one of you has it?

MARTIRIO   No one.

AMELIA   You'd think he was a silver St. Bartholomew.

ANGUSTIAS   Where's the picture?

Poncia, Magdalena, and Adela enter.

ADELA   What picture?

ANGUSTIAS   One of you has hidden it on me.

MAGDALENA   Do you have the effrontery to say that?

ANGUSTIAS   I had it in my room, and now it isn't there.

MARTIRIO   But couldn't it have jumped out into the yard at midnight? Pepe likes to walk around in the moonlight.

ANGUSTIAS   Don't joke with me! When he comes I'll tell him.

PONCIA   Don't do that! Because it'll turn up.

Looking at Adela.

ANGUSTIAS   I'd like to know which one of you has it.

ADELA (*looking at Martirio*)   Somebody has it! But not me!

MARTIRIO (*with meaning*)   Of course not you!

BERNARDA (*entering, with her cane*)   What scandal is this in my house in the heat's heavy silence? The neighbors must have their ears glued to the walls.

ANGUSTIAS   They've stolen my sweetheart's picture!

BERNARDA (*fiercely*)   Who? Who?

ANGUSTIAS   They have!

BERNARDA   Which one of you?

Silence.

Answer me!

Silence.

To La Poncia.

Search their rooms! Look in their beds. This comes of not tying you up with shorter leashes. But I'll teach you now!

To Angustias.

Are you sure?

ANGUSTIAS   Yes.

BERNARDA   Did you look everywhere?

ANGUSTIAS   Yes, Mother.

They all stand in an embarrassed silence.

BERNARDA   At the end of my life—to make me drink the bitterest poison a mother knows.

To Poncia.

Did you find it?

PONCIA   Here it is.

BERNARDA   Where did you find it?

PONCIA   It was . . .

BERNARDA   Say it! Don't be afraid.

PONCIA (*wonderingly*)   Between the sheets in Martirio's bed.

BERNARDA (*to Martirio*)   Is that true?

MARTIRIO   It's true.

BERNARDA (*advancing on her, beating her with her cane*)   You'll come to a bad end yet, you hypocrite! Trouble maker!

MARTIRIO (*fiercely*)   Don't hit me, Mother!

BERNARDA   All I want to!

MARTIRIO   If I let you! You hear me? Get back!

PONCIA   Don't be disrespectful to your mother!

ANGUSTIAS (*holding Bernarda*)   Let her go, please!

BERNARDA   Not even tears in your eyes.

MARTIRIO   I'm not going to cry just to please you.

BERNARDA   Why did you take the picture?

MARTIRIO   Can't I play a joke on my sister? What else would I want it for?

ADELA (*leaping forward, full of jealousy*)   It wasn't a joke! You never liked to play jokes. It was something else bursting in her breast—trying to come out. Admit it openly now.

MARTIRIO   Hush, and don't make me speak; for if I should speak the walls would close together one against the other with shame.

ADELA   An evil tongue never stops inventing lies.

BERNARDA   Adela!

MAGDALENA   You're crazy.

AMELIA   And you stone us all with your evil suspicions.

MARTIRIO   But some others do things more wicked!

ADELA   Until all at once they stand forth stark naked and the river carries them along.

BERNARDA   Spiteful!

ANGUSTIAS   It's not my fault Pepe el Romano chose me!

ADELA   For your money.

ANGUSTIAS   Mother!

BERNARDA   Silence!

MARTIRIO   For your fields and your orchards.

MAGDALENA   That's only fair.

BERNARDA   Silence, I say! I saw the storm coming but I didn't think it'd burst so soon. Oh, what an avalanche of hate you've thrown on my heart! But I'm not old yet—I have five chains for you, and this house my father built, so not even the weeds will know of my desolation. Out of here!

They go out. Bernarda sits down desolately. La Poncia is standing close to the wall. Bernarda recovers herself, and beats on the floor.

I'll have to let them feel the weight of my hand! Bernarda, remember your duty!

PONCIA   May I speak?

BERNARDA   Speak. I'm sorry you heard. A stranger is always out of place in a family.

PONCIA   What I've seen, I've seen.

BERNARDA   Angustias must get married right away.

PONCIA   Certainly. We'll have to get her away from here.

BERNARDA   Not her, him!

PONCIA   Of course. He's the one to get away from here. You've thought it all out.

BERNARDA   I'm not thinking. There are things that shouldn't and can't be thought out. I give orders.

PONCIA   And you think he'll be satisfied to go away?

BERNARDA (*rising*)   What are you imagining now?

PONCIA   He will, of course, marry Angustias.

BERNARDA   Speak up! I know you well enough to see that your knife's out for me.

PONCIA   I never knew a warning could be called murder.

BERNARDA   Have you some "warning" for me?

PONCIA   I'm not making any accusations, Bernarda. I'm only telling you to open your eyes and you'll see.

BERNARDA   See what?

PONCIA   You've always been smart, Bernarda. You've seen other people's sins a hundred miles away. Many times I've thought you could read minds. But, your children are your children, and now you're blind.

BERNARDA Are you talking about Martirio?

PONCIA Well, yes—about Martirio . . .

With curiosity.

I wonder why she hid the picture?

BERNARDA (*shielding her daughter*) After all, she says it was a joke. What else could it be?

PONCIA (*scornfully*) Do you believe that?

BERNARDA (*sternly*) I don't merely believe it. It's so!

PONCIA Enough of this. We're talking about your family. But if we were talking about your neighbor across the way, what would it be?

BERNARDA Now you're beginning to pull the point of the knife out.

PONCIA (*always cruelly*) No, Bernarda. Something very grave is happening here. I don't want to put the blame on your shoulders, but you've never given your daughters any freedom. Martirio is lovesick, I don't care what you say. Why didn't you let her marry Enrique Humanas? Why, on the very day he was coming to her window did you send him a message not to come?

BERNARDA (*loudly*) I'd do it a thousand times over! My blood won't mingle with the Humanas' while I live! His father was a shepherd.

PONCIA And you see now what's happening to you with these airs!

BERNARDA I have them because I can afford to. And you don't have them because you know where you came from!

PONCIA (*with hate*) Don't remind me! I'm old now. I've always been grateful for your protection.

BERNARDA (*emboldened*) You don't seem so!

PONCIA (*with hate, behind softness*) Martirio will forget this.

BERNARDA And if she doesn't—the worse for her. I don't believe this is that "very grave thing" that's happening here. Nothing's happening here. It's just that you wish it would! And if it should happen one day, you can be sure it won't go beyond these walls.

PONCIA I'm not so sure of that! There are people in town who can also read hidden thoughts, from afar.

BERNARDA   How you'd like to see me and my daughters on our way to a whorehouse!

PONCIA   No one knows her own destiny!

BERNARDA   I know my destiny! And my daughters! The whorehouse was for a certain woman, already dead. . . .

PONCIA (*fiercely*)   Bernarda, respect the memory of my mother!

BERNARDA   Then don't plague me with your evil thoughts!

Pause.

PONCIA   I'd better stay out of everything.

BERNARDA   That's what you ought to do. Work and keep your mouth shut. The duty of all who work for a living.

PONCIA   But we can't do that. Don't you think it'd be better for Pepe to marry Martirio or . . . yes! . . . Adela?

BERNARDA   No, I *don't* think so.

PONCIA (*with meaning*)   Adela! She's Romano's real sweetheart!

BERNARDA   Things are never the way we want them!

PONCIA   But it's hard work to turn them from their destined course. For Pepe to be with Angustias seems wrong to me—and to other people—and even to the wind. Who knows if they'll get what they want?

BERNARDA   There you go again! Sneaking up on me—giving me bad dreams. But I won't listen to you, because if all you say should come to pass—I'd scratch your face.

PONCIA   Frighten someone else with that.

BERNARDA   Fortunately, my daughters respect me and have never gone against my will!

PONCIA   That's right! But, as soon as they break loose they'll fly to the rooftops!

BERNARDA   And I'll bring them down with stones!

PONCIA   Oh, yes! You were always the bravest one!

BERNARDA   I've always enjoyed a good fight!

PONCIA   But aren't people strange. You should see Angustias' enthusiasm for her lover, at her age! And he seems very smitten too. Yesterday my oldest son told me that when he passed by with the oxen at four-thirty in the morning they were still talking.

BERNARDA   At four-thirty?

ANGUSTIAS (*entering*)   That's a lie!

PONCIA   That's what he told me.

BERNARDA (*to Angustias*)   Speak up!

ANGUSTIAS   For more than a week Pepe has been leaving at one. May God strike me dead if I'm lying.

MARTIRIO (*entering*)   I heard him leave at four too.

BERNARDA   But did you see him with your eyes?

MARTIRIO   I didn't want to look out. Don't you talk now through the side window?

ANGUSTIAS   We talk through my bedroom window.

Adela appears at the door.

MARTIRIO   Then . . .

BERNARDA   What's going on here?

PONCIA   If you're not careful, you'll find out! At least. Pepe was at *one* of your windows—and at four in the morning too!

BERNARDA   Are you sure of that?

PONCIA   You can't be sure of anything in this life!

ADELA   Mother, don't listen to someone who wants us to lose everything we have.

BERNARDA   I know how to take care of myself! If the townspeople want to come bearing false witness against me, they'll run into a stone wall! Don't any of you talk about this! Sometimes other people try to stir up a wave of filth to drown us.

MARTIRIO   I don't like to lie.

PONCIA   So there must be something.

BERNARDA   There won't be anything. I was born to have my eyes always open. Now I'll watch without closing them 'til I die.

ANGUSTIAS   I have the right to know.

BERNARDA   You don't have any right except to obey. No one's going to fetch and carry for me.

To La Poncia

And don't meddle in our affairs. No one will take a step without my knowing it.

SERVANT (*entering*)   There's a big crowd at the top of the street, and all the neighbors are at their doors!

BERNARDA (*to Poncia*)   Run see what's happening!

The Girls are about to run out.

Where are you going? I always knew you for window-watching women and breakers of your mourning. All of you, to the patio!

They go out. Bernarda leaves. Distant shouts are heard. Martirio and Adela enter and listen, not daring to step farther than the front door.

MARTIRIO   You can be thankful I didn't happen to open my mouth.

ADELA   I would have spoken too.

MARTIRIO   And what were you going to say? Wanting isn't doing!

ADELA   I do what I can and what happens to suit me. You've wanted to, but haven't been able.

MARTIRIO   You won't go on very long.

ADELA   I'll have everything!

MARTIRIO   I'll tear you out of his arms!

ADELA (*pleadingly*)   Martirio, let me be!

MARTIRIO   None of us will have him!

ADELA   He wants me for his house!

MARTIRIO   I saw how he embraced you!

ADELA   I didn't want him to. It's as if I were dragged by a rope.

MARTIRIO   I'll see you dead first!

Magdalena and Angustias look in. The tumult is increasing. A Servant enters with Bernarda. Poncia also enters from another door.

PONCIA   Bernarda!

BERNARDA   What's happening?

PONCIA   Librada's daughter, the unmarried one, had a child and no one knows whose it is!

ADELA   A child?

PONCIA   And to hide her shame she killed it and hid it under the rocks, but the dogs, with more heart than most Christians, dug it out and, as though directed by the hand of God, left it at her door. Now they want to kill her. They're dragging her through the streets—and down the paths and across the olive groves the men are coming, shouting so the fields shake.

BERNARDA   Yes, let them all come with olive whips and hoe handles—let them all come and kill her!

ADELA   No, not to kill her!

MARTIRIO   Yes—and let us go out too!

BERNARDA   And let whoever loses her decency pay for it!

Outside a woman's shriek and a great clamor is heard.

ADELA   Let her escape! Don't you go out!
MARTIRIO (*looking at Adela*)   Let her pay what she owes!
BERNARDA (*at the archway*)   Finish her before the guards come!
    Hot coals in the place where she sinned!
ADELA (*holding her belly*)   No! No!
BERNARDA   Kill her! Kill her!

CURTAIN

ACT THREE

*Four white walls, lightly washed in blue, of the interior patio of
Bernarda Alba's house. The doorways, illumined by the lights inside the
rooms, give a tenuous glow to the stage.*

*At the center there is a table with a shaded oil lamp about which
Bernarda and her Daughters are eating. La Poncia serves them.
Prudencia sits apart. When the curtain rises, there is a great silence
interrupted only by the noise of plates and silverware.*

PRUDENCIA   I'm going. I've made you a long visit.

She rises.

BERNARDA   But wait, Prudencia. We never see one another.
PRUDENCIA   Have they sounded the last call to rosary?
PONCIA   Not yet.

Prudencia sits down again.

BERNARDA   And your husband, how's he getting on?
PRUDENCIA   The same.
BERNARDA   We never see him either.
PRUDENCIA   You know how he is. Since he quarrelled with his
    brothers over the inheritance, he hasn't used the front door.
    He takes a ladder and climbs over the back wall.
BERNARDA   He's a real man! And your daughter?
PRUDENCIA   He's never forgiven her.
BERNARDA   He's right.
PRUDENCIA   I don't know what he told you. I suffer because of
    it.

BERNARDA A daughter who's disobedient stops being a daughter and becomes an enemy.

PRUDENCIA I let water run. The only consolation I've left is to take refuge in the church, but, since I'm losing my sight, I'll have to stop coming so the children won't make fun of me.

A heavy blow is heard against the walls.

What's that?

BERNARDA The stallion. He's locked in the stall and he kicks against the wall of the house.

Shouting.

Tether him and take him out in the yard!

In a lower voice.

He must be too hot.

PRUDENCIA Are you going to put the new mares to him?

BERNARDA At daybreak.

PRUDENCIA You've known how to increase your stock.

BERNARDA By dint of money and struggling.

PONCIA (*interrupting*) And she has the best herd in these parts. It's a shame that prices are low.

BERNARDA Do you want a little cheese and honey?

PRUDENCIA I have no appetite.

The blow is heard again.

PONCIA My God!

PRUDENCIA It quivered in my chest!

BERNARDA (*rising, furiously*) Do I have to say things twice? Let him out to roll on the straw.

Pause. Then, as though speaking to The Stableman.

Well then, lock the mares in the corral, but let him run free or he may kick down the walls.

She returns to the table and sits again.

Ay, what a life!

PRUDENCIA You have to fight like a man.

BERNARDA That's it.

Adela gets up from the table.

Where are you going?

ADELA   For a drink of water.

BERNARDA (*raising her voice*)   Bring a pitcher of cool water.

To Adela.

You can sit down.

Adela sits down.

PRUDENCIA   And Angustias, when will she get married?

BERNARDA   They're coming to ask for her within three days.

PRUDENCIA   You must be happy.

ANGUSTIAS   Naturally!

AMELIA (*to Magdalena*)   You've spilled the salt!

MAGDALENA   You can't possibly have worse luck than you're having.

AMELIA   It always brings bad luck.

BERNARDA   That's enough!

PRUDENCIA (*to Angustias*)   Has he given you the ring yet?

ANGUSTIAS   Look at it.

She holds it out.

PRUDENCIA   It's beautiful. Three pearls. In my day, pearls signified tears.

ANGUSTIAS   But things have changed now.

ADELA   I don't think so. Things go on meaning the same. Engagement rings should be diamonds.

PONCIA   The most appropriate.

BERNARDA   With pearls or without them, things are as one proposes.

MARTIRIO   Or as God disposes.

PRUDENCIA   I've been told your furniture is beautiful.

BERNARDA   It cost sixteen thousand *reales*.

PONCIA (*interrupting*)   The best is the wardrobe with the mirror.

PRUDENCIA   I never saw a piece like that.

BERNARDA   We had chests.

PRUDENCIA   The important thing is that everything be for the best.

ADELA   And that you never know.

BERNARDA   There's no reason why it shouldn't be.

Bells are heard very distantly.

PRUDENCIA   The last call.

To Angustias.

I'll be coming back to have you show me your clothes.

ANGUSTIAS   Whenever you like.

PRUDENCIA   Good evening—God bless you!

BERNARDA   Good-bye, Prudencia.

ALL FIVE DAUGHTERS (*at the same time*)   God go with you!

Pause. Prudencia goes out.

BERNARDA   Well, we've eaten.

They rise.

ADELA   I'm going to walk as far as the gate to stretch my legs and get a bit of fresh air.

Magdalena sits down in a low chair and leans against the wall.

AMELIA   I'll go with you.

MARTIRIO   I too.

ADELA (*with contained hate*)   I'm not going to get lost!

AMELIA   One needs company at night.

They go out. Bernarda sits down. Angustias is clearing the table.

BERNARDA   I've told you once already! I want you to talk to your sister Martirio. What happened about the picture was a joke and you must forget it.

ANGUSTIAS   You know she doesn't like me.

BERNARDA   Each one knows what she thinks inside. I don't pry into anyone's heart, but I want to put up a good front and have family harmony. You understand?

ANGUSTIAS   Yes.

BERNARDA   Then that's settled.

MAGDALENA (*she is almost asleep*)   Besides, you'll be gone in no time.

She falls asleep.

ANGUSTIAS   Not soon enough for me.

BERNARDA   What time did you stop talking last night?

ANGUSTIAS   Twelve-thirty.

BERNARDA   What does Pepe talk about?

ANGUSTIAS   I find him absent-minded. He always talks to me as though he were thinking of something else. If I ask him what's the matter, he answers—"We men have our worries."

BERNARDA You shouldn't ask him. And when you're married, even less. Speak if he speaks, and look at him when he looks at you. That way you'll get along.

ANGUSTIAS But, Mother, I think he's hiding things from me.

BERNARDA Don't try to find out. Don't ask him, and above all, never let him see you cry.

ANGUSTIAS I should be happy, but I'm not.

BERNARDA It's all the same.

ANGUSTIAS Many nights I watch Pepe very closely through the window bars and he seems to fade away—as though he were hidden in a cloud of dust like those raised by the flocks.

BERNARDA That's just because you're not strong.

ANGUSTIAS I hope so!

BERNARDA Is he coming tonight?

ANGUSTIAS No, he went into town with his mother.

BERNARDA Good, we'll get to bed early. Magdalena!

ANGUSTIAS She's asleep.

Adela, Martirio and Amelia enter.

AMELIA What a dark night!

ADELA You can't see two steps in front of you.

MARTIRIO A good night for robbers, for anyone who needs to hide.

ADELA The stallion was in the middle of the corral. White. Twice as large. Filling all the darkness.

AMELIA It's true. It was frightening. Like a ghost.

ADELA The sky has stars as big as fists.

MARTIRIO This one stared at them till she almost cracked her neck.

ADELA Don't you like them up there?

MARTIRIO What goes on over the roof doesn't mean a thing to me. I have my hands full with what happens under it.

ADELA Well, that's the way it goes with you!

BERNARDA And it goes the same for you as for her.

ANGUSTIAS Good night.

ADELA Are you going to bed now?

ANGUSTIAS Yes, Pepe isn't coming tonight.

She goes out.

ADELA Mother, why, when a star falls or lightning flashes, does one say:

> Holy Barbara, blessed on high
> May your name be in the sky
> With holy water written high?

BERNARDA The old people know many things we've forgotten.

AMELIA I close my eyes so I won't see them.

ADELA Not I. I like to see what's quiet and been quiet for years on end, running with fire.

MARTIRIO But all that has nothing to do with us.

BERNARDA And it's better not to think about it.

ADELA What a beautiful night! I'd like to stay up till very late and enjoy the breeze from the fields.

BERNARDA But we have to go to bed. Magdalena!

AMELIA She's just dropped off.

BERNARDA Magdalena!

MAGDALENA (*annoyed*) Leave me alone!

BERNARDA To bed!

MAGDALENA (*rising, in a bad humor*) You don't give anyone a moment's peace!

She goes off grumbling.

AMELIA Good night!

She goes out.

BERNARDA You two get along, too.

MARTIRIO How is it Angustias' sweetheart isn't coming tonight?

BERNARDA He went on a trip.

MARTIRIO (*looking at Adela*) Ah!

ADELA I'll see you in the morning!

She goes out. Martirio drinks some water and goes out slowly, looking at the door to the yard. La Poncia enters.

PONCIA Are you still here?

BERNARDA Enjoying this quiet and not seeing anywhere the "very grave thing" that's happening here—according to you.

PONCIA   Bernarda, let's not go any further with this.

BERNARDA   In this house there's no question of a yes or a no. My watchfulness can take care of anything.

PONCIA   Nothing's happening outside. That's true, all right. Your daughters act and are as though stuck in a cupboard. But neither you nor anyone else can keep watch inside a person's heart.

BERNARDA   My daughters breathe calmly enough.

PONCIA   That's your business, since you're their mother. I have enough to do just with serving you.

BERNARDA   Yes, you've turned quiet now.

PONCIA   I keep my place—that's all.

BERNARDA   The trouble is you've nothing to talk about. If there were grass in this house, you'd make it your business to put the neighbors' sheep to pasture here.

PONCIA   I hide more than you think.

BERNARDA   Do your sons still see Pepe at four in the morning? Are they still repeating this house's evil litany?

PONCIA   They say nothing.

BERNARDA   Because they can't. Because there's nothing for them to sink their teeth in. And all because my eyes keep constant watch!

PONCIA   Bernarda, I don't want to talk about this because I'm afraid of what you'll do. But don't you feel so safe.

BERNARDA   Very safe!

PONCIA   Who knows, lightning might strike suddenly. Who knows but what all of a sudden, in a rush of blood, your heart might stop.

BERNARDA   Nothing will happen here. I'm on guard now against all your suspicions.

PONCIA   All the better for you.

BERNARDA   Certainly, all the better!

SERVANT (*entering*)   I've just finished with the dishes. Is there anything else, Bernarda?

BERNARDA (*rising*)   Nothing. I'm going to get some rest.

PONCIA   What time do you want me to call you?

BERNARDA   No time. Tonight I intend to sleep well.

She goes out.

PONCIA   When you're powerless against the sea, it's easier to turn your back on it and not look at it.

SERVANT She's so proud! She herself pulls the blindfold over her eyes.

PONCIA I can do nothing. I tried to head things off, but now they frighten me too much. You feel this silence?—in each room there's a thunderstorm—and the day it breaks, it'll sweep all of us along with it. But I've said what I had to say.

SERVANT Bernarda thinks nothing can stand against her, yet she doesn't know the strength a man has among women alone.

PONCIA It's not all the fault of Pepe el Romano. It's true last year he was running after Adela; and she was crazy about him—but she ought to keep her place and not lead him on. A man's a man.

SERVANT And some there are who believe he didn't have to talk many times with Adela.

PONCIA That's true.

In a low voice.

And some other things.

SERVANT I don't know what's going to happen here.

PONCIA How I'd like to sail across the sea and leave this house, this battleground, behind!

SERVANT Bernarda's hurrying the wedding and it's possible nothing will happen.

PONCIA Things have gone much too far already. Adela is set no matter what comes, and the rest of them watch without rest.

SERVANT Martirio too . . . ?

PONCIA That one's the worst. She's a pool of poison. She sees El Romano is not for her, and she'd sink the world if it were in her hand to do so.

SERVANT How bad they all are!

PONCIA They're women without men, that's all. And in such matters even blood is forgotten. Sh-h-h-h!

She listens.

SERVANT What's the matter?

PONCIA (*she rises*) The dogs are barking.

SERVANT Someone must have passed by the back door.

Adela enters wearing a white petticoat and corselet.

PONCIA   Aren't you in bed yet?

ADELA   I want a drink of water.

She drinks from a glass on the table.

PONCIA   I imagined you were asleep.

ADELA   I got thirsty and woke up. Aren't you two going to get some rest?

SERVANT   Soon now.

Adela goes out.

PONCIA   Let's go.

SERVANT   We've certainly earned some sleep. Bernarda doesn't let me rest the whole day.

PONCIA   Take the light.

SERVANT   The dogs are going mad.

PONCIA   They're not going to let us sleep.

They go out. The stage is left almost dark. Maria Josefa enters with a lamb in her arms.

MARIA JOSEFA (*singing*)

> Little lamb, child of mine,
> Let's go to the shore of the sea,
> The tiny ant will be at his doorway,
> I'll nurse you and give you your bread.
> Bernarda, old leopard-face,
> And Magdalena, hyena-face,
> Little lamb . . .
> Rock, rock-a-bye,
> Let's go to the palms at Bethlehem's gate.

She laughs.

> Neither you nor I would want to sleep
> The door will open by itself
> And on the beach we'll go and hide
> In a little coral cabin.
> Bernarda, old leopard-face,
> And Magdalena, hyena-face,
> Little lamb . . .
> Rock, rock-a-bye,
> Let's go to the palms at Bethlehem's gate.

She goes off singing.

Adela enters. She looks about cautiously and disappears out the door leading to the corral. Martirio enters by another door and stands in anguished watchfulness near the center of the stage. She also is in petticoats. She covers herself with a small black scarf. Maria Josefa crosses before her.

MARTIRIO Grandmother, where are you going?

MARIA JOSEFA You are going to open the door for me? Who are you?

MARTIRIO How did you get out here?

MARIA JOSEFA I escaped. You, who are you?

MARTIRIO Go back to bed.

MARIA JOSEFA You're Martirio. Now I see you. Martirio, face of a martyr. And when are you going to have a baby? I've had this one.

MARTIRIO Where did you get that lamb?

MARIA JOSEFA I know it's a lamb. But can't a lamb be a baby? It's better to have a lamb than not to have anything. Old Bernarda, leopard-face, and Magdalena, hyena-face!

MARTIRIO Don't shout.

MARIA JOSEFA It's true. Everything's very dark. Just because I have white hair you think I can't have babies, but I can—babies and babies and babies. This baby will have white hair, and I'd have *this* baby, and another, and this *one* other; and with all of us with snow white hair we'll be like the waves—one, then another, and another. Then we'll all sit down and all of us will have white heads, and we'll be seafoam. Why isn't there any seafoam here? Nothing but mourning shrouds here.

MARTIRIO Hush, hush.

MARIA JOSEFA When my neighbor had a baby, I'd carry her some chocolate and later she'd bring me some, and so on—always and always and always. You'll have white hair, but your neighbors won't come. Now I have to go away, but I'm afraid the dogs will bite me. Won't you come with me as far as the fields? I don't like fields. I like houses, but open houses, and the neighbor women asleep in their beds with their little tiny tots, and the men outside sitting in their chairs. Pepe el Romano is a giant. All of you love him. But

he's going to devour you because you're grains of wheat. No,
not grains of wheat. Frogs with no tongues!

MARTIRIO (*angrily*) Come, off to bed with you.

She pushes her.

MARIA JOSEFA Yes, but then you'll open the door for me,
won't you?

MARTIRIO Of course.

MARIA JOSEFA (*weeping*)

> Little lamb, child of mine,
> Let's go to the shore of the sea,
> The tiny ant will be at his doorway,
> I'll nurse you and give you your bread.

*Martirio locks the door through which Maria Josefa came out and
goes to the yard door. There she hesitates, but goes two steps farther.*

MARTIRIO (*in a low voice*) Adela!

Pause. She advances to the door. Then, calling.

Adela!

Adela enters. Her hair is disarranged.

ADELA And what are you looking for me for?

MARTIRIO Keep away from him.

ADELA Who are you to tell me that?

MARTIRIO That's no place for a decent woman.

ADELA How you wish *you'd* been there!

MARTIRIO (*shouting*) This is the moment for me to speak. This
can't go on.

ADELA This is just the beginning. I've had strength enough to
push myself forward—the spirit and looks you lack. I've
seen death under this roof, and gone out to look for what
was mine, what belonged to me.

MARTIRIO That soulless man came for another woman. You
pushed yourself in front of him.

ADELA He came for the money, but his eyes were always on
me.

MARTIRIO I won't allow you to snatch him away. He'll marry
Angustias.

ADELA   You know better than I he doesn't love her.

MARTIRIO   I know.

ADELA   You know because you've seen—he loves me, me!

MARTIRIO (*desperately*)   Yes.

ADELA (*close before her*)   He loves me, *me!* He loves me, *me!*

MARTIRIO   Stick me with a knife if you like, but don't tell me that again.

ADELA   That's why you're trying to fix it so I won't go away with him. It makes no difference to you if he puts his arms around a woman he doesn't love. Nor does it to me. He could be a hundred years with Angustias, but for him to have his arms around me seems terrible to you—because you too love him! You love him!

MARTIRIO (*dramatically*)   Yes! Let me say it without hiding my head. Yes! My breast's bitter, bursting like a pomegranate. I love him!

ADELA (*impulsively, hugging her*)   Martirio, Martirio, I'm not to blame!

MARTIRIO   Don't put your arms around me! Don't try to smooth it over. My blood's no longer yours, and even though I try to think of you as a sister, I see you as just another woman.

She pushes her away.

ADELA   There's no way out here. Whoever has to drown—let her drown. Pepe is mine. He'll carry me to the rushes along the river bank. . . .

MARTIRIO   He won't!

ADELA   I can't stand this horrible house after the taste of his mouth. I'll be what he wants me to be. Everybody in the village against me, burning me with their fiery fingers; pursued by those who claim they're decent, and I'll wear, before them all, the crown of thorns that belongs to the mistress of a married man.

MARTIRIO   Hush!

ADELA   Yes, yes.

In a low voice.

Let's go to bed. Let's let him marry Angustias. I don't care any more, but I'll go off alone to a little house where he'll come to see me whenever he wants, whenever he feels like it.

MARTIRIO   That'll never happen! Not while I have a drop of blood left in my body.

ADELA   Not just weak you, but a wild horse I could force to his knees with just the strength of my little finger.

MARTIRIO   Don't raise that voice of yours to me. It irritates me. I have a heart full of a force so evil that, without my wanting to be, I'm drowned by it.

ADELA   You show us the way to love our sisters. God must have meant to leave me alone in the midst of darkness, because I can see you as I've never seen you before.

A whistle is heard and Adela runs toward the door, but Martirio gets in front of her.

MARTIRIO   Where are you going?

ADELA   Get away from that door!

MARTIRIO   Get by me if you can!

ADELA   Get away!

They struggle.

MARTIRIO (*shouts*)   Mother! Mother!

ADELA   Let me go!

Bernarda enters. She wears petticoats and a black shawl.

BERNARDA   Quiet! Quiet! How poor I am without even a man to help me!

MARTIRIO (*pointing to Adela*)   She was with him. Look at those skirts covered with straw!

BERNARDA (*going furiously toward Adela*)   That's the bed of a bad woman!

ADELA (*facing her*)   There'll be an end to prison voices here!

Adela snatches away her mother's cane and breaks it in two.

This is what I do with the tyrant's cane. Not another step. No one but Pepe commands me!

Magdalena enters.

MAGDALENA   Adela!

La Poncia and Angustias enter.

ADELA   I'm his.

To Angustias.

Know that—and go out in the yard and tell him. He'll be master in this house.

ANGUSTIAS My God!

BERNARDA The gun! Where's the gun?

She rushes out. La Poncia runs ahead of her. Amelia enters and looks on frightened, leaning her head against the wall. Behind her comes Martirio.

ADELA No one can hold me back!

She tries to go out.

ANGUSTIAS (*holding her*) You're not getting out of here with your body's triumph! Thief! Disgrace of this house!

MAGDALENA Let her go where we'll never see her again!

A shot is heard.

BERNARDA (*entering*) Just try looking for him now!

MARTIRIO (*entering*) That does away with Pepe el Romano.

ADELA Pepe! My God! Pepe!

She runs out.

PONCIA Did you kill him?

MARTIRIO No. He raced away on his mare!

BERNARDA It was my fault. A woman can't aim.

MAGDALENA Then, why did you say . . . ?

MARTIRIO For her! I'd like to pour a river of blood over her head!

PONCIA Curse you!

MAGDALENA Devil!

BERNARDA Although it's better this way!

A thud is heard.

Adela! Adela!

PONCIA (*at her door*) Open this door!

BERNARDA Open! Don't think the walls will hide your shame!

SERVANT (*entering*) All the neighbors are up!

BERNARDA (*in a low voice, but like a roar*) Open! Or I'll knock the door down!

Pause. Everything is silent.

Adela!

She walks away from the door.

A hammer!

La Poncia throws herself against the door. It opens and she goes in. As she enters, she screams and backs out.

What is it?

PONCIA (*she puts her hands to her throat*)   May we never die like that!

The Sisters fall back. The Servant crosses herself. Bernarda screams and goes forward.

Don't go in!

BERNARDA   No, not I! Pepe, you're running now, alive, in the darkness, under the trees, but another day you'll fall. Cut her down! My daughter died a virgin. Take her to another room and dress her as though she were a virgin. No one will say anything about this! She died a virgin. Tell them, so that at dawn, the bells will ring twice.

MARTIRIO   A thousand times happy she, who had him.

BERNARDA   And I want no weeping. Death must be looked at face to face. Silence!

To one daughter.

Be still, I said!

To another daughter.

Tears when you're alone! We'll drown ourselves in a sea of mourning. She, the youngest daughter of Bernarda Alba, died a virgin. Did you hear me? Silence, silence, I said. Silence!

Athaliah   (1691)*

Jean Racine   (*1639-1699*)

Based on the Bible (Kings IV, ix and Chronicles I, xxiii
and Chronicles II, xxiii), *Athaliah* shows the last attempts by its
aged namesake, daughter of the infamous Jezebel, to shore up
her power in the ninth-century Kingdom of Judah. She had
ordered all her own progeny slaughtered, but was unaware
that the High Priest, Joad, had preserved her grandchild, Joas
(aged nine in the time of the play), from the knife. Though
Racine insists here, as in all of his plays, on his fidelity to his
sources, he elaborates on the Biblical *données* to create powerful
portraits not only of the principals but of the secondary
characters as well.

Written during the playwright's semi-retirement from the
theater, undertaken more than a decade earlier just after his
"profane" masterpiece, *Phèdre* (1677), this play, like his other
"sacred" play, *Esther* (1689), was intended as an exemplary
dramatic exercise for the young women at the convent of
Saint-Cyr. *Athaliah* was, in fact, first produced at the convent
(three performances, early 1691) with music by Jean-Baptiste
Moreau and with the young women of the convent playing the
parts in an excessively simple staging. The enclosure of the
convent thus corresponded perfectly to the informing struc-
tural and symbolic motif of the action.

ATHALIAH
Jean Racine

TRANSLATED FROM THE FRENCH
BY KENNETH MUIR

Author's Preface

Everyone knows that the kingdom of Judah was composed of the two tribes of Judah and Benjamin, and that the other ten tribes who rebelled against Rehoboam composed the kingdom of Israel. As the kings of Judah were of the house of David, and as they had in their territory the town and Temple of Jerusalem, all the priests and Levites settled near them and remained attached to them: for, since the building of Solomon's Temple, it was not permitted to sacrifice elsewhere; and all those other altars which were erected to God on the mountains, called in the Scriptures for that reason the high places, were not agreeable to Him. So the legitimate cult existed no longer except in Judah. The ten tribes, except for a very few people, were either idolaters or schismatics.

Yet these priests and Levites were themselves a very numerous tribe. They were divided into different classes to serve in turn in the Temple, from one sabbath to another. The priests were of the family of Aaron; and only those of this family could perform the office of sacrificer. The Levites were subordinate to them, and had the task, among other things, of singing, of the preparation of the victims, and of guarding the Temple. This name of Levite is sometimes given indifferently to all those of the tribe. Those who were on their weekly turn of duty had, together with the High Priest, their lodging in the porches or galleries with which the Temple was surrounded, and which were a part of the Temple itself. All the building was called in general the holy place; but that part of the inner temple where the golden candlestick, the altar of the incense, and the tables of the shewbread were, was called more particularly by that name; and that part was again distinguished from the Holy of Holies, where the Ark was, and where the High Priest alone had the right to enter once a year. There was a tradition, almost without a break, that the mountain on which the Temple was built was the same mountain where Abraham had once offered his son Isaac in sacrifice.

I thought I should explain these details, so that those to whom the story of the Old Testament is not familiar will not be held up in reading this tragedy. Its subject is Joas recognized and placed on the throne; and according to the rules I should have entitled it *Joas*; but most people having heard of it only under the name of *Athaliah*, I have not thought it proper to offer it to them under another title, since in addition Athaliah plays so considerable a part in it, and since it is her death which concludes the play. She is a party to the principal events which precede this great action.

Joram,[1] King of Judah, son of Jehoshaphat, and the seventh king of the race of David, married Athaliah, daughter of Ahab and Jezebel, who reigned in Israel, both famous, but especially Jezebel, for their bloody persecutions of the prophets. Athaliah, not less impious than her mother, soon drew the King, her husband, into idolatry, and even had a temple built in Jerusalem to Baal, who was the god of the country of Tyre and Sidon, where Jezebel was born. Joram, after having seen perish by the hands of Arabs and Philistines all the princes, his children, except Ahaziah, died himself of a long malady which burnt up his entrails. His dreadful death did not prevent Ahaziah from imitating his impiety and that of Athaliah, his mother. But this prince, after reigning for only a year, while on a visit to the King of Israel, brother of Athaliah, was enveloped in the ruin of the house of Ahab, and killed by the orders of Jehu, whom God had anointed to reign over Israel and to be the minister of his vengeance. Jehu exterminated all the posterity of Ahab and caused Jezebel to be thrown from the window, who, according to the prophecy of Elijah, was eaten by the dogs in the vineyard of the same Naboth who had

1. Jehoram in the King James Bible.

been slain formerly so as to deprive him of his inheritance. Athaliah, having learned of all these massacres at Jerusalem, undertook on her part to extinguish completely the royal race of David, by causing to be slain all the children of Ahaziah, her own grandsons. But luckily Josabeth, sister of Ahaziah and daughter of Joram, but a different sort of mother from Athaliah, arriving during the massacres of the princes, her nephews, found means to snatch from the midst of the dead the infant Joas, still at the breast, and entrusted him with his nurse to the care of the High Priest, her husband, who hid them both in the Temple, where the child was brought up secretly till the day he was proclaimed King of Judah. The Book of Kings says that this was seven years afterwards. But the Greek text of Chronicles, which Severus Sulpicius has followed, says it was eight. It is this which authorizes me to make the prince nine or ten, to make him old enough to reply to the questions put to him.

I believe I have made him say nothing beyond the capacity of a child of this age with a good intelligence and memory. But even if I have, it must be considered that this is a quite exceptional child, brought up in the Temple by a High Priest who, looking on him as the unique hope of his nation, has instructed him from an early age in all the duties of religion and royalty. It was not the same with the children of the Jews as with most of ours: they were taught the sacred writings, not merely before they had attained the use of reason, but, to use Saint Paul's expression, from the breast. Every Jew was obliged to write once in his life, with his own hand, the whole book of the Law. The kings were even obliged to write it twice, and enjoined to have it continually before their eyes. I can say here that France sees in the person of a prince of eight and a half years, who delights us even now, an illustrious example of what a child, of natural ability aided by an excellent education, can do; and that if I had given to the child Joas the same vivacity and the same discernment which shines in the repartees of this young prince, I should have been accused with reason of having transgressed the rules of verisimilitude.

The age of Zachariah, son of the High Priest, not having been mentioned, one can suppose him, if one likes, to be two or three years older than Joas.

I have followed the explanation of several skillful commentators, who prove by the actual text of Scripture, that all the soldiers whom Jehoiada (or Joad, as he is called in Josephus) armed with the weapons consecrated to God by David, were as much priests and Levites as the five centurions who commanded them. Indeed, say the interpreters, everyone had to be holy in so holy an action, and no profane person should be employed. What was at stake was not merely keeping the scepter in the house of David, but also keeping for that great king the line of descendants of whom the Messiah should be born. "For this Messiah promised so many times as the son of Abraham, should also be the son of David and of all the kings of Judah." From this it follows that the illustrious and learned prelate from whom I have borrowed these words calls Joas the precious remnant of the house of David. Josephus speaks of him in the same terms; and Scripture states expressly that God did not exterminate all the family of Joram, wishing to conserve for David the lamp which he had promised him. For what else was this lamp but the light which should one day be revealed to the gentiles?

History does not specify at all the day on which Joas was proclaimed. Some interpreters claim that it was a feast day. I have chosen that of Pentecost, which was one of the three great feasts of the Jews. In it was celebrated the memory of the publication of the Law on Mount Sinai, and in it was also offered to God the first loaves of the new harvest: which made it called still the feast of the first fruits. I thought that these circumstances would furnish me with some variety for the songs of the chorus.

This chorus is composed of maidens of the tribe of Levi, and I have put at their head a girl whom I have given as sister to Zachariah. It is she who introduces the chorus into her mother's house. She sings with them, speaks for them, and performs the functions of the person of the ancient choruses who was called the coryphaeus. I have also tried to imitate from the ancients that continuity of action which makes their stage never left empty, the intervals between the acts being marked by the hymns and moralizing of the chorus, who are in touch with all that passes.

I shall perhaps be found a little audacious in having dared to put on the stage a prophet inspired by God, who predicts the future. But I have taken the precaution to put into his mouth only expressions taken from the prophets themselves. Although the Scriptures do not state expressly that Jehoiada had had a spirit of prophecy, as they do of his son, they represent him as a man full of the spirit of God. And besides, would it not appear by the gospel that he would have been able to prophecy in the capacity of sovereign pontiff? I suppose, therefore, that he sees the fatal change of Joas who, after twenty years of a reign of great piety, abandoned himself to the evil counsels of flatterers, and stained himself with the blood of Zachariah, son and successor of the High Priest. This murder, committed in the Temple, was one of the principal causes of the wrath of God against the Jews and of all the misfortunes which happened to them afterwards. It is even maintained that since that day the responses of God ceased entirely in the sanctuary. That has given me the opportunity to make Joad depict the destruction of the Temple and the ruin of Jerusalem. But as the prophets ordinarily joined consolations to their threats, and as also the action was concerned with putting on the throne one of the ancestors of the Messiah, I have taken occasion to give a glimpse of the coming of this comforter, for whom all the righteous men of ancient times sighed. This scene, which is a kind of episode, brings in music very naturally, by the custom which several prophets had of entering into their holy trances to the sound of instruments: witness that troop of prophets who came before Saul with the harps and lyres which were borne before them; and witness Elisha himself, who being consulted on the future by the King of Judah and the King of Israel, said, as Joad does here: *Adducite mihi psaltem.*[2] Add to that, that this prophecy

2. Bring me a harp-player.

serves greatly to augment the tension of the drama, by the consternation it causes and by the different reactions of the chorus and the principal actors.

CHARACTERS

ABNER, *one of Athaliah's principal officers*

JOAD, *High Priest*

JOSABETH, *his wife, aunt to Joas*

ZACHARIAH ⎱ *their children*
SALOMITH ⎰

AGAR, *woman of Athaliah's suite*

MATHAN, *priest of Baal*

ATHALIAH, *widow of Joram*

JOAS, *her grandson, the rightful King, called Eliacin*

NABAL, *confidant of Mathan*

AZARIAS, ISMAEL, *and other* LEVITES

NURSE *of Joas*

ATHALIAH'S GUARDS

CHORUS *of girls of the Tribe of Levi*

SCENE—*The Temple of Jerusalem, in a vestibule of the apartment of the High Priest*

ACT ONE

Scene 1

Abner and Joad discovered.

ABNER   Yes, I have come into this Temple now
To adore the Everlasting; I have come,
According to our old and solemn custom,
To celebrate with you the famous day
When on Mount Sinai the Law was given us.
How times have changed! As soon as the trumpet blast
Proclaimed the day's return, the chosen people
Poured into the sacred porticos in crowds,
And in the Temple, garlanded with flowers,
They stood before the altar rank by rank,
And to the God of the universe they offered
The first fruits of their fields. The sacrifices
By priests alone were not sufficient then.
A woman's presumption now has put a stop

To that great concourse; and to days of darkness
Has changed those happy days. Only a handful
Of zealous worshippers enable us
To trace a shadow of those former times;
While for their God the rest of them display
Fatal forgetfulness. They even flock
To Baal's altars, there to be initated
Into his shameful mysteries, and blaspheme
The name their sires invoked. I tremble now
That Athaliah—I will hide nothing from you—
Has not yet perfected her dire revenge.
She plans to snatch you from the altar, and . . .

JOAD   Whence comes this black presentiment of yours?

ABNER   Do you imagine that you can be just
And holy with impunity? For long
She has detested that rare constancy
Which gives a double glory to your crown;
For long she's looked on your religious zeal
As rank sedition; and this jealous queen
Hates above all the faithful Josabeth,
Your wife, even for her virtues. If you are
Aaron's successor, Josabeth's the sister
Of our last king. Mathan, moreover, Mathan,
That sacrilegious priest, who is more vile
Than Athaliah herself, at every hour
Besieges her—Mathan, the foul deserter
From the Lord's altars, ever the zealous foe
Of every virtue. 'Tis little that this Levite,
His brows encircled with an alien miter,
Now ministers to Baal: to him this Temple
Is a reproach, and his impiety
Would bring to nought the God that he has left.
There are no means to which he'll not resort
To ruin you; at times he'll pity you
And often he will even sing your praises;
Affecting for you a false tenderness,
And screening so the blackness of his rancor,
He paints you to the Queen as terrible;
Or else, insatiable for gold, he feigns
That in some place that's known to you alone
You hide King David's treasure. But Athaliah

Has seemed for two days to be plunged in gloom.
I watched her yesterday, and saw her eyes
Dart furious glances on the holy place,
As if within this mighty edifice
God hid an avenger, armed for her destruction.
Believe me, Joad, the more I think of it,
The more I am convinced her wrath is ready
To burst upon you, that the bloody daughter
Of Jezebel will soon attack our God,
Even in His sanctuary.

JOAD   He who can bridle
The fury of the waves knows how to foil
The plots of the wicked. Submissive to His will,
I fear the Lord, and have no other fear.
Yet, Abner, I am grateful for the zeal
Which has awakened you to all my perils.
I see injustice vexes you in secret;
That you are still an Israelite at heart.
Heaven be praised! But can you be content
With secret wrath and with an idle virtue?
And can the faith that acts not be sincere?
Eight years ago an impious foreigner
Usurped all the rights of David's scepter,
And with impunity imbrued herself
In the blood of our true kings—foul murderess
Of the children of her son, and even against God
Her treacherous arm is raised:
While you a pillar of this tottering State,
Brought up within the camps of Jehoshaphat,
That holy king, and under his son, Joram,
Commander of his hosts, who reassured
Our fearful towns when Ahaziah was slain,
And all his army at the sight of Jehu
Scattered in panic—"I fear the Lord," you say;
"His truth concerns me." By me that God replies:
"For what use is the zeal that you profess?
Think'st thou to honor me with barren vows?
What do I get from all your sacrifices?
Do I require the blood of goats and heifers?
The blood of your kings cries out and is not heard.
Break off all compact with impiety!

Root out the evil from among my people
And then approach me with your burnt offerings."

ABNER   What can I do among this beaten people?
Judah and Benjamin are powerless now:
The day that saw their race of kings extinguished
Extinguished too their ancient bravery.
God, they say, has withdrawn Himself from us:
He, who was jealous of the Hebrews' honor,
Now, careless, sees their greatness overthrown,
And in the end His mercy is exhausted.
The countless miracles He worked for us
To terrify mankind are seen no more.
The holy Ark is dumb, and renders now
Its oracles no longer.

JOAD   And what time
Was e'er so fertile in its miracles?
When has God shown His power to such effect?
Will you forever, O ungrateful people,
Have eyes which see not? Will great miracles
Forever strike your ears, but leave your heart
Untouched? Abner, must I recall the course
Of prodigies accomplished in our days?
The woes that fell on Israel's tyrants—God
Found faithful in his threats! The impious Ahab
Destroyed, and that field sprinkled with his blood,
Which he usurped by murder; and nearby
Jezebel slain and trampled by the horses,
So that the dogs lapped up her savage blood
And tore her frightful body limb from limb;
The troop of lying prophets all confounded,
And fire from heaven descended on the altar;
Elijah speaking to the elements
As sovereign master; the skies by him locked up
And turned to brass, so that the earth three years
Had neither rain nor dew; at Elisha's voice
The dead reanimated? Recognize,
Abner, in these deeds that still resound,
A God who is indeed the same today
As in the days of old. He manifests
His glory when He wills; His chosen people
Is always present to His memory.

ABNER   But where are those honors oft to David promised,
 And prophecied for Solomon, his son?
 Alas! we hoped that of their happy race
 There would descend a line of kings, of whom
 One would at last establish his dominion
 Over all tribes and nations, who would make
 Discord and war to cease, and at his feet
 Behold all kings of the earth.
JOAD   Wherefore renounce
 The promises of heaven?
ABNER   Where shall we find
 The royal son of David? Can heaven itself
 Repair the ruins of this tree that's withered
 Even to the very roots? For Athaliah
 Stifled the child in his cradle. Can the dead,
 Now eight years have gone by, come from the grave?
 If in her rage she had mistook her aim,
 If of our royal blood there had escaped
 One drop to . . .
JOAD   Well, what would you do?
ABNER   O joyous day for me! How ardently
 I'd recognize my king. You need not doubt
 The tribes would hasten at his feet to lay
 Their tribute. But why delude myself
 With such vain thoughts? The lamentable heir
 Of those triumphant monarchs, Ahaziah
 Alone remained—he and his children only.
 I saw the father stabbed by Jehu; you
 Beheld the sons all butchered by the mother.
JOAD   I'll not explain; but when the star of day
 Has traced a third of its course across the sky,
 And when the third hour summons us to prayer,
 Return to the Temple with the selfsame zeal,
 And God may show, by signal benefits,
 His word is firm, and never can deceive.
 Go now, I must prepare for this great day,
 And even now the pinnacle of the Temple
 Is whitened by the dawn.
ABNER   What will this be—
 This blessing that I cannot comprehend?
 The noble Josabeth is coming towards you.

I'll join the faithful flock the solemn rite
Of this day has attracted.

Exit Abner.

Scene 2

Enter Josabeth.

JOAD   The time is ripe,
Princess, and we must speak. Your happy theft
No longer can be hidden. The insolence
Of the Lord's foes who take His name in vain
From this deep silence has accused too long
His promises of error. What do I say?
Success has fanned their fury; and on our altar
Your evil stepmother would offer Baal
Idolatrous incense. Let us show this king—
The boy your hands have saved, to be brought up
Beneath the Lord's protecting wing. He'll have
Our Hebrew princes' courage, and already
His mind's outstripped his age. Before I speak
Of his high destiny, I'll offer him
To the God by whom kings reign, and soon before
The assembled priests and Levites, I'll declare
Their master's heir.

JOSABETH   Has he himself been told
Of his real name and noble destiny?

JOAD   Not yet. He answers only to the name
Of Eliacin, and thinks he is a child
Abandoned by his mother, to whom I deigned
To act as father.

JOSABETH   Alas! from what dire peril
I rescued him, and into what more peril
Is he about to enter!

JOAD   Is your faith
Already wavering?

JOSABETH   To your wise advice,
My lord, I do submit. For from the day
I snatched this child from death, into your hands

His life and fate were placed. I even feared
The violence of my love; and therefore tried
To shun his presence, lest in seeing him,
My tears for some grief not to be suppressed
Would let my secret out. To tears and prayers
I've consecrated three whole days and nights,
As duty bid; but may I ask today
What friends you have prepared to give you aid?
Will Abner, the brave Abner, fight for us?
And has he sworn that he'll be near his king?

JOAD Although his faith is sure, he does not yet
Know that we have a king.

JOSABETH   To whom will you
Entrust the guard of Joas? Obed or Amnon?
My father showered his benefits upon them. . . .

JOAD They're sold to Athaliah.

JOSABETH   Whom have you then
To oppose her satellites?

JOAD   Have I not told you?
Our priests, our Levites.

JOSABETH   I know indeed
That by your foresight secretly assembled
Their number is redoubled; that, full of love
For you, and full of hate for Athaliah,
A solemn oath has bound them in advance
To this son of David who will be revealed.
But though a noble ardor burns in them,
Can they alone their king's cause vindicate?
Can zeal alone for such a work suffice?
Do you doubt that Athaliah—when first 'tis bruited
That Ahaziah's son is cloistered here—
Will mass her foreign cohorts, to surround
The Temple and break in the doors. 'Gainst them
Will these your holy ministers suffice,
Who lifting innocent hands unto the Lord
Can only weep and pray for all our sins,
And ne'er shed blood, save of the sacrifice?
Joas, perhaps, pierced through with hostile spears,
Will in their arms . . .

JOAD   Is God who fights for us
By you accounted nothing? God who protects

The orphan's innocence, and makes his power
Displayed in weakness; God who hates the tyrant;
Who in Jezreel did vow to extirpate
Ahab and Jezebel; God, who striking Joram,
Their son-in-law, pursued the family,
Even to his son; God, whose avenging arm,
Suspended for a time, is still outstretched
Over this impious race?

JOSABETH   And His stern justice
Meted to all these kings is cause for me
To fear for my unlucky brother's son,
For who can tell, if by their crime enmeshed,
This child from birth was not condemned with them?
If God, for David's sake, dividing him
From all that odious race would grant him favor?
Alas! the horrible scene when heaven offered
The child to me again and again returns
To terrify my soul. The room was filled
With murdered princes. Relentless Athaliah,
A dagger in her hand, urged to the kill
Her barbarous soldiers, and pursued the course
Of all her murders. Joas, left for dead,
Suddenly struck my eyes; and even now
I see his frightened nurse throwing herself
In vain before his butchers, holding him
Head downwards on her breast. I took him, steeped
In blood. I bathed his face in tears. And then
I felt his innocent arms go round my neck,
In fear, or to caress me. O great God!
Let not my love be fatal to him now—
This precious relic of the faithful David
Here in thy house nourished upon the love
Of thy great Law. He knows as yet no father
Save Thee alone. Though in the face of peril,
When we're about to attack a murderous queen,
My faith begins to waver, though flesh and blood,
Faltering today, have some part in the tears
I shed for him, preserve the heritage
Of Thy sacred promises, and do not punish
Any save me for all my weaknesses.

JOAD   Your tears are guiltless, Josabeth; but God

Wills us to hope in his paternal care.
He is not wont to visit in his rage
The impiety of the father on the son
Who fears him. The faithful remnant of the Jews
Come to renew their vows to him today.
Even as David's race is still respected,
So is the daughter of Jezebel detested.
Joas will touch them with his innocence
In which the splendor of his blood reshines;
And God by His voice upholding our example
Will speak unto their hearts. Two faithless kings
Successively have braved Him. To the throne
A king must now be raised who'll not forget
God, by his priests, has placed him in the rank
Of his great ancestors, by their hand snatched him
From the tomb's oblivion, and lit again
The torch of David. Great God, if Thou foreseest
He'll be unworthy of his race, and leave
The ways of David, let him be as the fruit
Torn from the branch, or withered in its flower
By a hostile wind! But if this child should prove
Docile to Thy commands, an instrument
Useful to Thy designs, then hand the scepter
To the rightful heir; deliver into my hands
His powerful enemies; frustrate the counsels
Of this cruel queen; and grant, O grant, my God,
That upon her and Mathan shall be poured
Error and rashness, of the fall of kings
Fatal vaunt-courier! The time is short.
Farewell! Your son and daughter bring you now
The damsels of the holiest families.

Exit Joad.

Scene 3

Enter Zachariah, Salomith, and Chorus.
JOSABETH   Dear Zachariah, go now. Do not stop.
   Accompany your noble father's steps. (*Exit Zachariah.*)

Daughters of Levi, young and faithful flock,
Kindled already by the zeal of the Lord,
Who come so often all my sighs to share,
Children, my only joy in my long sorrows,
These garlands and these flowers upon your heads
Once suited with our solemn festivals;
But now, alas, in times of shame and sorrow,
What offering suits better than our tears?
I hear already, I hear the sacred trumpet;
The Temple soon will open. While I prepare,
Sing, praise the Lord whom you have come to seek.

Exeunt Josabeth and Salomith.

Scene 4

ALL THE CHORUS   All the universe is full of His glory!
Let us adore this God, and call upon Him!
His Empire was before the birth of Time!
O let us sing, his benefits to praise!
A VOICE   In vain unrighteous violence
Upon his worshippers imposeth silence:
His name will live always.
Day telleth day of His magnificence.
All the universe is full of His glory:
O let us sing, His benefits to praise.
ALL   All the universe is full of His glory:
O let us sing, His benefits to praise.
A VOICE   He gives unto the flowers their lovely hues,
He slowly ripens fruits upon the tree,
And gives them warmth by day and nightly dews;
The field repays his gifts with usury.
ANOTHER   The sun all nature doth reanimate
At His command; He gives the blessed light;
But His best gift to those He did create
Is still His holy Law, our pure delight.
ANOTHER   O Sinai, preserve the memory
Renowned forevermore of that great day
When from a thick cloud on thy flaming peak

The Lord made shine to mortal eyes a ray
Of His eternal glory! Why those flames,
The lightning flash, the eddying clouds of smoke,
Trumpets and thunder in the resounding air?
Came He to overturn the elemental order,
And shake the earth upon its ancient base?

ANOTHER   No, no, He came to reveal the eternal light
Of His holy laws to the children of the Jews;
He came to that happy people, to command them
To love Him with an everlasting love.

ALL   Divine and lovely Law,
O bounteous and just!
How right, how sweet to pledge
To God our love and trust!

A VOICE   He freed our fathers from the tyrant's yoke;
Fed them on manna in the wilderness;
He gives His laws, He gives Himself to us:
And for these blessings asks for love alone.

ALL   O bounteous and just!

A VOICE   For them He cleft the waters of the sea;
He made streams gush out from the arid rock.
He gives His laws, He gives Himself to us,
And for these blessings asks for love alone.

CHORUS   Divine and lovely Law!
How right, how sweet to pledge
To God our love and trust!

A VOICE   Ingrates, who only know a servile fear,
Cannot a God so gracious touch your heart?
Is love so stony and so hard a path?
It is the slave who fears the tyrant's wrath,
But filial love remains the children's part.
You wish this God to shower His gifts on you,
And never give the love that is His due.

CHORUS   Divine and lovely Law!
O bounteous and just!
How right, how sweet to pledge
To God our love and trust.

ACT TWO

Scene 1

Josabeth, Salomith, and Chorus.

JOSABETH   Enough, my daughters. Cease your canticles.
'Tis time to join us now in public prayers.
The hour is come. Let's celebrate this day
And appear before the Lord. But what do I see?

Scene 2

Enter Zachariah.

JOSABETH   My son, what brings you here? Where do you run,
All pale and out of breath?
ZACHARIAH   O Mother . . .
JOSABETH   Well?
What is it?
ZACHARIAH   The Temple is profaned. . . .
JOSABETH   How?
ZACHARIAH   The altar of the Lord abandoned!
JOSABETH   I tremble.
Hasten to tell me all.
ZACHARIAH   Even now my father,
The High Priest, had offered, according to the Law,
The first loaves of the harvest to our God
Who feeds us all. And then he held aloft
The smoking entrails of the sacrifice
In bloodstained hands, while young Eliacin,
Like me, stood by his side and ministered,
Clad in a linen robe, and while the priests
Sprinkled the altar and the congregation
With blood of the offerings—suddenly there was
A noise which made the people turn their eyes.
A woman . . . Can I name her without blasphemy?
A woman . . . It was Athaliah herself.
JOSABETH   Great heaven!

ZACHARIAH   Into a sanctuary reserved for men
  Entered that haughty woman, head held high,
  And made to pass into the holy precincts
  Open to Levites only. Struck with terror
  The people fled away. My father— Ah! what wrath
  Shone in his countenance, more terrible
  Than Moses before Pharaoh. "Queen," he said
  "Go from this holy place, from whence thy sex
  And thy impiety alike are banished.
  Com'st thou indeed to brave the majesty
  Of the living God?" Forthwith the Queen, upon him
  Turning a fierce glance, opened her mouth to speak,
  And doubtless to blaspheme. I know not whether
  The Angel of the Lord appeared to her
  Bearing a flaming sword; but this I know—
  Her tongue was frozen in her mouth, and all
  Her boldness seemed to crumble; while her eyes,
  Affrighted, dared not turn away. She seemed
  Amazed by Eliacin.

JOSABETH   How so? Did he
  Appear before her?

ZACHARIAH   Both of us beheld
  This cruel queen, and with an equal dread
  Our hearts were struck. But soon the priests stood round us,
  And led us forth. And that is all I know
  Of this ominous disorder.

JOSABETH   Ah! from our arms
  She comes to snatch him; and 'tis he her fury
  Seeks even at the altar. Perhaps even now
  The object of so many tears . . . O! God,
  Who seest my fears, remember David now.

SALOMITH   For whom do you weep?

ZACHARIAH   Is Eliacin's life
  In danger now?

SALOMITH   Could he have attracted
  The anger of the Queen?

ZACHARIAH   How could they fear
  A child without defense, and fatherless?

JOSABETH   She's here. Come, let us go. We must avoid her.

  Exeunt.

Scene 3

Enter Athaliah, Abner, Agar, and Guards.

AGAR   Your Majesty, why do you stay within
These precincts, where all objects vex and wound you?
O leave this Temple to the priests who dwell
Within its walls. Flee all this tumult now,
And in your palace strive to give back peace
To your o'ertroubled senses.

ATHALIAH   No. I cannot.
You see my weakness and disquiet. Go,
Send Mathan hither: let him come with speed. . . .
Happy if I by his aid can obtain
The peace I seek, which still eludes my grasp.

Exit Agar. Athaliah sits.

Scene 4

ABNER   Forgive me, madam, if I dare defend
The zeal of Joad, which should not surprise you.
Such is the eternal order of our God,
For He himself marked out for us His Temple,
To Aaron's children only did entrust
His sacrifices; both their place and functions
Appointed to the Levites; and forbad
To their posterity all intercourse
With any other God. Are you, O Queen,
The daughter and the mother of our kings,
So alien to us? Know you not our laws?
And is it necessary that today . . . ?
But here is Mathan. I will leave you with him.

ATHALIAH   I need your presence, Abner. Leave at that
The reckless insolence of Joad, and all
That empty heap of superstitions
Which bars your Temple to all other peoples.
Something more urgent has aroused my fears.

I know that Abner, raised from infancy
To be a soldier, has a noble heart;
And that he renders what he owes to God,
And renders what he owes unto his kings.
Remain with us.

Scene 5

Enter Mathan.

MATHAN   Great Queen, is here your place?
What has disquieted you? What terror now
Turned you to ice? What have you come to seek
Among your enemies? Do you dare approach
This impious Temple? Have you shed your hatred?

ATHALIAH   Both of you lend me an attentive ear.
I do not wish here to recall the past,
Nor give you reasons for the blood I've shed.
What I have done I thought was necessary.
Abner, I'll not accept a headstrong people
To be my judge. Whatever their insolence
Has dared to claim, I have been justified
By heaven itself. My power that is established
On my successful deeds has made the name
Of Athaliah held in great respect
From sea to sea. By me Jerusalem
Enjoys an absolute peace. The Jordan sees
No more the wandering Arab, and no more
The haughty Philistine with endless raids
(As in your kings' days) desolate her banks.
The Syrian treats me as a queen and sister:
At last the vile oppressor of my house,
Whose savagery I myself have felt,
Jehu, proud Jehu, trembles in Samaria,
On every side hemmed in by neighboring powers
Which I have raised against that murderer.
In these domains he leaves me sovereign mistress.
I now enjoy in peace my wisdom's fruits.
But yet, for some days past, a nagging fear
Has stopped the course of my prosperity.

A dream (why should a dream disturb me so?)
Brought to my heart a gnawing pain. I tried
To escape, but everywhere it followed me:
Methought that in the dreadful deep of night
My mother Jezebel rose up before me,
All gorgeously arrayed as when she died.
Her sorrows had not quenched her pride, but still
Her face was decked and painted to repair
The irreparable ravages of time.
"Tremble, my daughter, worthy of me," she said;
"The cruel God of the Jews will soon prevail
Over you also, and I mourn that you
Are falling into His relentless hands,
My child." In uttering these frightful words,
Her ghost, it seemed, bent down towards my bed;
But when I stretched my hands out to embrace her,
I found instead a horrible heap of bones,
And mangled flesh, and tatters soaked in blood
Dragged through the mire, and limbs unspeakable
For which voracious dogs were wrangling there.

ABNER   Great God!

ATHALIAH   In this confusion there appeared
Before my eyes a child with shining robes,
Like those of the Hebrew priests. On seeing him
My spirits revived, my deadly fear subsided.
But while I wondered at his noble bearing,
His charm and modesty, then all at once
I felt a murderous dagger which the traitor
Plunged deep into my heart. Perhaps you think
This mingling of such diverse images
In my strange dream was but the work of chance.
And I myself, ashamed of my own fear,
Have thought at times they must be the effect
Of some dark vapor. But my soul, possessed
With this remembrance, saw the selfsame sights
Twice visit me in sleep. Twice did my eyes
Behold this child prepare again to stab me,
Until worn down by these pursuing terrors
I went to pray to Baal for his protection,
And seek for peace of mind before his altars.
What cannot panic do to mortal minds?

Urged by a sudden impulse to this Temple
I came instead, thus hoping to appease
The Jewish God, and calm His wrath with gifts.
I thought that God, whoever He may be,
Might become merciful. Pontiff of Baal,
Forgive this strange infirmity of purpose.
I entered; the people fled; the sacrifice ceased.
The High Priest came towards me white with fury.
While he was speaking to me, I beheld—
With terror and astonishment beheld—
The very child of whom I had been warned
By such a fearful dream. I saw him there—
His air, his linen garments, his gait, his eyes,
And all his traits the same. 'Twas he. He walked
Beside the High Priest: but, on seeing me,
They made him disappear; and it is this
That troubles me and brings me to a stop.
It was on this I wished to consult you both.
What, Mathan,
Does this incredible prodigy presage?

MATHAN   Your dream and story fill me with amazement.

ATHALIAH   But, Abner, have you seen this fatal child?
    What is he? Of what blood? And of what tribe?

ABNER   Two children at the altar ministered:
    One is the son of Joad and Josabeth,
    The other I know not.

MATHAN   Why hesitate?
    Of both, madam, you need to be assured.
    You know the moderation and respect
    I have for Joad, that I do not seek
    To avenge my wrongs, that equity alone
    Reigns ever in my counsels. But, after all,
    Would he himself permit a criminal
    To live a moment, were it his own child?

ABNER   Of what crime can a child be capable?

MATHAN   Heaven made us see him brandishing a dagger
    Heaven is wise, and nothing does in vain.
    What more do you seek?

ABNER   But on the evidence
    Of a mere dream, will you imbrue your hands
    In a child's blood? You do not even know

His parentage, or what he is.

MATHAN   We fear him.
That's all we need to know. For if he stems
From famous stock, the splendor of his lot
Should hasten now his ruin; and if fate
Has given him humble birth, what does it matter
If a vile blood at random should be spilt?
Should kings be slow in justice, when their safety
Often depends on speedy punishment?
Let us not hamper them with awkward caution;
For from the moment one is suspect to them,
He's innocent no longer.

ABNER   What! Mathan!
Is this the language of a priest? 'Tis I,
Inured to slaughter in my trade of war,
Stern minister of royal vengeances,
Who lend a voice for the unfortunate child;
While you who owe him a paternal kindness,
You, minister of peace in times of wrath,
Covering resentment with a specious zeal—
Blood flows not fast enough in your opinion.
You have commanded me, O Queen, to speak
Without reserve. What then is the great cause
Of all your fear? A dream, a harmless child
Your eye, forewarned, believed to recognize,
Perhaps mistakenly.

ATHALIAH   I wish to think so.
I well may be mistaken. An empty dream
May too much have obsessed me. Ah, well! I must
See once again this child at closer view,
And at my leisure scrutinize his traits.
Let both appear before me.

ABNER   I am afraid . . .

ATHALIAH   That they will not comply? But what could be
Their reasons for refusal? That would cast me
Into some strange suspicions. Let Josabeth
Or Joad bring them. I can, when I wish,
Speak as a queen. Abner, I must avow
Your priests have every reason to extol
Athaliah's favors. I know that in their preaching
They abuse my power and conduct. Yet they live,

And still their Temple stands. But now I feel
My kindness nears its end. Let Joad bridle
His savage zeal, and not provoke my heart
By a second outrage. Go.

Exit Abner.

Scene 6

MATHAN   Now I can speak
 Freely, and put the truth as clear as day.
 Some newborn monster, Queen, is being raised
 Within this Temple. Wait not for the cloud
 To burst. I know that Abner before daybreak
 Came to the High Priest's house. You know his love
 For the blood of his kings; and who knows if Joad
 Has not some plan to place upon the throne
 This child with whom the heavens have menaced you,
 His own son, or some other?
ATHALIAH   Yes, you open
 My eyes, and clearly I begin to see
 The meaning of this portent. But I wish
 To clear my mind of doubt. A child's unable
 To hide his thoughts, and oft a single word
 Will let us guess at mighty purposes.
 Let me, dear Mathan, see and question him.
 And you meanwhile, without causing alarm,
 Order my Tyrians to take up arms.

Exit Mathan.

Scene 7

Enter Joas, Josabeth, Abner, Chorus, etc.
JOSABETH O servants of the Lord, upon these children,
 So dear, so precious, keep your eyes.
ABNER   Princess,

Assure yourself, I will protect them.

ATHALIAH   O Gods!
The more I scrutinize him . . . It is he!
And all my senses now are seized with horror.
Wife of Joad, is this boy your son?

JOSABETH   Who? He, madam?

ATHALIAH   He.

JOSABETH   I am not his mother.
There is my son.

ATHALIAH   And you, who is your father?
Answer me, child.

JOSABETH   Heaven, until this day . . .

ATHALIAH   Why do you hasten to reply for him?
I speak to him.

JOSABETH   From such a tender age
What information can you hope to get?

ATHALIAH   This age is innocent; his artlessness
Will not pervert the simple truth. Leave him
To answer freely everything I ask.

JOSABETH (*aside*) O put Thy wisdom in his mouth, O Lord!

ATHALIAH   What is your name?

JOAS   Eliacin.

ATHALIAH   Your father?

JOAS   They tell me I'm an orphan, thrown since birth
Upon the arms of God. I never knew
My parents.

ATHALIAH   You have no parents?

JOAS   No:
They abandoned me.

ATHALIAH   Since when?

JOAS   Since I was born.

ATHALIAH   Do you not know, at least, which is your country?

JOAS   This Temple is my country. I know no other.

ATHALIAH   Where did they find you?

JOAS   Among the cruel wolves
Ready to eat me up.

ATHALIAH   Who brought you here?

JOAS   An unknown woman, who did not tell her name
And was not seen again.

ATHALIAH   In your earliest years
Who looked after you?

JOAS   Has God ever left
His children in want? He feeds the tiniest birds;
His bounty stretches to the whole of nature.
I pray to him daily, and with a father's care
He feeds me with the gifts placed on his altar.
ATHALIAH   What new prodigy disturbs me now?
The sweetness of his voice, his childlike ways,
His grace, make to my enmity succeed . . .
Could I be moved by pity?
ABNER   Is this, madam,
Your terrible foe? Your dreams are plainly liars,
Unless your pity is the deadly stroke
Which made you tremble.
ATHALIAH   You're going?
JOSABETH   You've heard his fortunes.
He need intrude no longer on your presence.
ATHALIAH   No. Come back. What do you do each day?
JOAS   I worship the Lord and listen to His Law.
I have been taught to read His holy book,
And I am learning now to copy it.
ATHALIAH   What says this Law?
JOAS   That God demands our love
That He takes vengeance, soon or late, on those
Who take His name in vain; that He defends
The timid orphan; that He resists the proud
And punishes the murderer.
ATHALIAH   I see.
But all the people shut up in this place,
How do they spend their time?
JOAS   They praise and bless
The Lord.
ATHALIAH   Does God exact continual prayer
And worship?
JOAS   Everything profane is banished
Out of His Temple.
ATHALIAH   What are your pleasures then?
JOAS   Sometimes to the High Priest at the altar
I offer salt or incense. I hear songs
Of the infinite greatness of Almighty God;
I see the stately order of His rites.
ATHALIAH   Have you no sweeter pastime? I am sorry

That such a child should lead so sad a life.
Come to my palace! See my glory there!

JOAS   And lose the memory of God's benefits?

ATHALIAH   Why, no. I would not force you to forget them.

JOAS   You do not pray to Him.

ATHALIAH   But you could pray.

JOAS   I should see people pray to other gods.

ATHALIAH   I have my god, and serve him. You would serve
    yours.
There are two powerful gods.

JOAS   Mine must be feared:
He is God alone, madam, and yours is none.

ATHALIAH   Near me you'd find a host of pleasures, boy.

JOAS   The happiness of the wicked passeth away
    Even as a torrent.

ATHALIAH   Who are these wicked?

JOSABETH   Oh, madam,
Excuse a child . . .

ATHALIAH   I like to see your teaching.
So, Eliacin, you please me. You are not
An ordinary child. I am the Queen,
And have no heir. Take off this robe, and leave
This mean employment. I would have you share
In all my riches. From this very day
Make trial of my promises. At my table,
Everywhere, seated at my side, I mean
To treat you as my son.

JOAS   As your son?

ATHALIAH   Yes?
You're silent?

JOAS   What a father I should leave!
And for . . .

ATHALIAH   Well?

JOAS   For what a mother!

ATHALIAH   His memory is faithful; and in all
That he has said I recognize the spirit
Of you and Joad. This is how you use
(Infecting his simple youth) the peace wherein
I leave you; and you cultivate so young
Their hate and fury. You pronounce my name
Only with horror to them.

JOSABETH   Can we conceal
  From them the story of our woes? The world
  Knows them; and you yourself take glory in them.
ATHALIAH   Yes, my just fury—and I boast of it—
  Avenged my parents' deaths upon my sons.
  I saw my father and my brother butchered,
  My mother cast down from her palace window,
  And in one day (what a spectacle of horror!)
  Saw eighty princes murdered! For what reason?
  To avenge some prophets whose immoderate frenzies
  My mother justly punished; and I, a queen
  Without a heart, a girl without a friend,
  Slave to a cowardly and futile pity,
  Would not, transported by blind rage, commit
  Murder for murder, outrage for outrage,
  And treat all the posterity of David
  As they have treated Ahab's luckless sons?
  Where would I be today had I not conquered
  My weakness, stifled a mother's tenderness,
  Had I not shed a stream of my own blood
  With my own hand, and by this dauntless stroke
  Have quelled your plots? And now the vengeance
  Of your implacable God has snapped forever
  All bonds between our houses. David I hold
  Abhorred, and that king's sons, yea even those
  Born of my blood, are strangers to me.
JOSABETH   All
  Has prospered for you. May God see and judge us!
ATHALIAH   This God, who has been long your only refuge
  What will become of his predictions?
  Let Him give you this king, this child of David,
  Your hope and expectation, who is promised
  To all the nations. . . . But we shall see. Farewell.
  I leave you, satisfied. I wished to see.
  I have seen.
ABNER   As I have promised you
  I give you back what you entrusted me.

  Exeunt Athaliah with her Guards.

Scene 8

Enter Joad.

JOSABETH   Did you o'erhear this haughty queen, my lord?

JOAD   Yes, I heard all, and shared your grief and fears.
These Levites and myself, prepared to help you,
Resolved to perish with you. (*To Joas.*) May the Lord
Watch over you, my child, whose courage gives
A noble witness to your name. I'm grateful,
Abner, for what you've done. Do not forget
The hour when Joad expects you. As for us,
Whose looks are sullied and whose prayer's disturbed
By this impious murderess, let us go in,
And with a pure blood that my hands will shed
Cleanse even the marble where her feet have touched.

Exeunt All, except Chorus.

Scene 9

ONE OF THE CHORUS   What star is shining on us now?
What will this wondrous child become one day?
He braved the splendor of the proud,
And not allowed
Its perilous lures to lead his feet astray.

ANOTHER   While others are to alien altars hasting
To offer incense, this child, indomitable,
Proclaims that God alone is everlasting,
A new Elias before a Jezebel.

ANOTHER   Who will reveal to us your secret birth,
Dear child? Are you some holy prophet's son?

ANOTHER   So in the shadow of the tabernacle
Beloved Samuel grew,
Till he became our hope and oracle;
O may thou too
Console the children of Israel!

ANOTHER (*singing*)   O bless'd a thousand times

The child whom the Lord loveth,
Who hears his voice betimes,
     And whom that God instructeth.
Secluded from the world, from infancy,
     With all the gifts of heaven graced,
     The contagion of wickedness has not defaced
His spotless innocency.

ALL   Happy, O happy, is the infancy
The Lord doth teach and takes beneath his wing!

THE SAME VOICE (*alone*)   Thus in a sheltered valley
     A crystal stream beside,
There grows a tender lily,
     Kind Nature's love and pride.
Secluded from the world from infancy,
     With all the gifts of heaven graced,
     The contagion of wickedness has not defaced
His spotless innocency.

ALL   O bless'd a thousand times the child
Whom the Lord makes obedient to his laws!

A VOICE (*alone*)   O God! that virtue humble
          Down perilous paths must stumble;
That he who seeks Thee, longing to preserve
          His innocence of mind,
          Such obstacles should find,
Pitfalls and perils that may make him swerve.
          How manifold are Thy foes!
          Where can Thy saints repose?
The wicked cover all the face of the earth.

ANOTHER   Palace of David, and his city dear!
     O famous mount where God so long has dwelt,
     Why hast thou felt
The wrath of heaven? Zion, what dost thou say
     When thou beholdst an impious foreigner
Seated upon thy true kings' throne today?

ALL   Zion, dear Zion, what dost thou say,
When thou beholdst an impious foreigner
Seated upon thy true kings' throne today?

THE SAME VOICE (*continuing*)   Instead of beauteous songs, expressing
     The holy joys of David, blessing
          His God, his father, and his Lord,

Dear Zion, thou beholdst men hymning
The impious stranger's god, blaspheming
    The holy name thy kings adored.
A VOICE (*alone*)   How long, O Lord, how long shall we behold
    The wicked rise up against Thee?
    For in Thy Temple, impiously bold,
        They dare to come before Thee,
        Treating as mad the people who adore Thee.
    How long, O Lord, how long shall we behold
        The wicked rise up against Thee?
ANOTHER   What is the use (they say)
    Of your harsh virtue? And why should you shun
    Countless sweet pleasures? Since your God has done
    Nothing for you, 'tis foolish to obey.
ANOTHER   Come, let us sing (they say)
    And take the flowery way,
        From pleasure unto pleasure, as they fly;
        Mad is it on the future to rely,
        For the uncertain-numbered years slip by,
            Bringing their inevitable sorrow:
    Then let us hasten while we may
    To enjoy this life today:
        Who knows if we shall live tomorrow?
ALL   They shall weep, O God, and they shall tremble,
    Those wretches who will never once behold
    Thy holy city's splendor long foretold.
    It is for us to sing, here in Thy Temple,
        To whom Thou hast shown Thy everlasting light,
        To sing of all Thy gifts, and praise Thy might.
A VOICE (*alone*)   Of all these vain delights in which they swim
    What will remain? The memory of a dream
        Whose fond deceit is known.
    When they awake—awakening full of horror!—
        While the poor at Thy throne
    Shall taste the ineffable sweetness of Thy peace,
    They'll drink in the day of Thy wrath the cup of terror
    Thou shalt present to all that guilty race.
ALL   Awakening full of horror!
    O dream that quickly fades!
    O blind and dangerous error!

ACT THREE

Scene 1

Enter Mathan and Nabal to Chorus.

MATHAN   Go, children. One of you tell Josabeth
  Mathan would speak with her, in secret, here.
ONE OF THE CHORUS   Mathan! O God of heaven, may'st thou
    confound him!
NABAL   What! fled without response?
MATHAN   Let us approach.

Exit Chorus.

Scene 2

Enter Zachariah.

ZACHARIAH   Presumptuous man, where would you pass?
    Approach
  No further. This is the sacred dwelling place
  Of holy ministers. The laws forbid
  Any profane to enter. Whom do you seek?
  Upon this solemn day my father shuns
  The criminal sight of curst idolaters;
  And prostrate now before the Lord, my mother
  Fears to be interrupted.
MATHAN   We will wait.
  Cease to perturb yourself, my son. I wish
  To speak with your noble mother. I have come here
  Bearing the Queen's command.

Exit Zachariah.

Scene 3

NABAL   Even their children
  Display their haughty boldness. But tell me now:

What does the Queen desire on this occasion?
And whence has sprung confusion in her counsels?
Insulted by the insolent Joad today,
And in a nightmare threatened by a child,
She would have slaughtered Joad in her wrath,
And in this Temple set both Baal and you.
You told me of your joy, and I had hoped
To have my share of the spoils. What then has changed
Her wavering will?

MATHAN   My friend, these last two days
I have not known her. She is now no more
That bold, clear-sighted Queen, uplifted high
Above her timid sex, who crushed her foes
At once and unawares, and knew the price
Of a lost instant. Now fear of vain remorse
Troubles that lofty soul. She hesitates;
She drifts, and (in a word) she is a woman.
With bitterness and rancor I had filled
Her heart, already struck by heaven's threats;
Entrusting her revenge to me, she bade me
Muster the guard. But whether that same child—
A luckless waif, they say—when brought before her,
Appeased the terror of her dream, or whether
She found some charm in him, I've seen her wrath
Turn hesitant; and she postpones revenge
Until tomorrow. All her plans, it seems,
Destroy each other. "I have made inquiries,"
I told her, "of this child. They have begun
To boast his ancestry. From time to time,
Joad displays him to the factious mob,
Almost as though he were a second Moses,
And with false oracles supports his claims."
The blood at these words mounted to her face,
And never did a happy lie produce
Such prompt effect. "Is it for me to languish
In this uncertainty?" she said at once.
"Away with this disquietude! Go now:
Pronounce this sentence unto Josabeth:
The fires are kindled, and the sword prepared.
Nought can prevent the ravage of their Temple
Unless I have that child as hostage."

NABAL   Well,
For a child they do not know, whom chance perhaps
Has flung into their arms, would they permit
Their Temple to be razed? . . .

MATHAN   But Joad is
Proudest of mortals. Rather than deliver
Into my hands a child he has dedicated
Unto his God, you will see him undergo
The worst of deaths. Besides, it is apparent
They love this child; and if I've understood
The Queen's account, Joad knows something more
About the child's birth than he's yet revealed.
Whoever he is, he will be fatal to them—
That I can well foresee. They will deny him.
The rest is mine. And now I hope at last
That sword and fire will take away the sight
Of this obnoxious Temple.

NABAL   What can inspire
So strong a hatred in you? Does the zeal
Of Baal transport you? As for me, you know,
I am an Ishmaelite, and do not serve
Either Baal or the God of Israel.

MATHAN   Do you suppose, my friend, that with vain zeal
I let myself be blinded for an idol,
A fragile wooden idol which the worms
Upon his altar—in spite of all my care—
Consume each day? I was born a minister
Of the God they worship here, and I perhaps
Would serve Him still, could but the love of greatness,
The thirst for power, be accommodated
Within His narrow yoke. There is no need
For me to remind you of the famous quarrel
Between myself and Joad, when I strove
To supersede him—my intrigues, my struggles,
My tears, and my despair. Vanquished by him,
I entered then a new career: my soul
Attached itself entirely to the court,
Till, by degrees, I gained the ear of kings,
And soon became an oracle. I studied
Their hearts and flattered their caprice. For them
I sowed the precipice's edge with flowers;

Nothing, except their passions, was sacred to me:
I changed both weight and measure at their whim:
When Joad's harsh inflexibility
Wounded their proud and delicate ear, I charmed them
With my dexterity, veiling from their eyes
The dismal truth, depicting all their passions
In favorable colors, and, above all,
Prodigal with the blood of the poor. At last
To the new god the Queen had introduced
A temple was built by her. Jerusalem wept
To see herself profaned. The children of Levi
In consternation howled towards the heavens.
Myself alone, setting a good example
To the timid Jews, deserter from their Law,
Approved the enterprise—and thereby earned
The primacy of Baal. I became
Terrible to my rival: I too wore
The tiara on my brows, and went his equal.
Yet sometimes, I confess, in all my glory,
The memory of the God whom I have left
Importunes me with terror: this it is
Feeds and augments my fury. I shall be happy
If I achieve my vengeance on His Temple,
And thus convict His hate of impotence;
And amidst ruin, ravage, and the dead,
By deeds of horror lose all my remorse.
But here is Josabeth.

Scene 4

Enter Josabeth.

MATHAN   Sent by the Queen,
To re-establish peace and banish hatred,
Princess, whom heaven has given a gentle spirit,
Marvel not if I address you now.
A rumor I myself believe is false
Supports the warning she received in dreams,
And it has turned on Joad (who's accused
Of dangerous plots) the current of her wrath.

I will not brag here of my services.
Joad, I know, has treated me unjustly,
But one should always render good for evil.
So charged with words of peace I come to you.
Live, solemnize your feasts without reproof.
She only asks a pledge of your obedience.
It is—although I've done my best to dissuade her—
That orphan child she saw here.

JOSABETH   Eliacin?

MATHAN   I'm somewhat ashamed for her. Of an empty dream
She takes too much account, but nonetheless
You would declare yourselves her mortal foes
If in the hour this child is not delivered
Into my hands. The Queen, impatiently,
Awaits your answer.

JOSABETH   And that then is the peace
Which you announce?

MATHAN   How can you hesitate
To accept? And is the small compliance asked
Too much to pay?

JOSABETH   I would have been surprised
If Mathan, putting off deception, could
Have overcome the injustice of his heart,
And if the inventor of so many evils
Could now at last come forward as the author
Of even the shadow of good.

MATHAN   Of what do you complain?
Is someone coming in rage to tear your son
Out of your arms? What is this other child
Who seems so dear to you? This great attachment
Surprises me in turn. Is he a treasure
So precious and so rare? A liberator
That heaven prepares for you? Well, think of it.
Should you refuse, it would confirm for me
A rumor that begins to circulate.

JOSABETH   What rumor?

MATHAN   That this child is nobly born,
Destined for some great project by your husband.

JOSABETH   And by this rumor which must fan her fury
Mathan . . .

MATHAN   Princess, it is for you to draw me

Out of my error. I know that Josabeth,
The implacable foe of falsehood, would resign
Even her life, if saving it would cost
One word against the truth. Have you no trace
Of this child's origin? Does a dark night
Conceal his race? And are you ignorant
Both of his parents and from whose hands Joad
Received him to his arms? Speak. I am listening
And apt to give you credence. To the God
You serve, Princess, give glory!

JOSABETH   Wicked man,
'Tis fitting you should name in such a way
A God your mouth instructs men to blaspheme.
Is it possible His truth can be attested
By you who sit on the plague-ridden throne
Where falsehood reigns, disseminating poison;
You, villain, fed on perfidy and treason?

Scene 5

Enter Joad.

JOAD   Where am I? See I not the priest of Baal?
Daughter of David, speak you to this traitor?
Allow him speak with you? Do you not fear
That from the abyss which opens at his feet
Flames will rush out to set you in a blaze?
Or that the walls, in falling, crush you too?
What does he want? How dares the foe of God
Come to infect the air we breathe?

MATHAN   This rage
Is like you, Joad. Yet you ought to show
More prudence; and you should respect a queen,
And not insult the man she deigns to use
To bear her high commands.

JOAD   What evil tidings
Come from her now? What terrible command
That such an envoy brings?

MATHAN   I have conveyed
To Josabeth Queen Athaliah's will.

JOAD   Go from my presence then, thou impious monster:
  Heap up the measure of thy monstrous crimes.
  Go pile up all thy horrors. God prepares
  To join thee with the perjured race—with Doeg,
  Abiron, Dathan, and Achitophel.
  The dogs to whom He handed Jezebel,
  Awaiting but His rage to be unleashed,
  Are at the door and howling for their prey.
MATHAN   Before nightfall . . . it will be seen which one of us
  Will . . . But let us go, Nabal.
NABAL   Where are you going?
  What has bewildered and amazed your senses?
  There lies your way.

Exeunt Nabal and Mathan.

Scene 6

JOSABETH   The storm has broken.
  Now Athaliah in her fury asks
  For Eliacin. Already they have started
  To pierce the mystery of his birth, my lord,
  And of your plan—for Mathan nearly named
  His father.
JOAD   Who could have revealed his birth
  To the perfidious Mathan? Could he guess
  Too much from your confusion?
JOSABETH   I did my best
  To master it. But yet, my lord, believe me,
  The danger presses. Let us keep the child
  For a happier time: while the wicked confer,
  Before he is surrounded and they seize him,
  Let me hide him for a second time.
  The gates, the roads, are open still. If he
  Must be transported to most fearful deserts,
  I am prepared. I know a secret path
  By which with him unseeing and unseen
  I'll cross the falls of Kedron; I will go
  Into the desert where weeping once, and seeking

Safety in flight, as we do now, King David
Escaped pursuit by his rebellious son.
I shall, because of him, fear less the bears
And lions. But why refuse King Jehu's help?
I'll offer now some salutary advice:
Let Jehu now be the depositary
Of this our treasure. We could leave today.
The journey is but short. The heart of Jehu
Is neither savage nor inexorable
And he is well disposed to David's name.
Alas! is there a king so harsh and cruel—
Or one at least without a Jezebel
For mother—who'll not pity the misfortune
Of such a suppliant? Is not his cause
Common to every king?

JOAD   What timid counsels
Do you dare offer me? How could you hope
For Jehu's succor?

JOSABETH   Does the Lord forbid
All care and forethought? Does one not offend Him
By too much confidence? In His sacred plans
Employing human means, has He not armed
The hands of Jehu?

JOAD   Jehu, whom He chose
In His deep wisdom, Jehu, on whom I see
Your hope is founded, has repaid His blessings
With an ingrate forgetfulness. He leaves
Ahab's vile daughter in peace. He follows now
The ungodly example of the kings of Israel,
Preserves the temples of the god of Egypt;
And now at last in the high places dares
To offer an incense God cannot endure.
He has not served His cause, avenged His wrongs;
His heart's not upright, and his hands not pure.
No, no, in God alone must be our trust.
Let us show Eliacin openly—the royal
Circlet upon his head. I even wish
To advance the hour we had determined on,
Ere Mathan's plot is hatched.

Scene 7

Enter Azarias, Chorus, and Levites.

JOAD   Well, Azarias,
  Is the Temple closed?

AZARIAS   Yes, all the doors are shut.

JOAD   Only your sacred cohorts now remain?

AZARIAS   Twice have I gone through all the sacred courts.
  All, all have fled, and they will not return—
  A miserable troop dispersed with fear.
  The holy tribe alone remain to serve
  The Lord of Hosts. I think that since this people
  Escaped from Pharaoh, they have not been struck
  By such a terror.

JOAD   A coward race indeed,
  And born for slavery—brave against God alone.
  Let us pursue our task. But who has kept
  These children still among us?

A GIRL   Could we, my lord,
  Divide us from you? Are we strangers here
  In the Temple of God? You have beside you now
  Our fathers and our brothers.

ANOTHER   Alas, for us!
  If to avenge the shame of Israel
  Our hands cannot, as Jael's in former days,
  Pierce through the impious head of God's own foes,
  At least for Him we could give up our lives.
  When you, with arms, fight for His threatened Temple,
  We can at last invoke Him with our tears.

JOAD   See what avengers arm them for Thy quarrel,
  O everlasting Wisdom—priests and children!
  But if Thou dost uphold them, who can shake them?
  Thou canst, at pleasure, call us from the tomb;
  Strike us, and heal; destroy and resurrect.
  They do not trust now in their own deserts,
  But in Thy name, invoked so many times.
  And in Thine oaths, sworn to their holiest kings,
  And in this Temple, Thy holy dwelling place,
  Which shall endure as long as doth the sun.

Whence comes it that my heart with holy dread
Begins to tremble? Is it the Holy Spirit
Who takes possession of me? It is He.
He kindles me, and speaks. My eyes are opened,
And the dark centuries unroll before me.
You Levites, with the concord of your sounds,
Accompany the raptures He inspires.

CHORUS May the voice of the Lord be heard, His will
   revealed,
And as in springtime the sweet morning dew
   Refreshes the grass of the field,
May His oracle divine our hearts renew.

JOAD O heavens, hear my voice; O earth, give ear!
O Jacob, say no more the Lord doth sleep.
Sinners, begone. The Lord awakens now!

Music. Joad soon continues.

How is the pure gold turned to vilest lead?
Who is this High Priest slaughtered without pity
In the holy place? Weep, Jerusalem, weep!
Slayer of holy prophets, perfidious city!
Now God has turned away His love from thee:
Thy incense in His eyes is now polluted.
Where are these women and children led?
God has destroyed the queen of cities:
Her priests are captives, and her kings are fled.
Men come no more to her solemnities.
   The Temple overturns;
   The sacred cedar burns!
O Zion, that in vain my sorrow pities,
What hand has ravished all your loveliness?
My eyes have changed now into water-springs
   To weep for thy distress.

AZARIAS O holy Temple!
JOSABETH   O David!
CHORUS   O God of Zion,
Remember now Thy ancient promises.

Music again; after a moment Joad interrupts.

JOAD What new Jerusalem rises now
From out the desert shining bright,

Eternity upon her brow,
Triumphing over death and night?
Sing, peoples, Zion now is more
Lovely and glorious than before.
Whence come these children manifold
She did not carry at her breast?
Lift up thy head, O Zion, behold
These princes with thy fame possessed;
The earthly kings all prostrate bow
And kiss the dust before thee now.
Peoples to walk within thy light
Shall strive; and happy those who feel
Their souls for Zion burning bright
With fervent and with holy zeal;
Rain down, O heavens, thy sacred dew!
Earth, may a savior spring from you!

JOSABETH   How may this signal favor be vouchsafed
If David's line, from which this savior springs
Shall be . . .

JOAD   Prepare the gorgeous diadem
Which David wore upon his sacred brow.
And you, to arm yourselves, now follow me
To the secret chambers, far from eyes profane,
Where a great store is hid of swords and spears,
Once steeped in Philistinian blood, and then
By conquering David, laden with years and fame,
All consecrate to God. Could we employ them
In a nobler cause? Come, I myself desire
To share them now amongst you.

Exeunt All, except Salomith and Chorus

Scene 8

SALOMITH   Sisters, how many fears and mortal troubles!
Are these the first fruits, O omnipotent God,
Perfumes and sacrifices which should be
Offered upon Thy altar?

A VOICE   What a sight

For timorous eyes! For who would have believed
That we should ever see the murderous swords
And lances gleaming in the house of peace?

ANOTHER   Why does Jerusalem, to God indifferent,
Now hold her peace while pressing danger threatens?
Whence comes it, sisters, that to protect us all
Even brave Abner does not break his silence?

SALOMITH   But in a court where justice is unknown
And all the laws are force and violence,
Where honor's bought with base obedience,
Who will speak up for luckless innocence?

ANOTHER   In this peril and extreme confusion
For whom is the sacred diadem prepared?

SALOMITH   The Lord has deigned to speak unto His prophet:
But who can understand what is revealed?
Are they arming now in our defense?
Or will they bring destruction on us all?

ALL   O promise! O menace! O dark mystery!
According to the prophecy,
How many ills and blessings will there be?
How may the future for us prove
So much of anger with so much of love?

FIRST VOICE   Zion will be no more—a cruel flame
Will leave of all her glory but a name.

SECOND VOICE   Founded upon His everlasting word,
Zion will be protected by the Lord.

FIRST VOICE   My eyes behold her glory disappear.

SECOND VOICE   I see her brightness spreading everywhere.

FIRST VOICE   Zion has fallen into the abyss.

SECOND VOICE   Aspiring Zion and the heavens kiss.

FIRST VOICE   What sad abasement!

SECOND VOICE   What immortal glory!

FIRST VOICE   How many cries of sorrow!

SECOND VOICE   What songs of triumph!

THIRD VOICE   Peace, sisters, trouble not yourselves:
Some day the mystery will be revealed.

ALL THREE   Let us revere His wrath, hope in His love.

FOURTH VOICE   Who can disturb the peace,
Of a heart that loves Thee, Lord?
In Thy will is its peace,

Its trust is in Thy word.
Can there be happiness
In earth or heaven
Except the tranquil peace
That Thou hast given?

ACT FOUR

Scene 1

Joas, Josabeth, Zachariah, Salomith, a Levite, and Chorus.

SALOMITH   Beside his mother with majestic pace
    Young Eliacin advances with my brother.
    What do they bear between them in those cloths?
    What is that sword that's borne before them?
JOSABETH   My son,
    Upon that table reverently place
    The dread book of our Law. Dear Eliacin,
    Put the royal fillet near the holy book.
    Levite, the sword of David must be placed
    Beside his crown. So Joad has ordained.
JOAS   What is the meaning, Princess, of this sight?
    Wherefore the sword, the crown, the holy book?
    For since the Lord received me in His Temple,
    I have not seen a ceremony like it.
JOSABETH   All your doubts, my son, will soon be cleared.
JOAS   You wish to try this crown upon my brows?
    Princess, take care that you do not profane
    Its glory and respect the memory
    Of the King who wore it. I, a luckless child,
    Abandoned to the bears . . .
JOSABETH   Let be, my son.
    I know what is ordained.
JOAS   But yet I hear
    A sob escape you. You are weeping, Princess.
    What pity moves you? Must I, as Jepthah's daughter,
    Be sacrificed to appease the wrath of God?
    Alas! a son has nothing not his father's.

JOSABETH   Here comes the one who will expound heaven's
   will.
   Fear nothing. Now let all the rest depart.

Exeunt All, except Joas.

Scene 2

Enter Joad.

JOAS   Father!

JOAD   My son?

JOAS   What means this preparation?

JOAD   'Tis right, my son, that I should tell you all;
   You must be first to hear God's great designs
   For you and for His chosen. Arm yourself
   With courage and new faith. 'Tis time to show
   The ardor and the zeal which in your heart
   I have implanted, and to pay to God
   That which you owe him. Do you feel, my son,
   That generous desire?

JOAS   I am prepared,
   If he should wish, to give my life to Him.

JOAD   You've often heard the story of our kings.
   Do you recall, my son, what narrow laws
   A king who is worthy of the diadem
   Should self-impose?

JOAS   God himself has pronounced
   That a wise king does not rely on wealth.
   He fears the Lord his God, and walks before Him,
   Keeping His precepts, laws, and His strict judgments;
   And with excessive burdens does not load
   His brethren.

JOAD   But if you had to take as model
   One of our kings, my son, which would you choose
   To resemble?

JOAS   David, full of faithful love
   Of the Lord, appears to me the perfect model
   Of a great king.

JOAD   And so, in their excess,

You would not imitate the faithless Joram,
The impious Ahaziah?

JOAS   Oh, father!

JOAD   Go on:
How does it seem to you?

JOAS   May all like them
Perish as them! Why do you kneel before me?

JOAD   I render you the reverence that I owe
Unto my king. Make yourself worthy, Joas,
Of David, your great ancestor.

JOAS   Joas?
I?

JOAD   You shall know now by what signal grace
God overthrew the murderous design
Of a mad mother. Her knife was in your breast
When, choosing you, God saved you from the slaughter.
You have not yet escaped from her fierce rage;
Just as in former days she wished to kill
In you the last of her son's children, now
Her cruelty is bent to make you perish,
Pursuing you still under the name which hides you.
But now beneath your standards I have mustered
A loyal people, ready to avenge you.
Enter, you noble chiefs of sacred tribes,
Who have the honor to perform in turn
The holy ministry.

Scene 3

Enter Azarias, Ismael, and three Levites.

JOAD   King, these are
Thy champions against thy enemies.
Priests, here is the King that I have promised.

AZARIAS   What? Eliacin?

ISMAEL   This beloved child?

JOAD   Is of the kings of Judah the true heir,
Last born of the unhappy Ahaziah,
Named Joas, as you know. This tender flower,
Cut down so soon, all Judah mourned as you,

Believing that he shared his brothers' fate.
He was indeed struck with the treacherous knife,
But God preserved him from a fatal blow
And kept some warmth within his beating heart,
Let Josabeth deceive the vigilant eye
Of the assassins, bear him at her breast,
All bleeding, with myself the sole accomplice,
And in the Temple hide both child and nurse.

JOAS   Father, alas! How can I ever pay
So much of love and such great benefits?

JOAD   For other times reserve your thanks. Behold
Therefore, you ministers of God, your king,
Your cherished hope. For you I have preserved him,
Until this hour, and here begins your part.
As soon as the murderous daughter of Jezebel
Learns that our Joas sees the light of day,
She will return, to plunge him once again
Into the horror of the tomb. Already,
Before she knows him, she would murder him.
Now, holy priests, it is for you today
Her fury to forestall, and end at last
The shameful slavery of the Jews; avenge
Your murdered princes, raise again your Law,
And make the two tribes recognize their king.
The enterprise is great and perilous,
For I attack a proud queen on her throne.
Under her flag there is a numerous host
Of doughty foreigners and renegades:
But yet my strength is in the living God
Whose interest is my guide. Think, in this child
All Israel resides. The God of wrath
Already vexes her. Despite her spies,
Already I have gathered you together.
She thinks we have no arms, and no defense.
Let us crown Joas, and proclaim him King;
And then, intrepid warriors of your prince,
Let us invoke the arbiter of battles,
And, waking in our hearts our dormant faith,
Even in her palace let us seek our foe.
And then what hearts though sunk in cowardly slumber
On seeing us advance in this array

But will not haste to follow our example?
A king whom God has brought up in His Temple,
Aaron's successor followed by his priests,
Leading the sons of Levi to the combat,
And in these same hands, reverenced by the people,
The arms of the Lord by David consecrated!
God will spread terror in his enemies.
Now without horror in the infidel blood
Imbrue yourselves. Strike down the Tyrians,
And even Israelites: for are you not
Descended from those Levites, famed in story,
Who when the fickle Israelites in the desert
To the god of the Nile gave unlawful worship,
Their hands they sanctified in traitors' blood—
Holy murderers of their dearest kin—
And by this noble deed acquired for you
The signal honor to be alone employed
At the Lord's altars? But I see that you
Already burn to follow me. Swear then, first,
Upon this solemn book, to live, to fight,
And perish for this king whom heaven today
Has given back to you.

AZARIAS   Yes, here we swear
For us and for our brethren to restore
King Joas to his fathers' throne. We swear
Never to sheathe the sword till we've avenged him
On all his enemies. If one of us
Should break this vow, let him, great God, be struck
With Thy avenging wrath, that he and his children,
Excluded from Thy heritage, may be
Among the dead Thou dost not know!

JOAD   O King!
Wilt thou not swear to be forever faithful
Unto this Law, thy everlasting rule?

JOAS   Why should I not conform me to this Law?

JOAD   My son—I still dare call you by that name—
Suffer this tenderness; forgive the tears
That flow from me in thinking of your peril.
Nurtured far from the throne, you do not know
The poisonous enchantment of that honor.
You do not know yet the intoxication

Of absolute power, the bewitching voice
Of vilest flattery. Too soon they'll tell you
That sacred laws, though rulers of the rabble,
Must bow to kings; that a king's only bridle
Is his own will; that he should sacrifice
All to his greatness; that to tears and toil
The people are condemned, and must be ruled
With an iron scepter; that if they're not oppressed,
Sooner or later they oppress—and thus,
From snare to snare and from abyss to abyss,
Soiling the lovely purity of your heart,
They'll make you hate the truth, paint virtue for you
Under a hideous image. Alas! the wisest
Of all our kings was led astray by them.
Swear then upon this book, and before these
As witnesses, that God will always be
Your first of cares; that stern towards the wicked,
The refuge of the good, you'll always take
Between you and the poor the Lord for judge,
Remembering, my son, that in these garments
You once were poor and orphaned, even as they.

JOAS   I swear to keep that which the Law ordains.
Punish me, Lord, if I depart from You.

JOAD   Come:
We must anoint you with the holy oil.
Here, Josabeth: you now can show yourself. . . .

Scene 4

Enter Josabeth, Zachariah, and Chorus.

JOSABETH   O King! O son of David!

JOAS   My only mother!
Dear Zachariah, kiss your brother, come.

JOSABETH   Kneel down, my son, before your king.

Zachariah kneels.

JOAD   My children,
May you be always thus united.

JOSABETH   You know

What blood has given you life?
JOAS   I know as well
   What hand, except for you, had snatched it from me.
JOSABETH   I now can call you by your name—Joas.
JOAS   Joas will never cease to love you.
CHORUS   What!
   Is he . . . ?
JOSABETH   'Tis Joas.
JOAD   Let us hear this Levite.

Scene 5

Enter Levite
LEVITE   I do not know what project against God
   Is meditated; but the warning bronze
   Clangs everywhere; among the standards now
   They kindle fires; and doubtless Athaliah
   Musters her army. We are even now
   Cut off from succor; and the sacred mount
   On which the Temple stands is everywhere
   Hemmed in by insolent Tyrians. One of them,
   Blaspheming, has informed us even now
   That Abner is in irons and cannot shield us.
JOSABETH   Dear child, whom heaven in vain has given me,
   Alas! to save you I have done my best.
   God has forgotten now your father, David.
JOAD   Do you not fear to draw His wrath upon you
   And on the King you love? And should God tear him
   Forever from your arms, and seem to will
   That David's house should be extinguished quite,
   Are we not here upon the holy mount
   Where Abraham above his innocent son
   Lifted obedient arm without complaint,
   And placed upon a pyre the precious fruit
   Of his old age, leaving to God the task
   Of carrying out his promise, sacrificing
   All hope of issue with this son and heir
   In whom it was bound up? Friends, let us share
   The various posts between us. Let Ismael

Guard all the side that faces east. And you,
Take the north side; you the west; and you
The south. Let no one, whether priest or Levite,
Through hasty zeal discover my designs
Or leave before 'tis time. Let each one then,
Urged by a common ardor, guard the post
Where I have placed him, even to the death.
The foe in his blind rage regards us all
As flocks reserved for slaughter; and believes
He will meet nought but chaos and dismay.
Let Azarias accompany the King.
Come now, dear scion of a valiant race,
And fill your warriors with new bravery.
Put on the diadem before their eyes,
And die, if die you must, at least as King.
Follow him, Josabeth. Give me those arms.
Children, now offer God your innocent tears.

Exeunt All, except Salomith and Chorus.

Scene 6

CHORUS   Children of Aaron, go!
   Never did nobler cause
   Your fathers' zeal incite.
   Children of Aaron, go!
   'Tis for your rightful king
   And for your God you fight.
A VOICE   Where are the darts you throw,
   Great God, in Thy righteous anger?
   Wilt Thou not take vengeance on Thy foe?
   Art Thou a jealous God no longer?
ANOTHER   Where, God of Jacob, are Thy ancient blessings?
   In the horror which surrounds our lives
   Hear'st Thou but the voice of our transgressions?
   Art Thou no more the Lord God who forgives?
ALL   Where, God of Jacob, are Thy ancient blessings?
A VOICE   Against Thee, Lord, O even against Thee
      The wicked bends his bow.

The feasts of God (they say) shall cease to be
Upon the earth; men from His yoke we'll free;
    His altars overthrow;
His saints we'll slay; so that there will remain
    Of His name and of His glory
    Only a fading story,
And neither God nor His Anointed reign.

ALL   Where are the darts You throw,
Great God, in Thy righteous anger?
Wilt Thou not take vengeance on Thy foe?
Art Thou a jealous God no longer?

A VOICE   Sad remnant of our kings, the dear last bloom
Of a lovely stem, shall we behold you fall
Once more beneath a cruel mother's knife?
Did some bright angel then avert thy doom,
Or did the voice of the living God recall
From the night of the tomb thy spirit back to life?

ANOTHER   O God, dost Thou impute to him the sins
Of father and of grandfather? Has Thy pity
Abandoned him, and will it not return?

ALL   Where, God of Jacob, are Thy ancient blessings?
Art Thou no more the Lord God who forgives?

VOICE   Dear sisters, hear you not the trumpet sound
Of the cruel Tyrians?

SALOMITH   Yes, I also hear
The shouts of barbarous soldiers, and I shudder.
Quick, let us flee to the protecting shade
Of the strong sanctuary.

ACT FIVE

Scene 1

Zachariah, Salomith, and Chorus.

SALOMITH   Dear Zachariah, what can you tell us now?

ZACHARIAH   Redouble your ardent prayers to the Lord.
Perhaps our last hour's come. The order's given
For the dreadful battle.

SALOMITH   What is Joas doing?

ZACHARIAH   Joas has just been crowned, and the High Priest
   Has poured the consecrated oil upon him.
   O heavens! What joy in every eye was painted
   To see this king who from the tomb was snatched.
   Sister, the scar from the knife can still be seen.
   The faithful nurse is there, who had been hidden
   In this vast edifice, and kept her charge,
   And had no other witness of her cares
   Than Mother and our God. Our Levites wept
   With joy and tenderness, and mingled sobs
   With cries of joyfulness. Among it all,
   Friendly and without pride, he stretched a hand
   To one, and blessed another with his glance;
   He swore he would be ruled by their advice,
   And called them all his fathers and his brethren.
SALOMITH   But has the secret yet been spread abroad?
ZACHARIAH   No, it is kept within the Temple still.
   The Levites in deep silence guard the doors.
   Waiting to act together, and cry as signal
   "Long live King Joas." Our father forbids
   The King to risk his life, makes Azarias
   Remain with him as guard. Yet Athaliah,
   A dagger in her hand, now laughs to scorn
   The feeble ramparts of our brazen doors;
   To break them she awaits the fatal engines,
   And breathes forth blood and ruin. Some of the priests
   At first proposed that in a secret place,
   A subterranean cell our fathers hollowed,
   We should at least conceal our precious Ark.
   "O fear," my father cried, "unworthy of you,
   Insulting to our cause. The Ark which made
   So many lofty towers to fall, and forced
   Jordan to stay her course, so many times
   Triumphant over alien gods, to flee
   The aspect of an insolent woman!" Mother,
   Beside the King in terrible distress,
   Sometimes on him and sometimes on the altar
   Fastened her eyes, sinking beneath the weight
   Of her dumb fears. She would have made the eyes
   Of even the cruelest to weep. The King at whiles
   Embraced her, soothed her. Follow me, dear sisters,

And if today the King must perish, come,
Let us share his fate.
SALOMITH   What insolent hand is this
Redoubling knocks, which makes these Levites run
In apprehension? What precaution makes them
To hide their arms? O is the Temple forced?
ZACHARIAH   Banish your needless fears. God sends us Abner.

Scene 2

Enter Abner, Joad, Josabeth, Ismael, and Levites.
JOAD   Can I believe my eyes, dear Abner? By what path
Have you, despite the host that hems us in,
Gained access to this place? For it was said
That Ahab's sacrilegious daughter had,
To make assurance of her cruel purpose,
Laden with shameful irons your generous hands.
ABNER   Yes, my lord. She feared my zeal and courage;
This was the least reward she kept for me;
Shut in a horrid dungeon by her order,
I waited—when the Temple had been burnt
And streams of blood poured forth—for her to come
And free me from a weary life, to cut short
My days, and thus to end the pain I suffered,
That I'd outlived my kings.
JOAD   What miracle
Obtained for you your pardon?
ABNER   God only knows
What passes in that heart. She sent for me
And said distractedly: "You see this Temple
Encompassed by my host; the avenging sword
Stands poised above it, and your God's unable
Against me to defend it. But His priests
Can still—but time is short—redeem themselves.
On two conditions: that with Eliacin
Is put into my power the royal treasure—
I'm sure they know its hiding place—that treasure
Which David heaped together, and under pledge
Of secrecy, bequeathed to the High Priest:

Tell them that for this price I'll spare their lives.

JOAD   What counsel, Abner, should we follow now?

ABNER   If it is true you guard some secret hoard
Of David, give her all this gold, and all
You have been able from her greedy hands
To save of rich and rare, give it her now.
Would you that unclean murderers should break
The altar, burn the Cherubim, lay their hands
Upon the Ark, and with our proper blood
Pollute the sanctuary?

JOAD   But does it suit
Abner, with generous hearts, thus to deliver
A luckless child to death, a child which God
Confided to my care, redeem our lives
At the expense of his?

ABNER   God sees my heart:
And would that Athaliah, by His power,
Forgot this child, and that her cruelty,
Contented with my blood, thought thus to appease
Heaven which torments her. But what avails
Your useless care for him? When all will perish,
Will this boy perish less? Does God ordain
You should attempt the impossible? You know
That Moses, to obey a tyrant's law,
Was by his mother left beside the Nile,
Seeing himself from birth condemned to peril;
But God preserving him against all hope
Brought it to pass that he from infancy
Was nurtured by the tyrant. And who knows
What life he has reserved for Eliacin?
And if preparing for him a like fate,
He has made the implacable murderess of our kings
Already capable of pity? At least—
And Josabeth, perhaps, beheld it too—
I saw her so much moved at sight of him,
Her anger's violence declined. Princess,
You're silent in this peril. What! for a child
Who is a stranger to you, would you suffer
That Joad should allow you to be slain,
You, and your son, and all this people too,
And that the one place on the earth where God

Desires to be adored should be consumed
With fire? Were this young child a precious relic
Of the kings, your fathers, what would you do more?

JOSABETH (*aside*)   For his king's blood you see his tenderness.
Why don't you speak to him?

JOAD   'Tis not yet time,
Princess.

ABNER   Time is more precious than you think,
My lord. While you debate what to reply,
Mathan, near Athaliah, with flashing rage
Demands the signal, urges on the slaughter.
O must I kneel now at your sacred knees?
In the name of the holy place which you alone
May enter, where God's majesty resides,
However hard the law imposed on you
Let us consider how we may ward off
This unexpected blow. O give me but
The time to breathe! Tomorrow, even tonight,
I will take measures to assure the Temple
And to avenge its injuries. But I see
My tears and my vain words are means too weak
Your virtue to persuade. Well, find me then
Some sword, some weapon; at the Temple gates
Where the foe waits me, Abner can at least
Die fighting.

JOAD   I surrender. You have given
Advice that I embrace. Let us avert
The threat of all these ills. 'Tis true indeed
That there remains a treasure of King David
Committed to my trust—the final hope
Of the sad Jews, and I with vigilant care
Concealed it from the light. But since it must
To your queen be disclosed, I will content her.
Our doors will open to admit the Queen,
Her bravest captains too; but let her keep
Our holy altars from the open fury
Of a gang of foreigners. Spare me the horror
Of the pillage of the Temple. Would they fear
Children and priests? Let her arrange with you
The number of her suite. As for this child,
So feared, so dreadful, Abner, I know well

The justice of your heart; I will explain
About his birth before her, and to you.
You will see if we must put him in her power,
And you shall judge between the Queen and him.

ABNER   My lord, I take him under my protection.
Fear nothing, I return to her who sent me.

Exit Abner.

Scene 3

JOAD   O God! This is Thy hour. They bring to Thee
   Thy prey. Listen Ismael.

JOSABETH   Blindfold her eyes
   Once more, O master of the heavens, as when
   Thou rob'st her of the profit of her crime
   And hid that tender victim in my breast.

JOAD   Go, Ismael, lose no time, and carry out
   These orders to the letter; above all
   At her entry, and when she passes through,
   Show her the image of an absolute calm.
   You, children, make you ready now a throne
   For Joas. Accompanied by our sacred soldiers,
   Let him come forth. And tell his faithful nurse
   To come here also. Princess, may the source
   Of these your tears, dry up. (*To a Levite.*) You, when the Queen,
   Drunk with mad pride, has crossed the Temple threshold,
   That she may not retreat the way she came
   See that the warlike trumpet at that instant
   Startles the hostile camp with sudden fear.
   Call everyone to aid their king; and make
   Even to his ear the miracle resound,
   That Joas is preserved. Behold he comes.

Scene 4

Enter Joas.

JOAD   Ye holy Levites, priests of the living God,

Surround this place on every side. Keep hidden;
And leaving me to regulate your zeal,
Show not yourselves until you hear my voice.
King, I believe this hope may be allowed
In answer to your vows: that at your feet
Your enemies will fall. She who pursued
Your infancy with fury to this place
Now strives to kill you. But be not afraid:
Think that around you, and on our side, stands
The Angel of Death. Ascend your throne and wait. . . .
The door is opening. Allow this veil
To cover you a moment. You change color,
Princess.

JOSABETH   How can I see the Temple filled
With murderers, and not turn pale. Look now,
Do you not see with what a numerous escort . . . ?

JOAD   I see the Temple doors are closed again,
All is well.

Scene 5

Enter Athaliah and Soldiers.

ATHALIAH   There thou art, seducer,
Vile author of conspiracies and plots,
Who only in sedition set'st thy hopes,
Eternal enemy of absolute power;
Thou hast reposed upon thy God's support;
Art thou yet disabused of that vain hope?
He has put thy Temple and thy life itself
Into my power. On the altar where thy hand
Is wont to sacrifice, I should . . . But I must be
Contented with the price that's offered me.
What you have promised, see you execute.
This child, this treasure, you must now deliver
Into my hands—where are they?

JOAD   Immediately
Thou shalt be satisfied. I am going to show them
Both at one time.

The curtain is drawn. Joas is seen on his throne. His nurse on her knees, R. Azarias, sword in hand, stands L. Near him, Zachariah and Salomith are kneeling on the steps of the throne. Several Levites, sword in hand, are ranged on both sides.

JOAD   Appear, dear child,
Blood royal of our kings. Dost know, O Queen,
Our holiest monarch's heir? Dost know at least
These marks thy dagger made? There is thy king,
Thy grandson and the son of Ahaziah.
All people, and thou, Abner, recognize
King Joas!

ABNER   Heavens!

ATHALIAH   Traitor!

JOAD   Dost thou see
This faithful Jewess, at whose breast he fed,
As well thou knowest. He was by Josabeth
Delivered from thy rage; and in this Temple
God has preserved him. This is what remains
To me of David's treasure.

ATHALIAH   Thy knavery,
Thou traitor, will be fatal to the child.
Deliver me, soldiers, from an odious phantom!

JOAD Soldiers of the living God, defend your king.

The back of the stage opens. The inside of the Temple is seen; and the armed Levites enter from all sides.

ATHALIAH Where am I? Treason! O unlucky Queen!
With arms and enemies I am beset.

JOAD Thine eyes will seek in vain. There's no escape,
And God has hemmed thee in on every side.
That God thou bravedst has now delivered thee
Into our hands. Now render an account
To Him of the blood with which thou has been drunk.

ATHALIAH What! fear has frozen my unworthy soldiers!
Into what snare, base Abner, hast thou led me?

ABNER God is my witness, Queen . . .

ATHALIAH   Swear not by thy God,
Traitor! Avenge me.

ABNER   On whom? On Joas?
On my master?

ATHALIAH   He, Joas? He, thy king?

Know, wicked men, my arms besiege you still,
And all my camp is shouting for me now.
They are coming to my rescue. Tremble now,
You troop of rebels.

Scene 6

Enter Ismael.

ISMAEL   My lord, the Temple's freed
Of all its enemies. The stranger's fled;
The Jew submits. And even as the wind
Scatters the smoke, the voice of the Almighty
That army has dispersed. From the Temple gates
Our Levites have proclaimed the rightful King,
Have told how he was snatched in infancy
From the fatal sword, and how the daughter of Ahab
Is fallen in the snare. On every side
The trumpet sounded; mingled with its noise
The cries of the astounded host have spread
The sudden terror with which Gideon struck
The haughty Midian. The Tyrians,
Throwing away their swords and bucklers, fled
By diverse routes. They disappeared the first.
Some Jews, dumbfounded, also took to flight.
Wondering at God's mercy showered on Joas,
The rest, with acclamation, hailed him King.
Till all the people with the selfsame spirit
Inspired, women, old men, and children,
Embraced with joy, and blessed the Lord their God
For what He gave. All sing of David's son
Brought back to life; while in the holy city
Baal is struck with horror; and the doors
Of his sacrilegious temple are broke in.
Mathan is slain.
ATHALIAH   Thou hast conquered, O God of the Jews!
Yes, it is Joas, and I seek in vain
To deceive myself. I recognize the place
Where he was pierced. I see the mien and gesture
Of Ahaziah. Everything recalls

The blood which I detest. David has triumphed,
Ahab's alone destroyed. Remorseless God,
Thou hast brought everything to pass. 'Tis Thou,
Who flattering me with easy vengeance, made me
A score of times in a day oppose myself,
Sometimes arousing pity for a child,
And sometimes dazzling me with Thy rich treasures,
So that I've feared to give to flame and pillage
This Temple; so that this son reigns, Thy care
And the work of Thy hands; so that to signalize
His new gained empire, he will now be made
To plunge the dagger in my breast. This is
My dying wish for him. What said I? Wish?
Nay, I am confident that he will be
Repugnant to Thy yoke, tired with Thy Law,
Faithful to Ahab's blood he took from me;
That he will do what his grandfather did,
Be like his father. It shall come to pass
That this hated heir of David will abolish
Thy honors and profane Thy altar—to avenge
Ahab and Jezebel and Athaliah.

Exit Athaliah, guarded.

Scene 7

JOAD   Let her at once be taken from the Temple,
So that its sanctity is not profaned.
Go, you avengers of your murdered princes,
And stop their blood's cries even with her death.
If any rash men should embrace her quarrel,
Deliver him, too, to the fury of the sword.
JOAS (*descending*)   O God, who seest my trouble and affliction,
Turn far from me her curse. Suffer it not
To be accomplished, and let Joas die
Ere he forget You.
JOAD   Assemble all the people;
Show them their king, who comes to renew his oath.
King, priests, and people, filled with thankfulness,

Let us confirm the covenant of Jacob
With God, and penitent for our misdeeds,
Let us now re-engage ourselves to Him
With a new oath. Abner, beside the King
Take up your place again.

Scene 8

Enter a Levite.

JOAD   Well? Have they punished
   This rash and impious woman?

LEVITE   The sword has expiated
   The horrors of her life. Jerusalem,
   For long a prey to her unbridled rage,
   Freed from her odious yoke at last with joy
   Beheld her weltering in her blood.

JOAD   Her end
   Was terrible, but well deserved. Learn from it,
   King of the Jews, and ne'er forget that kings
   Have a stern judge in heaven, that innocence
   Has an avenger, the fatherless a father.

Awake and Sing!   (1935)*

Clifford Odets   (1906-1963)

The embryonic version of this fundamentally optimistic drama was a more depressing effort of 1932–33 that its twenty-six-year-old author called *I Got the Blues*—the "blues" that a whole country felt in those bottom years of the Great Depression that had followed so abruptly on the euphoric boom of the twenties. Some of this "depression"—economic and psychological—still informs the revision that the young playwright finally saw presented to the public for the first time on February 19, 1935, by the Group Theater (the company which, under Cheryl Crawford, Harold Clurman and Lee Strasberg, was to have an enormous influence on the theater of the subsequent decades). A bit actor with the Group since its first production in the fall of 1931, Odets had become more and more a part of its communal and almost familial spirit. As Mr. Weales has suggested in his study of the playwright, Odets may have found in the Group's friendly and reassuring "enclosure" that self-assurance as an artist that enabled him to depict the variety of human response to the enclosures of the spirit that are so obviously the informing motif of *Awake and Sing!* [1]

In the 1967–68 season the play was produced in Boston at

1. *Clifford Odets: Playwright* (New York: Pegasus, Bobbs-Merrill, 1971), pp. 29–30 and p. 78.

the Charles Playhouse (Michael Murray, artistic director), with Eda Reiss Merin as Bessie. It also ran for forty-one performances off-Broadway at the Bijou Theater in the spring of 1970 in a production by the Catalyst Company under the direction of Arthur A. Seidelman. In 1972, Hollywood Television Theater (Norman Lloyd and Robert Hopkins, producers, with Lewis Freedman as executive producer) distributed the play over National Education Television, under Mr. Lloyd's direction at N-C-E-T (Los Angeles), with Walter Matthau as Moe, Felicia Farr as Hennie, Ruth Storey as Bessie, Robert Lipton as Ralph, and Leo Fuchs as Jacob.

AWAKE AND SING!

Clifford Odets

CHARACTERS

All of the characters in Awake and Sing! *share a fundamental activity: a struggle for life amidst petty conditions.*

BESSIE BERGER, *as she herself states, is not only the mother in this home but also the father. She is constantly arranging and taking care of her family. She loves life, likes to laugh, has great resourcefulness and enjoys living from day to day. A high degree of energy accounts for her quick exasperation at inepititude. She is a shrewd judge of realistic qualities in people in the sense of being able to gauge quickly their effectiveness. In her eyes all of the people in the house are equal. She is naïve and quick in emotional response. She is afraid of utter poverty. She is proper according to her own standards, which are fairly close to those of most middle-class families. She knows that when one lives in the jungle one must look out for the wild life.*

MYRON, *her husband, is a born follower. He would like to be a leader. He would like to make a million dollars. He is not sad or ever depressed. Life is an even sweet event to him, but the "old days" were sweeter yet. He has a dignified sense of himself. He likes people. He likes everything. But he is heartbroken without being aware of it.*

HENNIE *is a girl who has had few friends, male or female. She is proud of her body. She won't ask favors. She travels alone. She is fatalistic about being trapped, but will escape if possible. She is self-reliant in the best sense. Till the day she dies she will be faithful to a loved man. She inherits her mother's sense of humor and energy.*

RALPH *is a boy with a clean spirit. He wants to know, wants to learn. He is ardent, he is romantic, he is sensitive. He is naïve too. He is trying to find why so much dirt must be cleared away before it is possible to "get to first base."*

JACOB, *too, is trying to find a right path for himself and the others. He is aware of justice, of dignity. He is an observer of the others, compares their activities with his real and ideal sense of life. This produces a reflective nature. In this home he is a constant boarder. He is a sentimental idealist with no power to turn ideal to action. With physical facts—such as housework—he putters. But as a barber he demonstrates the flair of an artist. He is an old Jew with living eyes in his tired face.*

UNCLE MORTY *is a successful American business man with five good senses. Something sinister comes out of the fact that the lives of others seldom touch him deeply. He holds to his own line of life. When he is generous, he wants others to be aware of it. He is pleased by attention—a rich relative to the Berger family. He is a shrewd judge of material values. He will die unmarried. Two and two make four, never five with him. He can blink in the sun for hours, a fat tomcat. Tickle him, he laughs. He lives in a penthouse with a real Japanese butler to serve him. He sleeps with dress models, but not from his own showrooms. He plays cards for hours on end. He smokes expensive cigars. He sees every Mickey Mouse cartoon that appears. He is a 32-degree Mason. He is really deeply intolerant finally.*

MOE AXELROD *lost a leg in the war. He seldom forgets that fact. He has killed two men in extra-martial activity. He is mordant, bitter. Life has taught him a disbelief in everything, but he will fight his way through. He seldom shows his feelings, fights against his own sensitivity. He has been everywhere and seen everything. All he wants is Hennie. He is very proud. He scorns the inability of others to make their way in life, but he likes people for whatever good qualities they possess. His passionate outbursts come from a strong but contained emotional mechanism.*

SAM FEINSCHREIBER *wants to find a home. He is a lonely man, a foreigner in a strange land, hypersensitive about this fact, conditioned by the humiliation of not making his way alone. He has a sense of others laughing at him. At night he gets up and sits alone in the dark. He hears acutely all the small sounds of life. He might have been a poet in another time and place. He approaches his wife as if he were always offering her a delicate flower. Life is a high chill wind weaving itself around his head.*

SCHLOSSER, *the janitor, is an overworked German whose wife ran away with another man and left him with a young daughter who in turn ran away and joined a burlesque show as chorus girl. The man suffers rheumatic pains. He has lost his identity twenty years before.*

Exposed on the stage are the dining room and adjoining front room of the Berger apartment. These two rooms are typically furnished. There is a curtain between them. A small door off the front room leads to Jacob's room. When his door is open one sees a picture of Sacco and Vanzetti[1] on the wall and several shelves of books. Stage left of this door presents the

---

1. Nicola Sacco and Bartolomeo Vanzetti, Italian immigrant anarchists and draft evaders, were accused of the murder of the paymaster of a shoe company in South Braintree, Mass., on April 15, 1920. Their case was a *cause célèbre* throughout the twenties, culminating in their execution on August 22, 1927 after a trial that has been considered a travesty of justice by many.

entrance to the foyer hall of the apartment. The two other bedrooms of the apartment are off this hall, but not necessarily shown.

Stage left of the dining room presents a swinging door which opens on the kitchen.

Awake and sing, ye that dwell in dust.

ISAIAH—26:19

ACT ONE

TIME: *The present; the family finishing supper.*

PLACE: *An apartment in the Bronx, New York City.*

RALPH   Where's advancement down the place? Work like crazy! Think they see it? You'd drop dead first.

MYRON   Never mind, son, merit never goes unrewarded. Teddy Roosevelt used to say—

HENNIE   It rewarded you—thirty years a haberdashery clerk!

Jacob laughs.

RALPH   All I want's a chance to get to first base!

HENNIE   That's all?

RALPH   Stuck down in that joint on Fourth Avenue—a stock clerk in a silk house! Just look at Eddie. I'm as good as he is—pulling in two-fifty a week for forty-eight minutes a day. A headliner, his name in all the papers.

JACOB   That's what you want, Ralphie? Your name in the paper?

RALPH   I wanna make up my own mind about things . . . be something! Didn't I want to take up tap dancing, too?

BESSIE   So take lessons. Who stopped you?

RALPH   On what?

BESSIE   On what? Save money.

RALPH   Sure, five dollars a week for expenses and the rest in the house. I can't save even for shoe laces.

BESSIE   You mean we shouldn't have food in the house, but you'll make a jig on the street corner?

RALPH   I mean something.

BESSIE   You also mean something when you studied on the drum, Mr. Smartie!

RALPH   I don't know. . . . Every other day to sit around with the blues and mud in your mouth.

MYRON   That's how it is—life is like that—a cake-walk.

RALPH   What's it get you?

HENNIE   A four-car funeral.

RALPH   What's it for?

JACOB   What's it for? If this life leads to a revolution it's a good life. Otherwise it's for nothing.

BESSIE   Never mind, Pop! Pass me the salt.

RALPH   It's crazy—all my life I want a pair of black and white shoes and can't get them. It's crazy!

BESSIE   In a minute I'll get up from the table. I can't take a bite in my mouth no more.

MYRON   (*restraining her*)   Now, Momma, just don't excite your-self——

BESSIE   I'm so nervous I can't hold a knife in my hand.

MYRON   Is that a way to talk, Ralphie? Don't Momma work hard enough all day?

Bessie allows herself to be reseated.

BESSIE   On my feet twenty-four hours?

MYRON   On her feet——

RALPH   (*jumps up*)   What do I do—go to night-clubs with Greta Garbo? Then when I come home can't even have my own room? Sleep on a day-bed in the front room! (*Choked, he exits to front room.*)

BESSIE   He's starting up that stuff again. (*Shouts to him.*) When Hennie here marries you'll have her room—I should only live to see the day.

HENNIE   Me, too. (*They settle down to serious eating.*)

MYRON   This morning the sink was full of ants. Where they come from I just don't know. I thought it was coffee grounds . . . and then they began moving.

BESSIE   You gave the dog eat?

JACOB   I gave the dog eat. (*Hennie drops a knife and picks it up again.*)

BESSIE   You got dropsy tonight.

HENNIE   Company's coming.

MYRON   You can buy a ticket for fifty cents and win fortunes. A man came in the store—it's the Irish Sweepstakes.

BESSIE   What?

MYRON   Like a raffle, only different. A man came in——

BESSIE   Who spends fifty-cent pieces for Irish raffles? They threw out a family on Dawson Street today. All the furniture on the sidewalk. A fine old woman with gray hair.

JACOB   Come eat, Ralph.

MYRON   A butcher on Beck Street won eighty thousand dollars.

BESSIE   Eighty thousand dollars! You'll excuse my expression, you're bughouse!

MYRON   I seen it in the paper—on one ticket—765 Beck Street.

BESSIE   Impossible!

MYRON   He did . . . yes he did. He says he'll take his old mother to Europe . . . an Austrian——

HENNIE   Europe . . .

MYRON   Six per cent on eighty thousand—forty-eight hundred a year.

BESSIE   I'll give you money. Buy a ticket in Hennie's name. Say, you can't tell—lightning never struck us yet. If they win on Beck Street we could win on Longwood Avenue.

JACOB (*ironically*)   If it rained pearls—who would work?

BESSIE   Another county heard from. (*Ralph enters and silently seats himself.*)

MYRON   I forgot, Beauty—Sam Feinschreiber sent you a present. Since I brought him for supper he just can't stop talking about you.

HENNIE   What's that "mockie" bothering about? Who needs him?

MYRON   He's a very lonely boy.

HENNIE   So I'll sit down and bust out crying " 'cause he's lonely."

BESSIE (*opening candy*)   He'd marry you one two three.

HENNIE   Too bad about him.

BESSIE (*naïvely delighted*)   Chocolate peanuts.

HENNIE   Loft's week-end special, two for thirty-nine.

BESSIE   You could think about it. It wouldn't hurt.

HENNIE (*laughing*)   To quote Moe Axelrod, "Don't make me laugh."

BESSIE   Never mind laughing. It's time you already had in your head a serious thought. A girl twenty-six don't grow younger. When I was your age it was already a big family with responsibilities.

HENNIE (*laughing*)   Maybe that's what ails you, Mom.

BESSIE   Don't you feel well?

HENNIE   'Cause I'm laughing? I feel fine. It's just funny—that poor guy sending me presents 'cause he loves me.

BESSIE   I think it's very, very nice.

HENNIE   Sure . . . swell!

BESSIE   Mrs. Marcus' Rose is engaged to a Brooklyn boy, a dentist. He came in his car today. A little dope should get such a boy. (*Finished with the meal, Bessie, Myron and Jacob rise. Both Hennie and Ralph sit silently at the table, he eating. Suddenly she rises.*)

HENNIE   Tell you what, Mom. I saved for a new dress, but I'll take you and Pop to the Franklin. Don't need a dress. From now on I'm planning to stay in nights. Hold everything!

BESSIE   What's the matter—a bedbug bit you suddenly?

HENNIE   It's a good bill—Belle Baker. Maybe she'll sing "Eli, Eli."

BESSIE   We was going to a movie.

HENNIE   Forget it. Let's go.

MYRON   I see in the papers (*as he picks his teeth*) Sophie Tucker took off twenty-six pounds. Fearful business with Japan.[2]

HENNIE   Write a book, Pop! Come on, we'll go early for good seats.

MYRON   Moe said you had a date with him for tonight.

BESSIE   Axelrod?

HENNIE   I told him no, but he don't believe it. I'll tell him no for the next hundred years, too.

MYRON   Don't break appointments, Beauty, and hurt people's feelings. (*Bessie exits.*)

HENNIE   His hands got free wheeling. (*She exits.*)

MYRON   I don't know . . . people ain't the same. N-O- The whole world's changing right under our eyes. Presto! No manners. Like the great Italian lover in the movies. What was his name? The Sheik. . . . No one remembers? (*Exits, shaking his head.*)

RALPH (*unmoving at the table*)   Jake . . .

JACOB   Noo?

---

2. Sophie Tucker (1884–1966) was a popular entertainer (obviously fat); beginning in 1932 Japan began a policy of military expansion.

RALPH   I can't stand it.

JACOB   There's an expression—"strong as iron you must be."

RALPH   It's a cock-eyed world.

JACOB   Boys like you could fix it some day. Look on the world, not on yourself so much. Every country with starving millions, no? In Germany and Poland a Jew couldn't walk in the street. Everybody hates, nobody loves.

RALPH   I don't get all that.

JACOB   For years, I watched you grow up. Wait! You'll graduate from my university. (*The others enter, dressed.*)

MYRON (*lighting*)   Good cigars now for a nickel.

BESSIE (*to Jacob*)   After take Tootsie on the roof. (*To Ralph.*) What'll you do?

RALPH   Don't know.

BESSIE   You'll see the boys around the block?

RALPH   I'll stay home every night!

MYRON   Momma don't mean for you——

RALPH   I'm flying to Hollywood by plane, that's what I'm doing.

Doorbell rings. Myron answers it.

BESSIE   I don't like my boy to be seen with those tramps on the corner.

MYRON (*without*)   Schlosser's here, Momma, with the garbage can.

BESSIE   Come in here, Schlosser. (*Sotto voce.*) Wait, I'll give him a piece of my mind. (*Myron ushers in Schlosser who carries a garbage can in each hand.*) What's the matter the dumbwaiter's broken again?

SCHLOSSER   Mr. Wimmer sends new ropes next week. I got a sore arm.

BESSIE   He should live so long your Mr. Wimmer. For seven years already he's sending new ropes. No dumbwaiter, no hot water, no steam—— In a respectable house, they don't allow such conditions.

SCHLOSSER   In a decent house dogs are not running to make dirty the hallway.

BESSIE   Tootsie's making dirty? Our Tootsie's making dirty in the hall?

SCHLOSSER (*to Jacob*)   I tell you yesterday again. You must not leave her——

BESSIE (*indignantly*) Excuse me! Please don't yell on an old man. He's got more brains in his finger than you got—I don't know where. Did you ever see—he should talk to you an old man?

MYRON Awful.

BESSIE From now on we don't walk up the stairs no more. You keep it so clean we'll fly in the windows.

SCHLOSSER I speak to Mr. Wimmer.

BESSIE Speak! Speak. Tootsie walks behind me like a lady any time, any place. So good-bye . . . good-bye, Mr. Schlosser.

SCHLOSSER I tell you dot—I verk verry hard here. My arms is . . .

Exits in confusion.

BESSIE Tootsie should lay all day in the kitchen maybe. Give him back if he yells on you. What's funny?

JACOB (*laughing*) Nothing.

BESSIE Come. (*Exits.*)

JACOB Hennie, take care. . . .

HENNIE Sure.

JACOB Bye-bye.

Hennie exits. Myron pops head back in door.

MYRON Valentino! That's the one! (*He exits.*)

RALPH I never in my life even had a birthday party. Every time I went and cried in the toilet when my birthday came.

JACOB (*seeing Ralph remove his tie*) You're going to bed?

RALPH No, I'm putting on a clean shirt.

JACOB Why?

RALPH I got a girl. . . . Don't laugh!

JACOB Who laughs? Since when?

RALPH Three weeks. She lives in Yorkville with an aunt and uncle. A bunch of relatives, but no parents.

JACOB An orphan girl—tch, tch.

RALPH But she's got me! Boy, I'm telling you I could sing! Jake, she's like stars. She's so beautiful you look at her and cry! She's like French words! We went to the park the other night. Heard the last band concert.

JACOB Music. . . .

RALPH (*stuffing shirt in trousers*) It got cold and I gave her my coat to wear. We just walked along like that, see, without a word, see. I never was so happy in all my life. It got late . . . we just sat there. She looked at me—you know what I mean, how a girl looks at you—right in the eyes? "I love you," she says, "Ralph." I took her home. . . . I wanted to cry. That's how I felt!

JACOB It's a beautiful feeling.

RALPH You said a mouthful!

JACOB Her name is——

RALPH Blanche.

JACOB A fine name. Bring her sometimes here.

RALPH She's scared to meet Mom.

JACOB Why?

RALPH You know Mom's not letting my sixteen bucks out of the house if she can help it. She'd take one look at Blanche and insult her in a minute—a kid who's got nothing.

JACOB Boychick!

RALPH What's the diff?

JACOB It's no difference—a plain bourgeois prejudice—but when they find out a poor girl—it ain't so kosher.

RALPH They don't have to know I've got a girl.

JACOB What's in the end?

RALPH Out I go! I don't mean maybe!

JACOB And then what?

RALPH Life begins.

JACOB What life?

RALPH Life with my girl. Boy, I could sing when I think about it! Her and me together—that's a new life!

JACOB Don't make a mistake! A new death!

RALPH What's the idea?

JACOB Me, I'm the idea! Once I had in *my* heart a dream, a vision, but came marriage and then you forget. Children come and you forget because——

RALPH Don't worry, Jake.

JACOB Remember, a woman insults a man's soul like no other thing in the whole world!

RALPH Why get so excited? No one——

JACOB Boychick, wake up! Be something! Make your life something good. For the love of an old man who sees in your young days his new life, for such love take the world in your two hands and make it like new. Go out and fight so life shouldn't be printed on dollar bills. A woman waits.

RALPH   Say, I'm no fool!

JACOB   From my heart I hope not. In the meantime—— (*Bell rings.*)

RALPH   See who it is, will you? (*Stands off.*) Don't want Mom to catch me with a clean shirt.

JACOB (*calls*)   Come in. (*Sotto voce.*) Moe Axelrod. (*Moe enters.*)

MOE   Hello girls, how's your whiskers? (*To Ralph.*) All dolled up. What's it, the weekly visit to the cat house?

RALPH   Please mind your business.

MOE   Okay, sweetheart.

RALPH (*taking a hidden dollar from a book*)   If Mom asks where I went——

JACOB   I know. Enjoy yourself.

RALPH   Bye-bye. (*He exits.*)

JACOB   Bye-bye.

MOE   Who's home?

JACOB   Me.

MOE   Good. I'll stick around a few minutes. Where's Hennie?

JACOB   She went with Bessie and Myron to a show.

MOE   She what?!

JACOB   You had a date?

MOE (*hiding his feelings*)   Here—I brought you some halavah.

JACOB   Halavah? Thanks. I'll eat a piece after.

MOE   So Ralph's got a dame? Hot stuff—a kid can't even play a card game.

JACOB   Moe, you're a no-good, a bum of the first water. To your dying day you won't change.

MOE   Where'd you get that stuff, a no-good?

JACOB   But I like you.

MOE   Didn't I go fight in France for democracy? Didn't I get my goddam leg shot off in that war the day before the armistice? Uncle Sam give me the Order of the Purple Heart, didn't he? What'd you mean, a no-good?

JACOB   Excuse me.

MOE   If you got an orange I'll eat an orange.

JACOB   No orange. An apple.

MOE   No oranges, huh?—what a dump!

JACOB   Bessie hears you once talking like this she'll knock your head off.

MOE   Hennie went with, huh? She wantsa see me squirm, only I don't squirm for dames.

JACOB   You came to see her?

MOE   What for? I got a present for our boy friend, Myron. He'll drop dead when I tell him his gentle horse galloped in fifteen to one. He'll die.

JACOB   It really won? The first time I remember.

MOE   Where'd they go?

JACOB   A vaudeville by the Franklin.

MOE   What's special tonight?

JACOB   Someone tells a few jokes . . . and they forget the street is filled with starving beggars.

MOE   What'll they do—start a war?

JACOB   I don't know.

MOE   You oughta know. What the hell you got all the books for?

JACOB   It needs a new world.

MOE   That's why they had the big war—to make a new world, they said—safe for democracy. Sure every big general laying up in a Paris hotel with a half dozen broads pinned on his mustache. Democracy! I learned a lesson.

JACOB   An imperial war. You know what this means?

MOE   Sure, I know everything!

JACOB   By money men the interests must be protected. Who gave you such a rotten haircut? Please (*fishing in his vest pocket*) give me for a cent a cigarette. I didn't have since yesterday——

MOE   (*giving one*)   Don't make me laugh. (*A cent passes back and forth between them, Moe finally throwing it over his shoulder.*) Don't look so tired all the time. You're a wow—always sore about something.

JACOB   And you?

MOE   You got one thing—you can play pinochle. I'll take you over in a game. Then you'll have something to be sore on.

JACOB   Who'll wash dishes? (*Moe takes deck from buffet drawer.*)

MOE   Do 'em after. Ten cents a deal.

JACOB   Who's got ten cents?

MOE   I got ten cents. I'll lend it to you.

JACOB   Commence.

MOE   (*shaking cards*)   The first time I had my hands on a pack in two days. Lemme shake up these cards. I'll make 'em talk. (*Jacob goes to his room where he puts on a Caruso[3] record.*)

JACOB You should live so long.

MOE Ever see oranges grow? I know a certain place—one summer I laid under a tree and let them fall right in my mouth.

JACOB (*off, the music is playing; the card game begins*) From "L'Africana" [4] . . . a big explorer comes on a new land—"O Paradiso." From act four this piece. Caruso stands on the ship and looks on a Utopia. You hear? "Oh paradise! Oh paradise on earth! Oh blue sky, oh fragrant air——"

MOE Ask him does he see any oranges? (*Bessie, Myron and Hennie enter.*)

JACOB You came back so soon?

BESSIE Hennie got sick on the way.

MYRON Hello, Moe. . . .

Moe puts cards back in pocket.

BESSIE Take off the phonograph, Pop. (*To Hennie.*) Lay down . . . I'll call the doctor. You should see how she got sick on Prospect Avenue. Two weeks already she don't feel right.

MYRON Moe . . . ?

BESSIE Go to bed, Hennie.

HENNIE I'll sit here.

BESSIE Such a girl I never saw! Now you'll be stubborn?

MYRON It's for your own good, Beauty. Influenza——

HENNIE I'll sit here.

BESSIE You ever seen a girl should say no to everything. She can't stand on her feet, so——

HENNIE Don't yell in my ears. I hear. Nothing's wrong. I ate tuna fish for lunch.

MYRON Canned goods. . . .

BESSIE Last week you also ate tuna fish?

HENNIE Yeah, I'm funny for tuna fish. Go to the show—have a good time.

BESSIE I don't understand what I did to God He blessed me with such children. From the whole world——

3. Enrico Caruso (1873–1921), Italian operatic tenor, one of the greatest singers in history.
4. Opera (1865) by Giacomo Meyerbeer (1791–1864), produced posthumously (1865).

MOE (*coming to aid of Hennie*) For Chris' sake, don't kibitz so much!

BESSIE You don't like it?

MOE (*aping*) No, I don't like it.

BESSIE That's too bad, Axelrod. Maybe it's better by your cigar-store friends. Here we're different people.

MOE Don't gimme that cigar-store line, Bessie. I walked up five flights——

BESSIE To take out Hennie. But my daughter ain't in your class, Axelrod.

MOE To see Myron.

MYRON Did he, did he, Moe?

MOE Did he what?

MYRON "Sky Rocket"?

BESSIE You bet on a horse!

MOE Paid twelve and a half to one.

MYRON There! You hear that, Momma? Our horse came in. You see, it happens, and twelve and a half to one. Just look at that!

MOE What the hell, a sure thing. I told you.

BESSIE If Moe said a sure thing, you couldn't bet a few dollars instead of fifty cents?

JACOB (*laughs*) "Aie, aie, aie."

MOE (*at his wallet*) I'm carrying six hundred "plunks" in big denominations.

BESSIE A banker!

MOE Uncle Sam sends me ninety a month.

BESSIE So you save it?

MOE Run it up, Run-it-up-Axelrod, that's me.

BESSIE The police should know how.

MOE (*shutting her up*) All right, all right—— Change twenty, sweetheart.

MYRON Can you make change?

BESSIE Don't be crazy.

MOE I'll meet a guy in Goldman's restaurant. I'll meet 'im and come back with change.

MYRON (*figuring on paper*) You can give it to me tomorrow in the store.

BESSIE (*acquisitive*) He'll come back, he'll come back!

MOE Lucky I bet some bucks myself. (*In derision to Hennie.*)

Let's step out tomorrow night, Par-a-dise. (*Thumbs his nose at her, laughs mordantly and exits.*)

MYRON   Oh, that's big percentage. If I picked a winner every day. . . .

BESSIE   Poppa, did you take Tootsie on the roof?

JACOB   All right.

MYRON   Just look at that—a cake walk. We can make——

BESSIE   It's enough talk. I got a splitting headache. Hennie, go in bed. I'll call Dr. Cantor.

HENNIE   I'll sit here . . . and don't call that old Ignatz 'cause I won't see him.

MYRON   If you get sick Momma can't nurse you. You don't want to go to a hospital.

JACOB   She don't look sick, Bessie, it's a fact.

BESSIE   She's got fever. I see in her eyes, so he tells me no. Myron, call Dr. Cantor.

Myron picks up phone, but Hennie grabs it from him.

HENNIE   I don't want any doctor. I ain't sick. Leave me alone.

MYRON   Beauty, it's for your own sake.

HENNIE   Day in and day out pestering. Why are you always right and no one else can say a word?

BESSIE   When you have your own children——

HENNIE   I'm not sick! Hear what I say? I'm not sick! Nothing's the matter with me! I don't want a doctor. (*Bessie is watching her with slow progressive understanding.*)

BESSIE   What's the matter?

HENNIE   Nothing, I told you!

BESSIE   You told me, but—— (*A long pause of examination follows.*)

HENNIE   See much?

BESSIE   Myron, put down the . . . the. . . . (*He slowly puts the phone down.*) Tell me what happened. . . .

HENNIE   Brooklyn Bridge fell down.

BESSIE (*approaching*)   I'm asking a question. . . .

MYRON   What's happened, Momma?

BESSIE   Listen to me!

HENNIE   What the hell are you talking?

BESSIE   Poppa—take Tootsie on the roof.

HENNIE (*holding Jacob back*)   If he wants he can stay here.

MYRON   What's wrong, Momma?

BESSIE (*her voice quivering slightly*)   Myron, your fine Beauty's in trouble. Our society lady. . . .

MYRON   Trouble? I don't under—is it——?

BESSIE   Look in her face. (*He looks, understands, and slowly sits in a chair, utterly crushed.*) Who's the man?

HENNIE   The Prince of Wales.

BESSIE   My gall is busting in me. In two seconds——

HENNIE (*in a violent outburst*)   Shut up! Shut up! I'll jump out the window in a minute! Shut up! (*Finally she gains control of herself, says in a low, hard voice.*) You don't know him.

JACOB   Bessie. . . .

BESSIE   He's a Bronx boy?

HENNIE   From out of town.

BESSIE   What do you mean?

HENNIE   From out of town!!

BESSIE   A long time you know him? You were sleeping by a girl from the office Saturday nights? You slept good, my lovely lady. You'll go to him . . . he'll marry you.

HENNIE   That's what you say.

BESSIE   That's what I say! He'll do it, take MY word he'll do it!

HENNIE   Where? (*To Jacob.*) Give her the letter. (*Jacob does so.*)

BESSIE   What? (*Reads.*) "Dear sir: In reply to your request of the 14th inst., we can state that no Mr. Ben Grossman has ever been connected with our organization . . ." You don't know where he is?

HENNIE   No.

BESSIE (*walks back and forth*)   Stop crying like a baby, Myron.

MYRON   It's like a play on the stage. . . .

BESSIE   To a mother you couldn't say something before. I'm old-fashioned—like your friends I'm not smart—I don't eat chop suey and run around Coney Island with tramps. (*She walks reflectively to buffet, picks up a box of candy, puts it down, says to Myron.*) Tomorrow night bring Sam Feinschreiber for supper.

HENNIE   I won't do it.

BESSIE   You'll do it, my fine beauty, you'll do it!

HENNIE   I'm not marrying a poor foreigner like him. Can't even speak an English word. Not me! I'll go to my grave without a husband.

BESSIE   You don't say! We'll find for you somewhere a

millionaire with a pleasure boat. He's going to night school, Sam. For a boy only three years in the country he speaks very nice. In three years he put enough in the bank, a good living.

JACOB   This is serious?

BESSIE   What then? I'm talking for my health? He'll come tomorrow night for supper. By Saturday they're engaged.

JACOB   Such a thing you can't do.

BESSIE   Who asked your advice?

JACOB   Such a thing——

BESSIE   Never mind!

JACOB   The lowest from the low!

BESSIE   Don't talk! I'm warning you! A man who don't believe in God—with crazy ideas——

JACOB   So bad I never imagined you could be.

BESSIE   Maybe if you didn't talk so much it wouldn't happen like this. You with your ideas—I'm a mother. I raise a family, they should have respect.

JACOB   Respect? (*Spits.*) Respect! For the neighbors' opinion! You insult me, Bessie!

BESSIE   Go in your room, Papa. Every job he ever had he lost because he's got a big mouth. He opens his mouth and the whole Bronx could fall in. Everybody said it——

MYRON   Momma, they'll hear you down the dumbwaiter.

BESSIE   A good barber not to hold a job a week. Maybe you never heard charity starts at home. You never heard it, Pop?

JACOB   All you know, I heard, and more yet. But Ralph you don't make like you. Before you do it, I'll die first. He'll find a girl. He'll go in a fresh world with her. This is a house? Marx said it—abolish such families.

BESSIE   Go in your room, Papa.

JACOB   Ralph you don't make like you!

BESSIE   Go lay in your room with Caruso and the books together.

JACOB   All right!

BESSIE   Go in the room!

JACOB   Some day I'll come out I'll—— (*Unable to continue, he turns, looks at Hennie, goes to his door and there says with an attempt at humor.*) Bessie, some day you'll talk to me so fresh . . . I'll leave the house for good! (*He exits.*)

BESSIE (*crying*) You ever in your life seen it? He should dare! He should just dare say in the house another word. Your gall could bust from such a man. (*Bell rings, Myron goes.*) Go to sleep now. It won't hurt.

HENNIE Yeah? (*Moe enters, a box in his hand. Myron follows and sits down.*)

MOE (*looks around first—putting box on table*) Cake. (*About to give Myron the money, he turns instead to Bessie.*) Six fifty, four bits change . . . come on, hand over half a buck. (*She does so. Of Myron.*) Who bit him?

BESSIE We're soon losing our Hennie, Moe.

MOE Why? What's the matter?

BESSIE She made her engagement.

MOE Zat so?

BESSIE Today it happened . . . he asked her.

MOE Did he? Who? Who's the corpse?

BESSIE It's a secret.

MOE In the bag, huh?

HENNIE Yeah. . . .

BESSIE When a mother gives away an only daughter it's no joke. Wait, when you'll get married you'll know. . . .

MOE (*bitterly*) Don't make me laugh—when I get married! What I think a women? Take 'em all, cut 'em in little pieces like a herring in Greek salad. A guy in France had the right idea—dropped his wife in a bathtub fulla acid. (*Whistles.*) Sss, down the pipe! Pfft—not even a corset button left!

MYRON Corsets don't have buttons.

MOE (*to Hennie*) What's the great idea? Gone big time, Paradise? Christ, it's suicide! Sure, kids you'll have, gold teeth, get fat, big in the tangerines——

HENNIE Shut your face!

MOE Who's it—some dope pullin' down twenty bucks a week? Cut your throat, sweetheart. Save time.

BESSIE Never mind your two cents, Axelrod.

MOE I say what I think—that's me!

HENNIE That's you—a lousy fourflusher who'd steal the glasses off a blind man.

MOE Get hot!

HENNIE My God, do I need it—to listen to this mutt shoot his mouth off?

MYRON Please. . . .

MOE   Now wait a minute, sweetheart, wait a minute. I don't have to take that from you.

BESSIE   Don't yell at her!

HENNIE   For two cents I'd spit in your eye.

MOE (*throwing coin to table*)   Here's two bits. (*Hennie looks at him and then starts across the room.*)

BESSIE   Where are you going?

HENNIE (*crying*)   For my beauty nap, Mussolini. Wake me up when it's apple blossom time in Normandy. (*Exits.*)

MOE   Pretty, pretty—a sweet gal, your Hennie. See the look in her eyes?

BESSIE   She don't feel well. . . .

MYRON   Canned goods. . . .

BESSIE   So don't start with her.

MOE   Like a battleship she's got it. Not like other dames— shove 'em and they lay. Not her. I got a yen for her and I don't mean a Chinee coin.

BESSIE   Listen, Axelrod, in my house you don't talk this way. Either have respect or get out.

MOE   When I think about it . . . maybe I'd marry her myself.

BESSIE (*suddenly aware of Moe*)   You could—— What do you mean, Moe?

MOE   You ain't sunburnt—you heard me.

BESSIE   Why don't you, Moe? An old friend of the family like you. It would be a blessing on all of us.

MOE   You said she's engaged.

BESSIE   But maybe she don't know her own mind. Say, it's——

MOE   I need a wife like a hole in the head. . . . What's to know about women, I know. Even if I asked her. She won't do it! A guy with one leg—it gives her the heebie-jeebies. I know what she's looking for. An arrow-collar guy, a hero, but with a wad of jack. Only the two don't go together. But I got what it takes . . . plenty, and more where it comes from. . . .

Breaks off, snorts and rubs his knee. A pause. In his room Jacob puts on Caruso singing the lament from "The Pearl Fishers." [5]

BESSIE   It's right—she wants a millionaire with a mansion on Riverside Drive. So go fight City Hall. Cake?

5. Opera (1863) by Georges Bizet (1838–75).

MOE Cake.

BESSIE I'll make tea. But one thing—she's got a fine boy with a business brain. Caruso! (*Exits into the front room and stands in the dark, at the window.*)

MOE No wet smack . . . a fine girl. . . . She'll burn that guy out in a month. (*Moe retrieves the quarter and spins it on the table.*)

MYRON I remember that song . . . beautiful. Nora Bayes sang it at the old Proctor's Twenty-third Street—"When It's Apple Blossom Time in Normandy."

MOE She wantsa see me crawl—my head on a plate she wants! A snowball in hell's got a better chance. (*Out of sheer fury he spins the quarter in his fingers.*)

MYRON (*as his eyes slowly fill with tears*) Beautiful . . .

MOE Match you for a quarter. Match you for any goddam thing you got. (*Spins the coin viciously.*) What the hell kind of house is this it ain't got an orange!!

SLOW CURTAIN

ACT TWO

Scene 1

One year later, a Sunday afternoon. The front room. Jacob is giving his son Mordecai (Uncle Morty) a haircut, newspapers spread around the base of the chair. Moe is reading a newspaper, leg propped on a chair. Ralph, in another chair, is spasmodically reading a paper. Uncle Morty reads colored jokes. Silence, then Bessie enters.

BESSIE Dinner's in half an hour, Morty.

MORTY (*still reading jokes*) I got time.

BESSIE A duck. Don't get hair on the rug, Pop. (*Goes to window and pulls down shade.*) What's the matter the shade's up to the ceiling?

JACOB (*pulling it up again*) Since when do I give a haircut in the dark? (*He mimics her tone.*)

BESSIE When you're finished, pull it down. I like my house to look respectable. Ralphie, bring up two bottles seltzer from Weiss.

RALPH I'm reading the paper.

BESSIE   Uncle Morty likes a little seltzer.

RALPH   I'm expecting a phone call.

BESSIE   Noo, if it comes you'll be back. What's the matter? (*Gives him money from apron pocket.*) Take down the old bottles.

RALPH (*to Jacob*)   Get that call if it comes. Say I'll be right back. (*Jacob nods assent.*)

MORTY (*giving change from vest*)   Get grandpa some cigarettes.

RALPH   Okay. (*Exits.*)

JACOB   What's new in the paper, Moe?

MOE   Still jumping off the high buildings like flies—the big shots who lost all their cocoanuts. Pfft!

JACOB   Suicides?

MOE   Plenty can't take it—good in the break, but can't take the whip in the stretch.

MORTY (*without looking up*)   I saw it happen Monday in my building. My hair stood up how they shoveled him together —like a pancake—a bankrupt manufacturer.

MOE   No brains.

MORTY   Enough . . . all over the sidewalk.

JACOB   If someone said five-ten years ago I couldn't make for myself a living, I wouldn't believe——

MORTY   Duck for dinner?

BESSIE   The best Long Island duck.

MORTY   I like goose.

BESSIE   A duck is just like a goose, only better.

MORTY   I like a goose.

BESSIE   The next time you'll be for Sunday dinner I'll make a goose.

MORTY (*sniffs deeply*)   Smells good. I'm a great boy for smells.

BESSIE   Ain't you ashamed? Once in a blue moon he should come to an only sister's house.

MORTY   Bessie, leave me live.

BESSIE   You should be ashamed!

MORTY   Quack quack!

BESSIE   No, better to lay around Mecca Temple playing cards with the Masons.

MORTY (*with good nature*)   Bessie, don't you see Pop's giving me a haircut?

BESSIE   You don't need no haircut. Look, two hairs he took off.

MORTY   Pop likes to give me a haircut. If I said no he don't forget for a year, do you, Pop? An old man's like that.

JACOB   I still do an A-1 job.

MORTY (*winking*)   Pop cuts hair to fit the face, don't you, Pop?

JACOB   For sure, Morty. To each face a different haircut. Custom built, no ready made. A round face needs special——

BESSIE (*cutting him short*)   A graduate from the B.M.T. (*Going.*) Don't forget the shade. (*The phone rings. She beats Jacob to it.*) Hello? Who is it, please? . . . Who is it please? . . . Miss Hirsch? No, he ain't here. . . . No, I couldn't say when. (*Hangs up sharply.*)

JACOB   For Ralph?

BESSIE   A wrong number. (*Jacob looks at her and goes back to his job.*)

JACOB   Excuse me!

BESSIE (*to Morty*)   Ralphie took another cut down the place yesterday.

MORTY   Business is bad. I saw his boss Harry Glicksman Thursday. I bought some velvets . . . they're coming in again.

BESSIE   Do something for Ralphie down there.

MORTY   What can I do? I mentioned it to Glicksman. He told me they squeezed out half the people. . . . (*Myron enters dressed in apron.*)

BESSIE   What's gonna be the end? Myron's working only three days a week now.

MYRON   It's conditions.

BESSIE   Hennie's married with a baby . . . money just don't come in. I never saw conditions should be so bad.

MORTY   Times'll change.

MOE   The only thing'll change is my underwear.

MORTY   These last few years I got my share of gray hairs. (*Still reading jokes without having looked up once.*) Ha, ha, ha—Popeye the sailor ate spinach and knocked out four bums.

MYRON   I'll tell you the way I see it. The country needs a great man now—a regular Teddy Roosevelt.

MOE   What this country needs is a good five-cent earthquake.[1]

---

1. A play on a familiar wisecrack of the period: "What this country needs is a good five-cent cigar."

JACOB   So long labor lives it should increase private gain——

BESSIE (*to Jacob*)   Listen, Poppa, go talk on the street corner. The government'll give you free board the rest of your life.

MORTY   I'm surprised. Don't I send a five-dollar check for Pop every week?

BESSIE   You could afford a couple more and not miss it.

MORTY   Tell me jokes. Business is so rotten I could just as soon lay all day in the Turkish bath.

MYRON   Why'd I come in here? (*Puzzled, he exits.*)

MORTY (*to Moe*)   I hear the bootleggers still do business, Moe.

MOE   Wake up! I kissed bootlegging bye-bye two years back.

MORTY   For a fact? What kind of racket is it now?

MOE   If I told you, you'd know something. (*Hennie comes from bedroom.*)

HENNIE   Where's Sam?

BESSIE   Sam? In the kitchen.

HENNIE (*calls*)   Sam. Come take the diaper.

MORTY   How's the Mickey Louse? Ha, ha, ha. . . .

HENNIE   Sleeping.

MORTY   Ah, that's life to a baby. He sleeps—gets it in the mouth—sleeps some more. To raise a family nowadays you must be a damn fool.

BESSIE   Never mind, never mind, a woman who don't raise a family—a girl—should jump overboard. What's she good for? (*To Moe—to change the subject.*) Your leg bothers you bad?

MOE   It's okay, sweetheart.

BESSIE (*to Morty*)   It hurts him every time it's cold out. He's got four legs in the closet.

MORTY   Four wooden legs?

MOE   Three.

MORTY   What's the big idea?

MOE   Why not? Uncle Sam gives them out free.

MORTY   Say, maybe if Uncle Sam gave out less legs we could balance the budget.

JACOB   Or not have a war so they wouldn't have to give out legs.

MORTY   Shame on you, Pop. Everybody knows war is necessary.

MOE   Don't make me laugh. Ask me—the first time you pack up a dead one in the trench—then you learn war ain't so damn necessary.

MORTY   Say, you should kick. The rest of your life Uncle Sam pays you ninety a month. Look, not a worry in the world.

MOE   Don't make me laugh. Uncle Sam can take his *seventy* bucks and—— (*Finishes with a gesture.*) Nothing good hurts. (*He rubs his stump.*)

HENNIE   Use a crutch, Axelrod. Give the stump a rest.

MOE   Mind your business, Feinschreiber.

BESSIE   It's a sensible idea.

MOE   Who asked you?

BESSIE   Look, he's ashamed.

MOE   So's your Aunt Fanny.

BESSIE (*naïvely*)   Who's got an Aunt Fanny? (*She cleans a rubber plant's leaves with her apron.*)

MORTY   It's a joke!

MOE   I don't want my paper creased before I read it. I want it fresh. Fifty times I said that.

BESSIE   Don't get so excited for a five-cent paper—our star boarder.

MOE   And I don't want no one using my razor either. Get it straight. I'm not buying ten blades a week for the Berger family. (*Furious, he limps out.*)

BESSIE   Maybe I'm using his razor too.

HENNIE   Proud!

BESSIE   You need luck with plants. I didn't clean off the leaves in a month.

MORTY   You keep the house like a pin and I like your cooking. Any time Myron fires you, come to me, Bessie. I'll let the butler go and you'll be my housekeeper. I don't like Japs so much—sneaky.

BESSIE   Say, you can't tell. Maybe any day I'm coming to stay. (*Hennie exits.*)

JACOB   Finished.

MORTY   How much, Ed. Pinaud? [2] (*Disengages self from chair.*)

JACOB   Five cents.

MORTY   Still five cents for a haircut to fit the face?

JACOB   Prices don't change by me. (*Takes a dollar.*) I can't change——

MORTY   Keep it. Buy yourself a Packard. Ha, ha, ha.

JACOB (*taking large envelope from pocket*)   Please, you'll keep this for me. Put it away.

2. The name of a strong-smelling hair tonic.

MORTY   What is it?

JACOB   My insurance policy. I don't like it should lay around where something could happen.

MORTY   What could happen?

JACOB   Who knows, robbers, fire . . . they took next door. Fifty dollars from O'Reilly.

MORTY   Say, lucky a Berger didn't lose it.

JACOB   Put it downtown in the safe. Bessie don't have to know.

MORTY   It's made out to Bessie?

JACOB   No, to Ralph.

MORTY   To Ralph?

JACOB   He don't know. Some day he'll get three thousand.

MORTY   You got good years ahead.

JACOB   Behind. (*Ralph enters.*)

RALPH   Cigarettes. Did a call come?

JACOB   A few minutes. She don't let me answer it.

RALPH   Did Mom say I was coming back?

JACOB   No. (*Morty is back at new jokes.*)

RALPH   She starting that stuff again? (*Bessie enters.*) A call come for me?

BESSIE (*waters pot from milk bottle*)   A wrong number.

JACOB   Don't say a lie, Bessie.

RALPH   Blanche said she'd call me at two—was it her?

BESSIE   I said a wrong number.

RALPH   Please, Mom, if it was her tell me.

BESSIE   You call me a liar next. You got no shame—to start a scene in front of Uncle Morty. Once in a blue moon he comes——

RALPH   What's the shame? If my girl calls I wanna know it.

BESSIE   You made enough mish mosh with her until now.

MORTY   I'm surprised, Bessie. For the love of Mike tell him yes or no.

BESSIE   I didn't tell him? No!

MORTY (*to Ralph*)   No! (*Ralph goes to a window and looks out.*)

BESSIE   Morty, I didn't say before—he runs around steady with a girl.

MORTY   Terrible. Should he run around with a foxie-woxie?

BESSIE   A girl with no parents.

MORTY   An orphan?

BESSIE   I could die from shame. A year already he runs

around with her. He brought her once for supper. Believe me, she didn't come again, no!

RALPH   Don't think I didn't ask her.

BESSIE   You hear? You raise them and what's in the end for all your trouble?

JACOB   When you'll lay in a grave, no more trouble. (*Exits.*)

MORTY   Quack quack!

BESSIE   A girl like that he wants to marry. A skinny consumptive-looking . . . six months already she's not working—taking charity from an aunt. You should see her. In a year she's dead on his hands.

RALPH   You'd cut her throat if you could.

BESSIE   That's right! Before she'd ruin a nice boy's life I would first go to prison. Miss Nobody should step in the picture and I'll stand by with my mouth shut.

RALPH   Miss Nobody! Who am I? Al Jolson? [3]

BESSIE   Fix your tie!

RALPH   I'll take care of my own life.

BESSIE   You'll take care? Excuse my expression, you can't even wipe your nose yet! He'll take care!

MORTY (*to Bessie*)   I'm surprised. Don't worry so much, Bessie. When it's time to settle down he won't marry a poor girl, will you? In the long run common sense is thicker than love. I'm a great boy for live and let live.

BESSIE   Sure, it's easy to say. In the meantime he eats out my heart. You know I'm not strong.

MORTY   I know . . . a pussy cat . . . ha, ha, ha.

BESSIE   You got money and money talks. But without the dollar who sleeps at night?

RALPH   I been working for years, bringing in money here—putting it in your hand like a kid. All right, I can't get my teeth fixed. All right, that a new suit's like trying to buy the Chrysler Building. You never in your life bought me a pair of skates even—things I died for when I was a kid. I don't care about that stuff, see. Only just remember I pay some of the bills around here, just a few . . . and if my girl calls me on the phone I'll talk to her any time I please. (*He exits. Hennie applauds.*)

BESSIE   Don't be so smart, Miss America! (*To Morty.*) He didn't have skates! But when he got sick, a twelve-year-old

3. Popular entertainer of stage, films, and radio, 1888–1950.

boy, who called a big specialist for the last $25 in the house? Skates!

JACOB (*Just in. Adjusts window shade.*)   It looks like snow today.

MORTY   It's about time—winter.

BESSIE   Poppa here could talk like Samuel Webster, too, but it's just talk. He should try to buy a two-cent pickle in the Burland Market without money.

MORTY   I'm getting an appetite.

BESSIE   Right away we'll eat. I made chopped liver for you.

MORTY   My specialty!

BESSIE   Ralph should only be a success like you, Morty. I should only live to see the day when he rides up to the door in a big car with a chauffeur and a radio. I could die happy, believe me.

MORTY   Success she says. She should see how we spend thousands of dollars making up a winter line and winter don't come—summer in January. Can you beat it?

JACOB   Don't live, just make success.

MORTY   Chopped liver—ha!

JACOB   Ha! (*Exits.*)

MORTY   When they start arguing, I don't hear. Suddenly I'm deaf. I'm a great boy for the practical side. (*He looks over to Hennie who sits rubbing her hands with lotion.*)

HENNIE   Hands like a raw potato.

MORTY   What's the matter? You don't look so well . . . no pep.

HENNIE   I'm swell.

MORTY   You used to be such a pretty girl.

HENNIE   Maybe I got the blues. You can't tell.

MORTY   You could stand a new dress.

HENNIE   That's not all I could stand.

MORTY   Come down to the place tomorrow and pick out a couple from the "eleven-eighty" line. Only don't sing me the blues.

HENNIE   Thanks. I need some new clothes.

MORTY   I got two thousand pieces of merchandise waiting in the stock room for winter.

HENNIE   I never had anything from life. Sam don't help.

MORTY   He's crazy about the kid.

HENNIE   Crazy is right. Twenty-one a week he brings in—a nigger don't have it so hard. I wore my fingers off on an

Underwood for six years. For what? Now I wash baby diapers. Sure, I'm crazy about the kid too. But half the night the kid's up. Try to sleep. You don't know how it is, Uncle Morty.

MORTY   No, I don't know. I was born yesterday. Ha, ha, ha. Some day I'll leave you a little nest egg. You like eggs? Ha?

HENNIE   When? When I'm dead and buried?

MORTY   No, when *I'm* dead and buried. Ha, ha, ha.

HENNIE   You should know what I'm thinking.

MORTY   Ha, ha, ha, I know. (*Myron enters.*)

MYRON   I never take a drink. I'm just surprised at myself, I——

MORTY   I got a pain. Maybe I'm hungry.

MYRON   Come inside, Morty. Bessie's got some schnapps.

MORTY   I'll take a drink. Yesterday I missed the Turkish bath.

MYRON   I get so bitter when I take a drink, it just surprises me.

MORTY   Look how fat. Say, you live once. . . . Quack, quack. (*Both exit, Moe stands silently in the doorway.*)

SAM (*entering*)   I'll make Leon's bottle now!

HENNIE   No, let him sleep, Sam. Take away the diaper. (*He does. Exits.*)

MOE (*advancing into the room*)   That your husband?

HENNIE   Don't you know?

MOE   Maybe he's a nurse you hired for the kid—it looks it—how he tends it. A guy comes howling to your old lady every time you look cock-eyed. Does he sleep with you?

HENNIE   Don't be so wise!

MOE (*indicating newspaper*)   Here's a dame strangled her hubby with wire. Claimed she didn't like him. Why don't you brain Sam with an axe some night?

HENNIE   Why don't you lay an egg, Axelrod?

MOE   I laid a few in my day, Feinschreiber. Hard-boiled ones too.

HENNIE   Yeah?

MOE   Yeah. You wanna know what I see when I look in your eyes?

HENNIE   No.

MOE   Ted Lewis playing the clarinet—some of those high

crazy notes! Christ, you coulda had a guy with some guts instead of a cluck stands around boilin' baby nipples.

HENNIE Meaning you?

MOE Meaning me, sweetheart.

HENNIE Think you're pretty good.

MOE You'd know if I slept with you again.

HENNIE I'll smack your face in a minute.

MOE You do and I'll break your arm. (*Holds up paper.*) Take a look. (*Reads.*) "Ten-day luxury cruise to Havana." That's the stuff you coulda had. Put up at ritzy hotels, frenchie soap, champagne. Now you're tied down to "Snake-Eye" here. What for? What's it get you? . . . a 2 x 4 flat on 108th Street . . . a pain in the bustle it gets you.

HENNIE What's it to you?

MOE I know you from the old days. How you like to spend it! What I mean! Lizard-skin shoes, perfume behind the ears. . . . You're in a mess, Paradise! Paradise—that's a hot one—yah, crazy to eat a knish at your own wedding.

HENNIE I get it—you're jealous. You can't get me.

MOE Don't make me laugh.

HENNIE Kid Jailbird's been trying to make me for years. You'd give your other leg. I'm hooked? Maybe, but you're in the same boat. Only it's worse for you. I don't give a damn no more, but you gotta yen makes you——

MOE Don't make me laugh.

HENNIE Compared to you I'm sittin' on top of the world.

MOE You're losing your looks. A dame don't stay young forever.

HENNIE You're a liar. I'm only twenty-four.

MOE When you comin' home to stay?

HENNIE Wouldn't you like to know?

MOE I'll get you again.

HENNIE Think so?

MOE Sure, whatever goes up comes down. You're easy—you remember—two for a nickel—a pushover! (*Suddenly she slaps him. They both seem stunned.*) What's the idea?

HENNIE Go on . . . break my arm.

MOE (*as if saying "I love you"*) Listen, lousy.

HENNIE Go on, do something!

MOE Listen——

HENNIE You're so damn tough!

MOE   You like me. (*He takes her.*)

HENNIE   Take your hand off! (*Pushes him away.*) Come around when it's a flood again and they put you in the ark with the animals. Not even then—if you was the last man!

MOE   Baby, if you had a dog I'd love the dog.

HENNIE   Gorilla! (*Exits. Ralph enters.*)

RALPH   Were you here before?

MOE (*sits*)   What?

RALPH   When the call came for me?

MOE   What?

RALPH   The call came. (*Jacob enters.*)

MOE (*rubbing his leg*)   No.

JACOB   Don't worry, Ralphie, she'll call back.

RALPH   Maybe not. I think somethin's the matter.

JACOB   What?

RALPH   I don't know. I took her home from the movie last night. She asked me what I'd think if she went away.

JACOB   Don't worry, she'll call again.

RALPH   Maybe not, if Mom insulted her. She gets it on both ends, the poor kid. Lived in an orphan asylum most of her life. They shove her around like an empty freight train.

JACOB   After dinner go see her.

RALPH   Twice they kicked me down the stairs.

JACOB   Life should have some dignity.

RALPH   Every time I go near the place I get heart failure. The uncle drives a bus. You oughta see him—like Babe Ruth.

MOE   Use your brains. Stop acting like a kid who still wets the bed. Hire a room somewhere—a club room for two members.

RALPH   Not that kind of proposition, Moe.

MOE   Don't be a bush leaguer all your life.

RALPH   Cut it out!

MOE (*on a sudden upsurge of emotion*)   Ever sleep with one? Look at 'im blush.

RALPH   You don't know her.

MOE   I seen her—the kind no one sees undressed till the undertaker works on her.

RALPH   Why give me the needles all the time? What'd I ever do to you?

MOE   Not a thing. You're a nice kid. But grow up! In life there's two kinds—the men that's sure of themselves and the ones who ain't! It's time you quit being a selling-plater[4] and got in the first class.

JACOB And you, Axelrod?

MOE (*to Jacob*) Scratch your whiskers! (*To Ralph.*) Get independent. Get what-it-takes and be yourself. Do what you like.

RALPH Got a suggestion? (*Morty enters, eating.*)

MOE Sure, pick out a racket. Shake down the cocoanuts. See what that does.

MORTY We know what it does—puts a pudding on your nose! Sing Sing! Easy money's against the law. Against the law don't win. A racket is illegitimate, no?

MOE It's all a racket—from horse racing down. Marriage, politics, big business—everybody plays cops and robbers. You, you're a racketeer yourself.

MORTY Who? Me? Personally I manufacture dresses.

MOE Horse feathers!

MORTY (*seriously*) Don't make such remarks to me without proof. I'm a great one for proof. That's why I made a success in business. Proof—put up or shut up, like a game of cards. I heard this remark before—a rich man's a crook who steals from the poor. Personally, I don't like it. It's a big lie!

MOE If you don't like it, buy yourself a fife and drum—and go fight your own war.

MORTY Sweatshop talk. Every Jew and Wop in the shop eats my bread and behind my back says, "a sonofabitch." I started from a poor boy who worked on an ice wagon for two dollars a week. Pop's right here—he'll tell you. I made it honest. In the whole industry nobody's got a better name.

JACOB It's an exception, such success.

MORTY Ralph can't do the same thing?

JACOB No, Morty, I don't think. In a house like this he don't realize even the possibilities of life. Economics comes down like a ton of coal on the head.

MOE Red rover, red rover, let Jacob come over!

JACOB In my day the propaganda was for God. Now it's for success. A boy don't turn around without having shoved in him he should make success.

MORTY Pop, you're a comedian, a regular Charlie Chaplin.

4. A racing term for a horse that runs in selling races—thus an "also-ran" or second-best.

JACOB   He dreams all night of fortunes. Why not? Don't it say in the movies he should have a personal steamship, pyjamas for fifty dollars a pair and a toilet like a monument? But in the morning he wakes up and for ten dollars he can't fix the teeth. And millions more worse off in the mills of the South—starvation wages. The blood from the worker's heart. (*Morty laughs loud and long.*) Laugh, laugh . . . tomorrow not.

MORTY   A real, a real Boob McNutt[5] you're getting to be.

JACOB   Laugh, my son. . . .

MORTY   Here is the North, Pop.

JACOB   North, south, it's one country.

MORTY   The country's all right. A duck quacks in every pot!

JACOB   You never heard how they shoot down men and women which ask a better wage? Kentucky 1932?

MORTY   That's a pile of chopped liver, Pop. (*Bessie and others enter.*)

JACOB   Pittsburgh, Passaic, Illinois—slavery—it begins where success begins in a competitive system. (*Morty howls with delight.*)

MORTY   Oh Pop, what are you bothering? Why? Tell me why? Ha ha ha. I bought you a phonograph . . . stick to Caruso.

BESSIE   He's starting up again.

MORTY   Don't bother with Kentucky. It's full of moonshiners.

JACOB   Sure, sure——

MORTY   You don't know practical affairs. Stay home and cut hair to fit the face.

JACOB   It says in the Bible how the Red Sea opened and the Egyptians went in and the sea rolled over them. (*Quotes two lines of Hebrew.*) In this boy's life a Red Sea will happen again. I see it!

MORTY   I'm getting sore, Pop, with all this sweatshop talk.

BESSIE   He don't stop a minute. The whole day, like a phonograph.

MORTY   I'm surprised. Without a rich man you don't have a roof over your head. You don't know it?

MYRON   Now you can't bite the hand that feeds you.

RALPH   Let him alone—he's right!

BESSIE   Another county heard from.

5. A cartoon character who wore a tin can on his head.

RALPH   It's the truth. It's——

MORTY   Keep quiet, snotnose!

JACOB   For sure, charity, a bone for an old dog. But in Russia an old man don't take charity so his eyes turn black in his head. In Russia they got Marx.

MORTY (*scoffingly*)   Who's Marx?

MOE   An outfielder for the Yanks. (*Morty howls with delight.*)

MORTY   Ha ha ha, it's better than the jokes. I'm telling you. This is Uncle Sam's country. Put it in your pipe and smoke it.

BESSIE   Russia, he says! Read the papers.

SAM   Here is opportunity.

MYRON   People can't believe in God in Russia. The papers tell the truth, they do.

JACOB   So you believe in God . . . you got something for it? You! You worked for all the capitalists. You harvested the fruit from your labor? You got God! But the past comforts you? The present smiles on you, yes? It promises you the future something? Did you found a piece of earth where you could live like a human being and die with the sun on your face? Tell me, yes, tell me. I would like to know myself. But on these questions, on this theme—the struggle for existence—you can't make an answer. The answer I see in your face . . . the answer is your mouth can't talk. In this dark corner you sit and you die. But abolish private property!

BESSIE (*settling the issue*)   Noo, go fight City Hall!

MORTY   He's drunk!

JACOB   I'm studying from books a whole lifetime.

MORTY   That's what it is—he's drunk. What the hell does all that mean?

JACOB   If you don't know, why should I tell you.

MORTY (*triumphant at last*)   You see? Hear him? Like all those nuts, don't know what they're saying.

JACOB   I know, I know.

MORTY   Like Boob McNutt you know! Don't go in the park, Pop—the squirrels'll get you. Ha, ha, ha. . . .

BESSIE   Save your appetite, Morty. (*To Myron.*) Don't drop the duck.

MYRON   We're ready to eat, Momma.

MORTY (*to Jacob*)   Shame on you. It's your second childhood. (*Now they file out. Myron first with the duck, the others behind him.*)

BESSIE   Come eat. We had enough for one day. (*Exits.*)

MORTY   Ha, ha, ha. Quack, quack. (*Exits.*)

Jacob sits there trembling and deeply humiliated. Moe approaches him and thumbs the old man's nose in the direction of the dining room.

MOE   Give 'em five. (*Takes his hand away.*) They got you pasted on the wall like a picture, Jake. (*He limps out to seat himself at the table in the next room.*)

JACOB   Go eat, boychick. (*Ralph comes to him.*) He gives me eat, so I'll climb in a needle. One time I saw an old horse in summer . . . he wore a straw hat . . . the ears stuck out on top. An old horse for hire. Give me back my young days . . . give me fresh blood . . . arms . . . give me—— (*The telephone rings. Quickly Ralph goes to it. Jacob pulls the curtains and stands there, a sentry on guard.*)

RALPH   Hello? . . . Yeah, I went to the store and came right back, right after you called. (*Looks at Jacob.*)

JACOB   Speak, speak. Don't be afraid they'll hear.

RALPH   I'm sorry if Mom said something. You know how excitable Mom is . . . Sure! What? . . . Sure, I'm listening. . . . Put on the radio, Jake. (*Jacob does so. Music comes in and up, a tango, grating with an insistent nostalgic pulse. Under the cover of the music Ralph speaks more freely.*) Yes . . . yes . . . What's the matter? Why're you crying? What happened? (*To Jacob.*) She's putting her uncle on. Yes? . . . Listen, Mr. Hirsch, what're you trying to do? What's the big idea? Honest to God. I'm in no mood for joking! Lemme talk to her! Gimme Blanche! (*Waits.*) Blanche? What's this? Is this a joke? Is that true? I'm coming right down! I know, but—— You wanna do that? . . . I know, but—— I'm coming down . . . tonight! Nine o'clock . . . sure . . . sure . . . sure. . . . (*Hangs up.*)

JACOB   What happened?

MORTY (*enters*)   Listen, Pop. I'm surprised you didn't—— (*He howls, shakes his head in mock despair, exits.*)

JACOB   Boychick, what?

RALPH   I don't get it straight. (*To Jacob.*) She's leaving. . . .

JACOB   Where?

RALPH   Out West—— To Cleveland.

JACOB   Cleveland?

RALPH ... In a week or two. Can you picture it? It's a put-up job. But they can't get away with that.

JACOB We'll find something.

RALPH Sure, the angels of heaven'll come down on her uncle's cab and whisper in his ear.

JACOB Come eat. . . . We'll find something.

RALPH I'm meeting her tonight, but I know—— (*Bessie throws open the curtain between the two rooms and enters.*)

BESSIE Maybe we'll serve for you a special blue plate supper in the garden?

JACOB All right, all right. (*Bessie goes over to the window, levels the shade and on her way out, clicks off the radio.*)

MORTY (*within*) Leave the music, Bessie. (*She clicks it on again, looks at them, exits.*)

RALPH I know . . .

JACOB Don't cry, boychick. (*Goes over to Ralph.*) Why should you make like this? Tell me why you should cry, just tell me. . . .

Jacob takes Ralph in his arms and both, trying to keep back the tears, trying fearfully not to be heard by the others in the dining room, begin crying.

You mustn't cry. . . .

The tango twists on. Inside the clatter of dishes and the clash of cutlery sound. Morty begins to howl with laughter.

CURTAIN

Scene 2

That night. The dark dining room.

At Rise Jacob is heard in his lighted room, reading from a sheet, declaiming aloud as if to an audience.

JACOB They are there to remind us of the horrors—under those crosses lie hundreds of thousands of workers and farmers who murdered each other in uniform for the greater glory of capitalism. (*Comes out of his room.*) The new imperialist war will send millions to their death, will bring prosperity to the pockets of the capitalist—aie, Morty—and will bring only greater hunger and misery to the masses of workers and farmers. The memories of the last world slaughter are still vivid in our minds. (*Hearing a noise he quickly retreats to his room. Ralph comes in from the street. He sits with hat and coat on. Jacob tentatively opens door and asks.*) Ralphie?

RALPH It's getting pretty cold out.

JACOB (*enters room fully, cleaning hair clippers*) We should have steam till twelve instead of ten. Go complain to the Board of Health.

RALPH It might snow.

JACOB It don't hurt . . . extra work for men.

RALPH When I was a kid I laid awake at nights and heard the sounds of trains . . . far-away lonesome sounds . . . boats going up and down the river. I used to think of all kinds of things I wanted to do. What was it, Jake? Just a bunch of noise in my head?

JACOB (*waiting for news of the girl*) You wanted to make for yourself a certain kind of world.

RALPH I guess I didn't. I'm feeling pretty, pretty low.

JACOB You're a young boy and for you life is all in front like a big mountain. You got feet to climb.

RALPH I don't know how.

JACOB So you'll find out. Never a young man had such opportunity like today. He could make history.

RALPH Ten P.M. and all is well. Where's everybody?

JACOB They went.

RALPH Uncle Morty too?

JACOB Hennie and Sam he drove down.

RALPH I saw her.

JACOB (*alert and eager*) Yes, yes, tell me.

RALPH I waited in Mount Morris Park till she came out. So cold I did a buck'n wing[1] to keep warm. She's scared to death.

JACOB They made her?

RALPH Sure. She wants to go. They keep yelling at her—they want her to marry a millionaire, too.

JACOB You told her you love her?

RALPH Sure. "Marry me," I said. "Marry me tomorrow." On

___

1. A brisk, complicated tap-dance step.

sixteen bucks a week. On top of that I had to admit Mom'd have Uncle Morty get me fired in a second. . . . Two can starve as cheap as one!

JACOB   So what happened?

RALPH   I made her promise to meet me tomorrow.

JACOB   Now she'll go in the West?

RALPH   I'd fight the whole goddam world with her, but not her. No guts. The hell with her. If she wantsa go—all right—I'll get along.

JACOB   For sure, there's more important things than girls. . . .

RALPH   You said a mouthful . . . and maybe I don't see it. She'll see what I can do. No one stops me when I get going. . . .

Near to tears, he has to stop. Jacob examines his clippers very closely.

JACOB   Electric clippers never do a job like by hand.

RALPH   Why won't Mom let us live here?

JACOB   Why? Why? Because in a society like this today people don't love. Hate!

RALPH   Gee, I'm no bum who hangs around pool parlors. I got the stuff to go ahead. I don't know what to do.

JACOB   Look on me and learn what to do, boychick. Here sits an old man polishing tools. You think maybe I'll use them again! Look on this failure and see for seventy years he talked, with good ideas, but only in the head. It's enough for me now I should see your happiness. This is why I tell you—DO! Do what is in your heart and you carry in yourself a revolution. But you should act. Not like me. A man who had golden opportunities but drank instead a glass tea. No. . . . (*A pause of silence.*)

RALPH   (*listening*)   Hear it? The Boston air mail plane. Ten minutes late. I get a kick the way it cuts across the Bronx every night. (*The bell rings: Sam, excited, disheveled, enters.*)

JACOB   You came back so soon?

SAM   Where's Mom?

JACOB   Mom? Look on the chandelier.

SAM   Nobody's home?

JACOB   Sit down. Right away they're coming. You went in the street without a tie?

SAM   Maybe it's a crime.

JACOB   Excuse me.

RALPH   You had a fight with Hennie again?

SAM   She'll fight once . . . some day. . . . (*Lapses into silence.*)

JACOB   In my day the daughter came home. Now comes the son-in-law.

SAM   Once too often she'll fight with me, Hennie. I mean it. I mean it like anything. I'm a person with a bad heart. I sit quiet, but inside I got a——

RALPH   What happened?

SAM   I'll talk to Mom. I'll see Mom.

JACOB   Take an apple.

SAM   Please . . . he tells me apples.

RALPH   Why hop around like a billiard ball?

SAM   Even in a joke she should dare say it.

JACOB   My grandchild said something?

SAM   To my father in the old country they did a joke . . . I'll tell you: One day in Odessa he talked to another Jew on the street. They didn't like it, they jumped on him like a wild wolf.

RALPH   Who?

SAM   Cossacks. They cut off his beard. A Jew without a beard! He came home—I remember like yesterday how he came home and went in bed for two days. He put like this the cover on his face. No one should see. The third morning he died.

RALPH   From what?

SAM   From a broken heart. . . . Some people are like this. Me too. I could die like this from shame.

JACOB   Hennie told you something?

SAM   Straight out she said it—like a lightning from the sky. The baby ain't mine. She said it.

RALPH   Don't be a dope.

JACOB   For sure, a joke.

RALPH   She's kidding you.

SAM   She should kid a policeman, not Sam Feinschreiber. Please . . . you don't know her like me. I wake up in the nighttime and she sits watching me like I don't know what. I make a nice living from the store. But it's no use—she looks for a star in the sky. I'm afraid like anything. You could go crazy from less even. What I shall do I'll ask Mom.

JACOB   "Go home and sleep," she'll say. "It's a bad dream."

SAM   It don't satisfy me more, such remarks, when Hennie
could kill in the bed. (*Jacob laughs.*) Don't laugh. I'm so
nervous—look, two times I weighed myself on the subway
station. (*Throws small cards to table.*)

JACOB (*examining one*)   One hundred and thirty-eight—also a
fortune. (*Turns it and reads.*) "You are inclined to deep
thinking, and have a high admiration for intellectual
excellence and inclined to be very exclusive in the selection
of friends." Correct! I think maybe you got mixed up in the
wrong family, Sam. (*Myron and Bessie now enter.*)

BESSIE   Look, a guest! What's the matter? Something wrong
with the baby? (*Waits.*)

SAM   No.

BESSIE   Noo?

SAM (*in a burst*)   I wash my hands from everything.

BESSIE   Take off your coat and hat. Have a seat. Excitement
don't help. Myron, make tea. You'll have a glass tea. We'll
talk like civilized people. (*Myron goes.*) What is it, Ralph,
you're all dressed up for a party? (*He looks at her silently and
exits. To Sam.*) We saw a very good movie, with Wallace
Beery. He acts like life, very good.

MYRON (*within*)   Polly Moran too.

BESSIE   Polly Moran too—a woman with a nose from here to
Hunts Point, but a fine player. Poppa, take away the tools
and the books.

JACOB   All right. (*Exits to his room.*)

BESSIE   Noo, Sam, why do you look like a funeral?

SAM   I can't stand it. . . .

BESSIE   Wait. (*Yells.*) You took up Tootsie on the roof.

JACOB (*within*)   In a minute.

BESSIE   What can't you stand?

SAM   She said I'm a second fiddle in my own house.

BESSIE   Who?

SAM   Hennie. In the second place, it ain't my baby, she said.

BESSIE   What? What are you talking? (*Myron enters with dishes.*)

SAM   From her own mouth. It went like a knife in my heart.

BESSIE   Sam, what're you saying?

SAM   Please, I'm making a story? I fell in the chair like a
dead.

BESSIE   Such a story you believe?

SAM   I don't know.

BESSIE   How you don't know?

SAM   She told me even the man.

BESSIE   Impossible!

SAM   I can't believe myself. But she said it. I'm a second fiddle, she said. She made such a yell everybody heard for ten miles.

BESSIE   Such a thing Hennie should say—impossible!

SAM   What should I do? With my bad heart such a remark kills.

MYRON   Hennie don't feel well, Sam. You see, she——

BESSIE   What then?—a sick girl. Believe me, a mother knows. Nerves. Our Hennie's got a bad temper. You'll let her she says anything. She takes after me—nervous. (*To Myron.*) You ever heard such a remark in all your life? She should make such a statement! Bughouse.

MYRON   The little one's been sick all these months. Hennie needs a rest. No doubt.

BESSIE   Sam don't think she means it——

MYRON   Oh, I know he don't, of course——

BESSIE   I'll say the truth, Sam. We didn't half the time understand her ourselves. A girl with her own mind. When she makes it up, wild horses wouldn't change her.

SAM   She don't love me.

BESSIE   This is sensible, Sam?

SAM   Not for a nickel.

BESSIE   What do you think? She married you for your money? For your looks? You ain't no John Barrymore,[2] Sam. No, she liked you.

SAM   Please, not for a nickel. (*Jacob stands in the doorway.*)

BESSIE   We stood right here the first time she said it. "Sam Feinschreiber's a nice boy," she said it, "a boy he's got good common sense, with a business head." Right here she said it, in this room. You sent her two boxes of candy together, you remember?

MYRON   Loft's candy.

BESSIE   This is when she said it. What do you think?

MYRON   You were just the only boy she cared for.

BESSIE   So she married you. Such a world . . . plenty of boy friends she had, believe me!

2. A matinee idol of the period, member of a family of distinguished actors and actresses.

JACOB A popular girl. . . .

MYRON Y-e-s.

BESSIE I'll say it plain out—Moe Axelrod offered her plenty —a servant, a house . . . she don't have to pick up a hand.

MYRON Oh, Moe? Just wild about her. . . .

SAM Moe Axelrod? He wanted to——

BESSIE But she didn't care. A girl like Hennie you don't buy. I should never live to see another day if I'm telling a lie.

SAM She was kidding me.

BESSIE What then? You shouldn't be foolish.

SAM The baby looks like my family. He's got Feinschreiber eyes.

BESSIE A blind man could see it.

JACOB Sure . . . sure. . . .

SAM The baby looks like me. Yes. . . .

BESSIE You could believe me.

JACOB Any day. . . .

SAM But she tells me the man. She made up his name too?

BESSIE Sam, Sam, look in the phone book—a million names.

MYRON Tom, Dick and Harry. (*Jacob laughs quietly, soberly.*)

BESSIE Don't stand around, Poppa. Take Tootsie on the roof. And you don't let her go under the water tank.

JACOB Schmah Yisroel.[3] Behold! (*Quietly laughing he goes back into his room, closing the door behind him.*)

SAM I won't stand he should make insults. A man eats out his——

BESSIE No, no, he's an old man—a second childhood. Myron, bring in the tea. Open a jar of raspberry jelly. (*Myron exits.*)

SAM Mom, you think——?

BESSIE I'll talk to Hennie. It's all right.

SAM Tomorrow, I'll take her by the doctor. (*Ralph enters.*)

BESSIE Stay for a little tea.

SAM No, I'll go home. I'm tired. Already I caught a cold in such weather. (*Blows his nose.*)

MYRON (*entering with stuffs*) Going home?

SAM I'll go in bed. I caught a cold.

MYRON Teddy Roosevelt used to say, "When you have a problem, sleep on it."

BESSIE My Sam is no problem.

---

3. Hear, O Israel (Deuteronomy 6:4).

MYRON   I don't mean . . . I mean he said——

BESSIE   Call me tomorrow. Sam.

SAM   I'll phone supper time. Sometime I think there's something funny about me. (*Myron sees him out. In the following
pause Caruso is heard singing within.*)

BESSIE   A bargain! Second fiddle. By me he don't even play in
the orchestra—a man like a mouse. Maybe she'll lay down
and die 'cause he makes a living?

RALPH   Can I talk to you about something?

BESSIE   What's the matter—I'm biting you?

RALPH   It's something about Blanche.

BESSIE   Don't tell me.

RALPH   Listen now——

BESSIE   I don't wanna know.

RALPH   She's got no place to go.

BESSIE   I don't want to know.

RALPH   Mom, I love this girl. . . .

BESSIE   So go knock your head against the wall.

RALPH   I want her to come here. Listen, Mom, I want you to
let her live here for a while.

BESSIE   You got funny ideas, my son.

RALPH   I'm as good as anyone else. Don't I have some rights
in the world? Listen, Mom, if I don't do something, she's
going away. Why don't you do it? Why don't you let her
stay here for a few weeks? Things'll pick up. Then we
can——

BESSIE   Sure, sure. I'll keep her fresh on ice for a wedding day.
That's what you want?

RALPH   No, I mean you should——

BESSIE   Or maybe you'll sleep here in the same bed without
marriage. (*Jacob stands in his doorway, dressed.*)

RALPH   Don't say that, Mom. I only mean. . . .

BESSIE   What you mean, I know . . . and what I mean I also
know. Make up your mind. For your own good, Ralphie. If
she dropped in the ocean I don't lift a finger.

RALPH   That's all, I suppose.

BESSIE   With me it's one thing—a boy should have respect for
his own future. Go to sleep, you look tired. In the morning
you'll forget.

JACOB   "Awake and sing, ye that dwell in dust, and the earth
shall cast out the dead." It's cold out?

MYRON   Oh, yes.

JACOB   I'll take up Tootsie now.

MYRON (*eating bread and jam*)   He come on us like the wild man of Borneo, Sam. I don't think Hennie was fool enough to tell him the truth like that.

BESSIE   Myron! (*A deep pause.*)

RALPH   What did he say?

BESSIE   Never mind.

RALPH   I heard him. I heard him. You don't needa tell me.

BESSIE   Never mind.

RALPH   You trapped that guy.

BESSIE   Don't say another word.

RALPH   Just have respect? That's the idea?

BESSIE   Don't say another word. I'm boiling over ten times inside.

RALPH   You won't let Blanche here, huh. I'm not sure I want her. You put one over on that little shrimp. The cat's whiskers, Mom?

BESSIE   I'm telling you something!

RALPH   I got the whole idea. I get it so quick my head's swimming. Boy, what a laugh! I suppose you know about this, Jake?

JACOB   Yes.

RALPH   Why didn't you do something?

JACOB   I'm an old man.

RALPH   What's that got to do with the price of bonds? Sits around and lets a thing like that happen! You make me sick too.

MYRON (*after a pause*)   Let me say something, son.

RALPH   Take your hand away! Sit in a corner and wag your tail. Keep on boasting you went to law school for two years.

MYRON   I want to tell you——

RALPH   You never in your life had a thing to tell me.

BESSIE (*bitterly*)   Don't say a word. Let him, let him run and tell Sam. Publish in the papers, give a broadcast on the radio. To him it don't matter nothing his family sits with tears pouring from the eyes. (*To Jacob.*) What are you waiting for? I didn't tell you twice already about the dog? You'll stand around with Caruso and make a bughouse. It ain't enough all day long. Fifty times I told you I'll break every record in the house. (*She brushes past him, breaks the records, comes out.*) The next time I say something you'll maybe believe it. Now maybe you learned a lesson. (*Pause.*)

JACOB (*quietly*) Bessie, new lessons . . . not for an old dog. (*Moe enters.*)

MYRON You didn't have to do it, Momma.

BESSIE Talk better to your son, Mr. Berger! Me, I don't lay down and die for him and Poppa no more. I'll work like a nigger? For what? Wait, the day comes when you'll be punished. When it's too late you'll remember how you sucked away a mother's life. Talk to him, tell him how I don't sleep at night. (*Bursts into tears and exits.*)

MOE (*sings*) "Good-by to all your sorrows. You never hear them talk about the war, in the land of Yama Yama. . . ." [4]

MYRON Yes, Momma's a sick woman, Ralphie.

RALPH Yeah?

MOE We'll be out of the trenches by Christmas. Putt, putt, putt . . . here, stinker. . . . (*Picks up Tootsie, a small, white poodle that just then enters from the hall.*) If there's reincarnation in the next life I wanna be a dog and lay in a fat lady's lap. Barrage over? How 'bout a little pinochle, Pop?

JACOB Nnno.

RALPH (*taking dog*) I'll take her up. (*Conciliatory.*)

JACOB No, I'll do it. (*Takes dog.*)

RALPH (*ashamed*) It's cold out.

JACOB I was cold before in my life. A man sixty-seven. . . . (*Strokes the dog.*) Tootsie is my favorite lady in the house. (*He slowly passes across the room and exits. A settling pause.*)

MYRON She cried all last night—Tootsie—I heard her in the kitchen like a young girl.

MOE Tonight I could do something. I got a yen . . . I don't know.

MYRON (*rubbing his head*) My scalp is impoverished.

RALPH Mom bust all his records.

MYRON She didn't have to do it.

MOE Tough tit! Now I can sleep in the morning. Who the hell wantsa hear a wop air his tonsils all day long!

RALPH (*handling the fragment of a record*) "O Paradiso!"

MOE (*gets cards*) It's snowing out, girls.

---

4. A line from a popular song of 1917. Note how Moe's bitter memory of the war informs almost everything he says.

MYRON   There's no more big snows like in the old days. I think the whole world's changing. I see it, right under our very eyes. No one hardly remembers any more when we used to have gaslight and all the dishes had little fishes on them.

MOE   It's the system, girls.

MYRON   I was a little boy when it happened—the Great Blizzard. It snowed three days without a stop that time. Yes, and the horse cars stopped. A silence of death was on the city and little babies got no milk . . . they say a lot of people died that year.

MOE (*singing as he deals himself cards*)

"Lights are blinking while you're drinking,
That's the place where the good fellows go.
Good-by to all your sorrows,
You never hear them talk about the war,
In the land of Yama Yama
Funicalee, funicala, funicalo. . . ."

MYRON   What can I say to you, Big Boy?

RALPH   Not a damn word.

MOE (*goes "ta ra ta ra" throughout*)

MYRON   I know how you feel about all those things, I know.

RALPH   Forget it.

MYRON   And your girl. . . .

RALPH   Don't soft soap me all of a sudden.

MYRON   I'm not foreign born. I'm an American, and yet I never got close to you. It's an American father's duty to be his son's friend.

RALPH   Who said that—Teddy R.?

MOE (*dealing cards*)   You're breaking his heart, "Litvak."[5]

MYRON   It just happened the other day. The moment I began losing my hair I just knew I was destined to be a failure in life . . . and when I grew bald I was. Now isn't that funny, Big Boy?

MOE   It's a pisscutter!

MYRON   I believe in Destiny.

MOE   You get what-it-takes. Then they don't catch you with your pants down. (*Sings out.*) Eight of clubs. . . .

5. Yiddish for "Lithuanian." The Lithuanian Jews are considered "high-minded."

MYRON   I really don't know. I sold jewelry on the road before I married. It's one thing to—— Now here's a thing the druggist gave me. (*Reads.*) "The Marvel Cosmetic Girl of Hollywood is going on the air. Give this charming little radio singer a name and win five thousand dollars. If you will send——"

MOE   Your old man still believes in Santy Claus.

MYRON   Someone's got to win. The government isn't gonna allow everything to be a fake.

MOE   It's a fake. There ain't no prizes. It's a fake.

MYRON   It says——

RALPH (*snatching it*)   For Christ's sake, Pop, forget it. Grow up. Jake's right—everybody's crazy. It's like a zoo in this house. I'm going to bed.

MOE   In the land of Yama Yama. . . . (*Goes on with ta ra.*)

MYRON   Don't think life's easy with Momma. No, but she means for your good all the time. I tell you she does, she——

RALPH   Maybe, but I'm going to bed. (*Downstairs doorbell rings violently.*)

MOE (*ring*)   Enemy barrage begins on sector eight seventy-five.

RALPH   That's downstairs.

MYRON   We ain't expecting anyone this hour of the night.

MOE   "Lights are blinking while you're drinking, that's the place where the good fellows go. Good-by to ta ra tara ra," etc.

RALPH   I better see who it is.

MYRON   I'll tick the button. (*As he starts, the apartment doorbell begins ringing, followed by large knocking. Myron goes out.*)

RALPH   Who's ever ringing means it. (*A loud excited voice outside.*)

MOE   "In the land of Yama Yama, Funicalee, funicalo, funic——"

Myron enters followed by Schlosser the janitor. Bessie cuts in from the other side.

BESSIE   Who's ringing like a lunatic?

RALPH   What's the matter?

MYRON   Momma. . . .

BESSIE   Noo, what's the matter? (*Downstairs bell continues.*)

RALPH   What's the matter?

BESSIE   Well, well . . . ?

MYRON   Poppa. . . .

BESSIE   What happened?

SCHLOSSER   He shlipped maybe in de snow.

RALPH   Who?

SCHLOSSER (*to Bessie*)   Your fadder fall off de roof. . . . Ja. (*A dead pause. Ralph then runs out.*)

BESSIE (*dazed*)   Myron. . . . Call Morty on the phone . . . call him. (*Myron starts for phone.*) No. I'll do it myself. I'll . . . do it. (*Myron exits.*)

SCHLOSSER (*standing stupidly*)   Since I was in dis country . . . I was pudding out de ash can . . . The snow is vet. . . .

MOE (*to Schlosser*)   Scram. (*Schlosser exits.*)

Bessie goes blindly to the phone, fumbles and gets it. Moe sits quietly, slowly turning cards over, but watching her.

BESSIE   He slipped. . . .

MOE (*deeply moved*)   Slipped?

BESSIE   I can't see the numbers. Make it, Moe, make it. . . .

MOE   Make it yourself. (*He looks at her and slowly goes back to his game of cards with shaking hands.*)

BESSIE   Riverside 7— . . . (*Unable to talk she dials slowly. The dial whizzes on.*)

MOE   Don't . . . make me laugh. . . . (*He turns over cards.*)

CURTAIN

ACT THREE

A week later in the dining room. Morty, Bessie and Myron eating. Sitting in the front room is Moe marking a "dope sheet," but really listening to the others.

BESSIE   You're sure he'll come tonight—the insurance man?

MORTY   Why not? I shtupped him a ten-dollar bill. Everything's hot delicatessen.

BESSIE   Why must he come so soon?

MORTY   Because you had a big expense. You'll settle once and for all. I'm a great boy for making hay while the sun shines.

BESSIE   Stay till he'll come, Morty. . . .

MORTY   No, I got a strike downtown. Business don't stop for personal life. Two times already in the past week those bastards threw stink bombs in the showroom. Wait! We'll give them strikes—in the kishkas[1] we'll give them. . . .

BESSIE   I'm a woman. I don't know about policies. Stay till he comes.

MORTY   Bessie—sweetheart, leave me live.

BESSIE   I'm afraid, Morty.

MORTY   Be practical. They made an investigation. Everybody knows Pop had an accident. Now we'll collect.

MYRON   Ralphie don't know Papa left the insurance in his name.

MORTY   It's not his business. And I'll tell him.

BESSIE   The way he feels. (*Enter Ralph into front room.*) He'll do something crazy. He thinks Poppa jumped off the roof.

MORTY   Be practical, Bessie. Ralphie will sign when I tell him. Everything is peaches and cream.

BESSIE   Wait for a few minutes. . . .

MORTY   Look, I'll show you in black on white what the policy says. *For God's sake, leave me live!* (*Angrily exits to kitchen. In parlor, Moe speaks to Ralph who is reading a letter.*)

MOE   What's the letter say?

RALPH   Blanche won't see me no more, she says. I couldn't care very much, she says. If I didn't come like I said. . . . She'll phone before she leaves.

MOE   She don't know about Pop?

RALPH   She won't ever forget me she says. Look what she sends me . . . a little locket on a chain . . . if she calls I'm out.

MOE   You mean it?

RALPH   For a week I'm trying to go in his room. I guess he'd like me to have it, but I can't. . . .

MOE   Wait a minute! (*Crosses over.*) They're trying to rook you—a freeze-out.

RALPH   Who?

MOE   That bunch stuffin' their gut with hot pastrami. Morty in particular. Jake left the insurance—three thousand dollars—for you.

RALPH   For me?

MOE   Now you got wings, kid. Pop figured you could use it. That's why. . . .

---

1. Kishka is Yiddish for "gut." Morty means they will "kick 'em in the gut."

RALPH   That's why what?

MOE   It ain't the only reason he done it.

RALPH   He done it?

MOE   You think a breeze blew him off? (*Hennie enters and sits.*)

RALPH   I'm not sure what I think.

MOE   The insurance guy's coming tonight. Morty shtupped [2] him.

RALPH   Yeah?

MOE   I'll back you up. You're dead on your feet. Grab a sleep for yourself.

RALPH   No!

MOE   Go on! (*Pushes boy into room.*)

SAM   (*whom Morty has sent in for the paper*)   Morty wants the paper.

HENNIE   So?

SAM   You're sitting on it. (*Gets paper.*) We could go home now, Hennie! Leon is alone by Mrs. Strasberg a whole day.

HENNIE   Go on home if you're so anxious. A full tub of diapers is waiting.

SAM   Why should you act this way?

HENNIE   'Cause there's no bones in ice cream. Don't touch me.

SAM   Please, what's the matter. . . .

MOE   She don't like you. Plain as the face on your nose. . . .

SAM   To me, my friend, you talk a foreign language.

MOE   A quarter you're lousy. (*Sam exits.*) Gimme a buck, I'll run it up to ten.

HENNIE   Don't do me no favors.

MOE   Take a chance. (*Stopping her as she crosses to doorway.*)

HENNIE   I'm a pushover.

MOE   I say lotsa things. You don't know me.

HENNIE   I know you—when you knock 'em down you're through.

MOE   (*sadly*)   You still don't know me.

HENNIE   I know what goes in your wise-guy head.

MOE   Don't run away. . . . I ain't got hydrophobia. Wait. I want to tell you. . . . I'm leaving.

HENNIE   Leaving?

MOE   Tonight. Already packed.

2. Yiddish for "screwed." Note earlier (p. 170) it means "slipped."

HENNIE   Where?

MORTY   (*as he enters followed by the others*)   My car goes through snow like a dose of salts.

BESSIE   Hennie, go eat. . . .

MORTY   Where's Ralphie?

MOE   In his new room. (*Moves into dining room.*)

MORTY   I didn't have a piece of hot pastrami in my mouth for years.

BESSIE   Take a sandwich, Hennie. You didn't eat all day. . . . (*At window.*) A whole week it rained cats and dogs.

MYRON   Rain, rain, go away. Come again some other day. (*Puts shawl on her.*)

MORTY   Where's my gloves?

SAM   (*sits on stool*)   I'm sorry the old man lays in the rain.

MORTY   Personally, Pop was a fine man. But I'm a great boy for an honest opinion. He had enough crazy ideas for a regiment.

MYRON   Poppa never had a doctor in his whole life. . . . (*Enter Ralph.*)

MORTY   He had Caruso. Who's got more from life?

BESSIE   Who's got more? . . .

MYRON   And Marx he had.

Myron and Bessie sit on sofa.

MORTY   Marx! Some say Marx is the new God today. Maybe I'm wrong. Ha ha ha. . . . Personally I counted my ten million last night. . . . I'm sixteen cents short. So tomorrow I'll go to Union Square and yell no equality in the country! Ah, it's a new generation.

RALPH   You said it!

MORTY   What's the matter, Ralphie? What are you looking funny?

RALPH   I hear I'm left insurance and the man's coming tonight.

MORTY   Poppa didn't leave no insurance for you.

RALPH   What?

MORTY   In your name he left it—but not for you.

RALPH   It's my name on the paper.

MORTY   Who said so?

RALPH   (*to his mother*)   The insurance man's coming tonight?

MORTY   What's the matter?

RALPH   I'm not talking to you. (*To his mother.*) Why?

BESSIE   I don't know why.

RALPH   He don't come in this house tonight.

MORTY   That's what *you* say.

RALPH   I'm not talking to you, Uncle Morty, but I'll tell you, too, he don't come here tonight when there's still mud on a grave. (*To his mother.*) Couldn't you give the house a chance to cool off?

MORTY   Is this a way to talk to your mother?

RALPH   Was that a way to talk to your father?

MORTY   Don't be so smart with me, Mr. Ralph Berger!

RALPH   Don't be so smart with *me*.

MORTY   What'll you do? I say he's coming tonight. Who says no?

MOE   (*suddenly, from the background*)   Me.

MORTY   Take a back seat, Axelrod. When you're in the family——

MOE   I got a little document here. (*Produces paper.*) I found it under his pillow that night. A guy who slips off a roof don't leave a note before he does it.

MORTY   (*starting for Moe after a horrified silence*)   Let me see this note.

BESSIE   Morty, don't touch it!

MOE   Not if you crawled.

MORTY   It's a fake. Poppa wouldn't——

MOE   Get the insurance guy here and we'll see how—— (*The bell rings.*) Speak of the devil. . . . Answer it, see what happens. (*Morty starts for the ticker.*)

BESSIE   Morty, don't!

MORTY   (*stopping*)   Be practical, Bessie.

MOE   Sometimes you don't collect on suicides if they know about it.

MORTY   You should let. . . . You should let him. . . . (*A pause in which all seem dazed. Bell rings insistently.*)

MOE   Well, we're waiting.

MORTY   Give me the note.

MOE   I'll give you the head off your shoulders.

MORTY   Bessie, you'll stand for this? (*Points to Ralph.*) Pull down his pants and give him with a strap.

RALPH   (*as bell rings again*)   How about it?

BESSIE Don't be crazy. It's not my fault. Morty said he should come tonight. It's not nice so soon. I didn't——

MORTY I said it? Me?

BESSIE Who then?

MORTY You didn't sing a song in my ear a whole week to settle quick?

BESSIE I'm surprised. Morty, you're a big liar.

MYRON Momma's telling the truth, she is!

MORTY Lissen. In two shakes of a lamb's tail, we'll start a real fight and then nobody won't like nobody. Where's my fur gloves? I'm going downtown. (*To Sam.*) You coming? I'll drive you down.

HENNIE (*to Sam, who looks questioningly at her*) Don't look at me. Go home if you want.

SAM If you're coming soon, I'll wait.

HENNIE Don't do me any favors. Night and day he pesters me.

MORTY You made a cushion——sleep!

SAM I'll go home. I know . . . to my worst enemy I don't wish such a life——

HENNIE Sam, keep quiet.

SAM (*quietly; sadly*) No more free speech in America? (*Gets his hat and coat.*) I'm a lonely person. Nobody likes me.

MYRON I like you, Sam.

HENNIE (*going to him gently; sensing the end*) Please go home, Sam. I'll sleep here. . . . I'm tired and nervous. Tomorrow I'll come home. I love you . . . I mean it. (*She kisses him with real feeling.*)

SAM I would die for you. . . . (*Sam looks at her. Tries to say something, but his voice chokes up with a mingled feeling. He turns and leaves the room.*)

MORTY A bird in the hand is worth two in the bush. Remember I said it. Good night. (*Exits after Sam.*) (*Hennie sits depressed. Bessie goes up and looks at the picture calendar again. Myron finally breaks the silence.*)

MYRON Yesterday a man wanted to sell me a saxophone with pearl buttons. But I——

BESSIE It's a beautiful picture. In this land, nobody works. . . . Nobody worries. . . . Come to bed, Myron. (*Stops at the door, and says to Ralph*) Please don't have foolish ideas about the money.

RALPH   Let's call it a day.

BESSIE   It belongs for the whole family. You'll get your teeth fixed——

RALPH   And a pair of black and white shoes?

BESSIE   Hennie needs a vacation. She'll take two weeks in the mountains and I'll mind the baby.

RALPH   I'll take care of my own affairs.

BESSIE   A family needs for a rainy day. Times is getting worse. Prospect Avenue, Dawson, Beck Street—every day furniture's on the sidewalk.

RALPH   Forget it, Mom.

BESSIE   Ralphie, I worked too hard all my years to be treated like dirt. It's no law we should be stuck together like Siamese twins. Summer shoes you didn't have, skates you never had, but I bought a new dress every week. A lover I kept—Mr. Gigolo! Did I ever play a game of cards like Mrs. Marcus? Or was Bessie Berger's children always the cleanest on the block?! Here I'm not only the mother, but also the father. The first two years I worked in a stocking factory for six dollars while Myron Berger went to law school. If I didn't worry about the family who would? On the calendar it's a different place, but here without a dollar you don't look the world in the eye. Talk from now to next year—this is life in America.

RALPH   Then it's wrong. It don't make sense. If life made you this way, then it's wrong!

BESSIE   Maybe you wanted me to give up twenty years ago. Where would you be now? You'll excuse my expression—a bum in the park!

RALPH   I'm not blaming you, Mom. Sink or swim—I see it. But it can't stay like this.

BESSIE   My foolish boy. . . .

RALPH   No, I see every house lousy with lies and hate. He said it, Grandpa— Brooklyn hates the Bronx. Smacked on the nose twice a day. But boys and girls can get ahead like that, Mom. We don't want life printed on dollar bills, Mom!

BESSIE   So go out and change the world if you don't like it.

RALPH   I will! And why? 'Cause life's different in my head. Gimme the earth in two hands. I'm strong. There . . . hear him? The air mail off to Boston. Day or night, he flies away, a job to do. That's us and it's no time to die. (*The airplane sound fades off as Myron gives alarm clock to Bessie which she begins to wind.)*

BESSIE "Mom, what does she know? She's old-fashioned!" But I'll tell you a big secret: My whole life I wanted to go away too, but with children a woman stays home. A fire burned in *my* heart too, but now it's too late. I'm no spring chicken. The clock goes and Bessie goes. Only my machinery can't be fixed.

She lifts a button: the alarm rings on the clock; she stops it, says "Good night" and exits.

MYRON I guess I'm no prize bag. . . .

BESSIE *(from within)* Come to bed, Myron.

MYRON *(tears page off calendar)* Hmmm. . . . *(Exits to her.)*

RALPH Look at him, draggin' after her like an old shoe.

MOE Punch drunk. *(Phone rings.)* That's for me. *(At phone.)* Yeah? . . . Just a minute. *(To Ralph.)* Your girl . . .

RALPH Jeez, I don't know what to say to her.

MOE Hang up? *(Ralph slowly takes phone.)*

RALPH Hello. . . . Blanche, I wish. . . . I don't know what to say. . . . Yes . . . Hello? . . . *(Puts phone down.)* She hung up on me . . .

MOE Sorry?

RALPH No girl means anything to me until. . . .

MOE Till when?

RALPH Till I can take care of her. Till we don't look out on an airshaft. Till we can take the world in two hands and polish off the dirt.

MOE That's a big order.

RALPH Once upon a time I thought I'd drown to death in bolts of silk and velour. But I grew up these last few weeks. Jake said a lot.

MOE Your memory's okay?

RALPH But take a look at this. *(Brings armful of books from Jacob's room—dumps them on table.)* His books, I got them too—the pages ain't cut in half of them.

MOE Perfect.

RALPH Does it prove something? Damn tootin'! A ten-cent nailfile cuts them. Uptown, downtown, I'll read them on the way. Get a big lamp over the bed. *(Picks up one.)* My eyes are good. *(Puts book in pocket.)* Sure, inventory tomorrow. Coletti to Driscoll to Berger[3]—that's how we work. It's a team down the warehouse. Driscoll's a show-off, a wiseguy, and Joe talks pigeons day and night. But they're like me, looking for a chance to get to first base too. Joe razzed me about my girl. But he don't know why. I'll tell him. Hell, he might tell me something I don't know. Get teams together all over. Spit on your hands and get to work. And with enough teams together maybe we'll get steam in the warehouse so our fingers don't freeze off. Maybe we'll fix it so life won't be printed on dollar bills.

MOE Graduation Day. .

RALPH (*starts for door of his room, stops*) Can I have . . . Grandpa's note?

MOE Sure you want it?

RALPH Please— (*Moe gives it.*) It's blank!

MOE (*taking note back and tearing it up*) That's right.

RALPH Thanks! (*Exits.*)

MOE The kid's a fighter! (*To Hennie.*) Why are you crying?

HENNIE I never cried in my life. (*She is now.*)

MOE (*starts for door, stops*) You told Sam you love him. . . .

HENNIE If I'm sore on life, why take it out on him?

MOE You won't forget me to your dyin' day—I was the first guy. Part of your insides. You won't forget. I wrote my name on you—indelible ink!

HENNIE One thing I won't forget—how you left me crying on the bed like I was two for a cent!

MOE Listen, do you think——

HENNIE Sure. Waits till the family goes to the open air movie. He brings me perfume. . . . He grabs my arms——

MOE You won't forget me!

HENNIE How you left the next week?

MOE So I made a mistake. For Chris' sake, don't act like the Queen of Roumania!

HENNIE Don't make me laugh!

MOE What the hell do you want, my head on a plate?! Was my life so happy? Chris', my old man was a bum. I supported the whole damn family—five kids and Mom. When they grew up they beat it the hell away like rabbits.

---

3. On the model of "Tinker to Evers to Chance," a famous double-play combination of the National League Chicago baseball team (1902–12).

Mom died. I went to the war; got clapped down like a bedbug; woke up in a room without a leg. What the hell do you think, anyone's got it better than you? I never had a home either. I'm lookin' too!

HENNIE   So what?!

MOE   So you're it—you're home for me, a place to live! That's the whole parade, sickness, eating out your heart! Sometimes you meet a girl—she stops it—that's love. . . . So take a chance! Be with me, Paradise. What's to lose?

HENNIE   My pride!

MOE   (*grabbing her*)   What do you want? Say the word—I'll tango on a dime. Don't gimme ice when your heart's on fire!

HENNIE   Let me go! (*He stops her.*)

MOE   WHERE?!!

HENNIE   What do you want, Moe, what do you want?

MOE   You!

HENNIE   You'll be sorry you ever started——

MOE   You!

HENNIE   Moe, lemme go—— (*Trying to leave.*) I'm getting up early—lemme go.

MOE   No! . . . I got enough fever to blow the whole damn town to hell. (*He suddenly releases her and half stumbles backwards. Forces himself to quiet down.*) You wanna go back to him? Say the word. I'll know what to do. . . .

HENNIE   (*helplessly*)   Moe, I don't know what to say.

MOE   Listen to me.

HENNIE   What?

MOE   Come away. A certain place where it's moonlight and roses. We'll lay down, count stars. Hear the big ocean making noise. You lay under the trees. Champagne flows like——(*Phone rings. Moe finally answers the telephone.*) Hello? . . . Just a minute. (*Looks at Hennie.*)

HENNIE   Who is it?

MOE   Sam.

HENNIE   (*starts for phone, but changes her mind*)   I'm sleeping. . . .

MOE   (*in phone*)   She's sleeping. . . . (*Hangs up. Watches Hennie who slowly sits.*) He wants you to know he got home O.K. . . . What's on your mind?

HENNIE   Nothing.

MOE   Sam?

HENNIE   They say it's a palace on those Havana boats.

MOE   What's on your mind?

HENNIE (*trying to escape*)   Moe, I don't care for Sam—I never loved him——

MOE   But your kid—?

HENNIE   All my life I waited for this minute.

MOE (*holding her*)   Me too. Made believe I was talkin' just bedroom golf, but you and me forever was what I meant! Christ, baby, there's one life to live! Live it!

HENNIE   Leave the baby?

MOE   Yeah!

HENNIE   I can't. . . .

MOE   You can!

HENNIE   No. . . .

MOE   But you're not sure!

HENNIE   I don't know.

MOE   Make a break or spend the rest of your life in a coffin.

HENNIE   Oh God, I don't know where I stand.

MOE   Don't look up there. Paradise, you're on a big boat headed south. No more pins and needles in your heart, no snake juice squirted in your arm. The whole world's green grass and when you cry it's because you're happy.

HENNIE   Moe, I don't know. . . .

MOE   Nobody knows, but you do it and find out. When you're scared the answer's zero.

HENNIE   You're hurting my arm.

MOE   The doctor said it—cut off your leg to save your life! And they done it—one thing to get another. (*Enter Ralph.*)

RALPH   I didn't hear a word, but do it, Hennie, do it!

MOE   Mom can mind the kid. She'll go on forever, Mom. We'll send money back, and Easter eggs.

RALPH   I'll be here.

MOE   Get your coat . . . get it.

HENNIE   Moe!

MOE   I know . . . but get your coat and hat and kiss the house good-by.

HENNIE   The man I love. . . . (*Myron entering.*) I left my coat in Mom's room. (*Exits.*)

MYRON   Don't wake her up, Beauty. Momma fell asleep as soon as her head hit the pillow. I can't sleep. It was a long day. Hmmm. (*Examines his tongue in buffet mirror.*) I was reading the other day a person with a thick tongue is feebleminded. I can do anything with my tongue. Make it thick, flat. No fruit in the house lately. Just a lone apple. (*He gets apple and paring knife and starts paring.*) Must be something wrong with me—I say I won't eat but I eat. (*Hennie enters dressed to go out.*) Where you going, little Red Riding Hood?

HENNIE   Nobody knows, Peter Rabbit.

MYRON   You're looking very pretty tonight. You were a beautiful baby too. 1910, that was the year you was born. The same year Teddy Roosevelt come back from Africa.

HENNIE   Gee, Pop; you're such a funny guy.

MYRON   He was a boisterous man, Teddy. Good night. (*He exits, paring apple.*)

RALPH   When I look at him, I'm sad. Let me die like a dog, if I can't get more from life.

HENNIE   Where?

RALPH   Right here in the house! My days won't be for nothing. Let Mom have the dough. I'm twenty-two and kickin'! I'll get along. Did Jake die for us to fight about nickels? No! "Awake and sing," he said. Right here he stood and said it. The night he died, I saw it like a thunderbolt! I saw he was dead and I was born! I swear to God, I'm one week old! I want the whole city to hear it—fresh blood, arms. We got 'em. We're glad we're living.

MOE   I wouldn't trade you for two pitchers and an outfielder. Hold the fort!

RALPH   So long.

MOE   So long.

They go and Ralph stands full and strong in the doorway seeing them off as the curtain slowly falls.

The Country Wife (1675)

William Wycherley (1640-1716)

This surprisingly modern play (first performed in January 1675) depends in part on Moliere for certain of its moments: the use of the wife to subvert her husband's messages to her lover (*L'Ecole des maris*, 1661) and the stern but vain precepts on marriage dictated by the husband to the wife he obviously cannot keep as well as the more general motif of the transformation of the innocent wife into a guileful mistress (*L'Ecole des femmes*, 1662). Yet the play is all Wycherley: satirically pungent, dramatically varied and rapid, at once blunt and elegant in its language, broad and subtle in its characterization. As we have noted in our Introduction, it is the least patently "enclosed" of our selections. The lodgings of the Pinchwifes, for example, are only the most tenuous of confinements. Yet in his amusing insistence on the fragility of these "enclosures," the dramatist creates a veritable filigree of symbolic play upon the theme.

In recent years, the play has been staged frequently and successfully—for example, in 1957 in New York at the Adelphi Theater by the Playwrights' Company (Malcolm Wells and Daniel Blum, general directors), with Julie Harris as Margery Pinchwife and Laurence Harvey as Mr. Horner, under the direction of George Devine. The Stratford Shakespearean Festival of Canada (summer 1964) staged the play under Michael Langham's direction with John Colicos as Horner and Helen Burns as Margery. In 1965, The Repertory Theater of Lincoln Center in New York City (Herbert Blau and Jules Irving, directors) produced the play, with Stacy Keach as Horner under direction by Robert Symonds.

THE COUNTRY WIFE

William Wycherley

Indignor quidquam reprehendi, non quia crasse
Compositum illepideve putetur, sed quia nuper:
Nec veniam antiquis, sed honorem et præmia posci.[1]

HORAT

CHARACTERS

MR. HORNER

MR. HARCOURT

MR. DORILANT

A BOY

A QUACK

WAITERS, SERVANTS, *and* ATTEND-
ANTS

MRS. MARGERY PINCHWIFE

ALITHEA, *Sister of* PINCHWIFE

MR. PINCHWIFE

MR. SPARKISH

SIR JASPER FIDGET

LADY FIDGET

MRS. DAINTY FIDGET, *Sister of* SIR
JASPER

MRS. SQUEAMISH

OLD LADY SQUEAMISH

LUCY, ALITHEA'S *Maid*

SCENE—*London.*

PROLOGUE

Spoken by Mr. Hart[2]

Poets, like cudgelled bullies, never do
At first or second blow submit to you;
But will provoke you still, and ne'er have done,
Till you are weary first with laying on.
The late so baffled scribbler of this day,[3]

1. I am out of patience when anything is blamed, not because it is thought coarsely and inelegantly composed, but because it is new: when for the ancients not indulgence, but honour and rewards are demanded.—Horace, *Epistles*, II. i. 76–8.
2. The actor playing Horner in the first production.
3. Wycherley is referring to his most recent play, *The Gentleman Dancing-Master*, which had failed three years earlier.

Though he stands trembling, bids me boldly say,
What we before most plays are used to do,
For poets out of fear first draw on you;
In a fierce prologue the still pit defy,
And, ere you speak, like Castril [4] give the lie.
But though our Bayes's[5] battles oft I've fought,
And with bruised knuckles their dear conquests bought;
Nay, never yet feared odds upon the stage,
In prologue dare not hector with the age;
But would take quarter from your saving hands,
Though Bayes within all yielding countermands,
Says, you confederate wits no quarter give,
Therefore his play shan't ask your leave to live.
Well, let the vain rash fop, by huffing so,
Think to obtain the better terms of you;
But we, the actors, humbly will submit,
Now, and at any time, to a full pit;
Nay, often we anticipate your rage,
And murder poets for you on our stage:
We set no guards upon our tiring-room,
But when with flying colours there you come,
We patiently, you see, give up to you
Our poets, virgins, nay, our matrons too.

ACT ONE

Horner's lodging.
Enter Horner, and Quack following him at a distance.

HORNER (*aside*) A quack is as fit for a pimp, as a midwife for a bawd; they are still but in their way, both helpers of nature.—(*Aloud.*) Well, my dear doctor, hast thou done what I desired?

QUACK I have undone you for ever with the women, and reported you throughout the whole town as bad as an eunuch, with as much trouble as if I had made you one in earnest.

4. Alternate spelling: Kastrill—a character in Ben Jonson's *The Alchemist* who tells Subtle "you lie" before that character even begins to speak.
5. The author in George Villiers' *The Rehearsal*.

HORNER   But have you told all the midwives you know, the orange wenches at the playhouses, the city husbands, and old fumbling keepers of this end of the town? for they'll be the readiest to report it.

QUACK   I have told all the chambermaids, waiting-women, tire-women, and old women of my acquaintance; nay, and whispered it as a secret to 'em, and to the whisperers of Whitehall; so that you need not doubt 'twill spread, and you will be as odious to the handsome young women, as—

HORNER   As the small-pox. Well—

QUACK   And to the married women of this end of the town, as—

HORNER   As the great one; nay, as their own husbands.

QUACK   And to the city dames, as aniseed Robin,[1] of filthy and contemptible memory; and they will frighten their children with your name, especially their females.

HORNER   And cry, Horner's coming to carry you away. I am only afraid 'twill not be believed. You told 'em it was by an English-French disaster, and an English-French chirurgeon, who has given me at once not only a cure, but an antidote for the future against that damned malady, and that worse distemper, love, and all other women's evils?

QUACK   Your late journey into France has made it the more credible, and your being here a fortnight before you appeared in public, looks as if you apprehended the shame, which I wonder you do not. Well, I have been hired by young gallants to belie 'em t'other way; but you are the first would be thought a man unfit for women.

HORNER   Dear Mr. Doctor, let vain rogues be contented only to be thought abler men than they are, generally 'tis all the pleasure they have; but mine lies another way.

QUACK   You take, methinks, a very preposterous way to it, and as ridiculous as if we operators in physic should put forth bills to disparage our medicaments, with hopes to gain customers.

HORNER   Doctor, there are quacks in love as well as physic, who get but the fewer and worse patients for their boasting; a good name is seldom got by giving it one's self; and women, no more than honour, are compassed by bragging.

1. A famous hermaphrodite, the subject of many obscene stories.

Come, come, Doctor, the wisest lawyer never discovers the merits of his cause till the trial; the wealthiest man conceals his riches, and the cunning gamester his play. Shy husbands and keepers, like old rooks, are not to be cheated but by a new unpractised trick: false friendship will pass now no more than false dice upon 'em; no, not in the city.

Enter Boy.

BOY   There are two ladies and a gentleman coming up.

Exit.

HORNER   A pox! some unbelieving sisters of my former acquaintance, who, I am afraid, expect their sense should be satisfied of the falsity of the report. No—this formal fool and women!

Enter Sir Jasper Fidget, Lady Fidget, and Mrs. Dainty Fidget.

QUACK   His wife and sister.

SIR JASPER   My coach breaking just now before your door, sir, I look upon as an occasional reprimand to me, sir, for not kissing your hands, sir, since your coming out of France, sir; and so my disaster, sir, has been my good fortune, sir; and this is my wife and sister, sir.

HORNER   What then, sir?

SIR JASPER   My lady, and sister, sir.—Wife, this is Master Horner.

LADY FIDGET   Master Horner, husband!

SIR JASPER   My lady, my Lady Fidget, sir.

HORNER   So, sir.

SIR JASPER   Won't you be acquainted with her, sir?—(*Aside.*) So, the report is true, I find, by his coldness or aversion to the sex; but I'll play the wag with him.—(*Aloud.*) Pray salute my wife, my lady, sir.

HORNER   I will kiss no man's wife, sir, for him, sir; I have taken my eternal leave, sir, of the sex already, sir.

SIR JASPER (*aside*)   Ha! ha! ha! I'll plague him yet.—(*Aloud.*) Not know my wife, sir?

HORNER   I do know your wife, sir; she's a woman, sir, and consequently a monster, sir, a greater monster than a husband, sir.

SIR JASPER   A husband! how, sir?

HORNER   So, sir; but I make no more cuckolds, sir. (*Makes horns.*)[2]

SIR JASPER   Ha! ha! ha! Mercury! Mercury! [3]

LADY FIDGET   Pray, Sir Jasper, let us be gone from this rude fellow.

MRS. DAINTY FIDGET   Who, by his breeding, would think he had ever been in France?

LADY FIDGET   Foh! he's but too much a French fellow, such as hate women of quality and virtue for their love to their husbands. Sir Jasper, a woman is hated by 'em as much for loving her husband as for loving their money. But pray let's be gone.

HORNER   You do well, madam; for I have nothing that you came for. I have brought over not so much as a bawdy picture, no new postures, nor the second part of the *Ecole des filles*;[4] nor—

QUACK (*apart to Horner*)   Hold, for shame, sir! what d'ye mean? you'll ruin yourself for ever with the sex—

SIR JASPER   Ha! ha! ha! he hates women perfectly, I find.

MRS. DAINTY FIDGET   What pity 'tis he should!

LADY FIDGET   Ay, he's a base fellow for't. But affectation makes not a woman more odious to them than virtue.

HORNER   Because your virtue is your greatest affectation, madam.

LADY FIDGET   How, you saucy fellow! Would you wrong my honour?

HORNER   If I could.

LADY FIDGET   How d'ye mean, sir?

SIR JASPER   Ha! ha! ha! no, he can't wrong your ladyship's honour, upon my honour. (*Whispers.*) He, poor man—hark you in your ear—a mere eunuch.

LADY FIDGET   O filthy French beast! foh! foh! why do we stay? let's be gone: I can't endure the sight of him.

SIR JASPER   Stay but till the chairs come; they'll be here presently.

LADY FIDGET   No.

2. The sign of the cuckold.
3. Mercury: a mineral used to treat venereal disease.
4. Horner is not referring to Moliere's *L'Ecole des femmes* but to *L'Ecole des filles, ou la philosophie des dames, divisée en deux dialogues* (1688) by an author known as Mililot or Milot or Millot or Hélot.

SIR JASPER   Nor can I stay longer. 'Tis, let me see, a quarter and half quarter of a minute past eleven. The council will be sat; I must away. Business must be preferred always before love and ceremony with the wise, Mr. Horner.

HORNER   And the impotent, Sir Jasper.

SIR JASPER   Ay, ay, the impotent, Master Horner; hah! hah! hah!

LADY FIDGET   What, leave us with a filthy man alone in his lodgings?

SIR JASPER   He's an innocent man now, you know. Pray stay, I'll hasten the chairs to you.—Mr. Horner, your servant; I should be glad to see you at my house. Pray come and dine with me, and play at cards with my wife after dinner; you are fit for women at that game yet, ha! ha!—(*Aside.*) 'Tis as much a husband's prudence to provide innocent diversion for a wife as to hinder her unlawful pleasures; and he had better employ her than let her employ herself.—(*Aloud.*) Farewell.

HORNER   Your servant, Sir Jasper.

Exit Sir Jasper.

LADY FIDGET   I will not stay with him, foh!—

HORNER   Nay, madam, I beseech you stay, if it be but to see I can be as civil to ladies yet as they would desire.

LADY FIDGET   No, no, foh! you cannot be civil to ladies.

MRS. DAINTY FIDGET   You as civil as ladies would desire?

LADY FIDGET   No, no, no, foh! foh! foh!

Exeunt Lady Fidget and Mrs. Dainty Fidget.

QUACK   Now, I think, I, or you yourself, rather, have done your business with the women.

HORNER   Thou art an ass. Don't you see already, upon the report, and my carriage, this grave man of business leaves his wife in my lodgings, invites me to his house and wife, who before would not be acquainted with me out of jealousy?

QUACK   Nay, by this means you may be the more acquainted with the husbands, but the less with the wives.

HORNER   Let me alone; if I can but abuse the husbands, I'll soon disabuse the wives. Stay—I'll reckon you up the advantages I am like to have by my stratagem. First, I shall be rid of all my old acquaintances, the most insatiable sort of duns, that invade our lodgings in a morning; and next to the pleasure of making a new mistress is that of being rid of an old one, and of all old debts. Love, when it comes to be so, is paid the most unwillingly.

QUACK Well, you may be so rid of your old acquaintances; but how will you get any new ones?

HORNER Doctor, thou wilt never make a good chemist, thou art so incredulous and impatient. Ask but all the young fellows of the town if they do not lose more time, like huntsmen, in starting the game, than in running it down. One knows not where to find 'em; who will or will not. Women of quality are so civil, you can hardly distinguish love from good breeding, and a man is often mistaken: but now I can be sure she that shows an aversion to me loves the sport, as those women that are gone, whom I warrant to be right. And then the next thing is, your women of honour, as you call 'em, are only chary of their reputations, not their persons; and 'tis scandal they would avoid, not men. Now may I have, by the reputation of an eunuch, the privileges of one, and be seen in a lady's chamber in a morning as early as her husband; kiss virgins before their parents or lovers; and may be, in short, the *passe-partout* of the town. Now, doctor.

QUACK Nay, now you shall be the doctor; and your process is so new that we do not know but it may succeed.

HORNER Not so new neither; *probatum est,* doctor.

QUACK Well, I wish you luck, and many patients, whilst I go to mine.

Exit.
Enter Harcourt and Dorilant.

HARCOURT Come, your appearance at the play yesterday, has, I hope, hardened you for the future against the women's contempt, and the men's raillery; and now you'll abroad as you were wont.

HORNER Did I not bear it bravely?

DORILANT With a most theatrical impudence, nay, more than the orange-wenches show there, or a drunken vizard-mask,[5]

5. Prostitute.

or a great-bellied actress; nay, or the most impudent of creatures, an ill poet; or what is yet more impudent, a second-hand critic.

HORNER   But what say the ladies? have they no pity?

HARCOURT   What ladies? The vizard-masks, you know, never pity a man when all's gone, though in their service.

DORILANT   And for the women in the boxes, you'd never pity them when 'twas in your power.

HARCOURT   They say 'tis pity but all that deal with common women should be served so.

DORILANT   Nay, I dare swear they won't admit you to play at cards with them, go to plays with 'em, or do the little duties which other shadows of men are wont to do for 'em.

HORNER   What do you call shadows of men?

DORILANT   Half-men.

HORNER   What, boys?

DORILANT   Ay, your old boys, old *beaux garçons,*[6] who, like superannuated stallions, are suffered to run, feed, and whinny with the mares as long as they live, though they can do nothing else.

HORNER   Well, a pox on love and wenching! Women serve but to keep a man from better company. Though I can't enjoy them, I shall you the more. Good fellowship and friendship are lasting, rational, and manly pleasures.

HARCOURT   For all that, give me some of those pleasures you call effeminate too; they help to relish one another.

HORNER   They disturb one another.

HARCOURT   No, mistresses are like books. If you pore upon them too much, they doze you, and make you unfit for company; but if used discreetly, you are the fitter for conversation by 'em.

DORILANT   A mistress should be like a little country retreat near the town; not to dwell in constantly, but only for a night and away, to taste the town the better when a man returns.

HORNER   I tell you, 'tis as hard to be a good fellow, a good friend, and a lover of women, as 'tis to be a good fellow, a good friend, and a lover of money. You cannot follow both, then choose your side. Wine gives you liberty, love takes it away.

6. Fops.

DORILANT   Gad, he's in the right on't.

HORNER   Wine gives you joy; love, grief and tortures, besides surgeons. Wine makes us witty; love, only sots. Wine makes us sleep; love breaks it.

DORILANT   By the world he has reason, Harcourt.

HORNER   Wine makes—

DORILANT   Ay, wine makes us—makes us princes; love makes us beggars, poor rogues, egad—and wine—

HORNER   So, there's one converted.—No, no, love and wine, oil and vinegar.

HARCOURT   I grant it; love will still be uppermost.

HORNER   Come, for my part, I will have only those glorious manly pleasures of being very drunk and very slovenly.

Enter boy.

BOY   Mr. Sparkish is below, sir.

Exit.

HARCOURT   What, my dear friend! a rogue that is fond of me only, I think, for abusing him.

DORILANT   No, he can no more think the men laugh at him than that women jilt him; his opinion of himself is so good.

HORNER   Well, there's another pleasure by drinking I thought not of,—I shall lose his acquaintance, because he cannot drink: and you know 'tis a very hard thing to be rid of him; for he's one of those nauseous offerers at wit, who, like the worst fiddlers, run themselves into all companies.

HARCOURT   One that, by being in the company of men of sense, would pass for one.

HORNER   And may so to the short-sighted world; as a false jewel amongst true ones is not discerned at a distance. His company is as troublesome to us as a cuckold's when you have a mind to his wife's.

HARCOURT   No, the rogue will not let us enjoy one another, but ravishes our conversation; though he signifies no more to't than Sir Martin Mar-all's gaping, and awkward thrumming upon the lute, does to his man's voice and music.[7]

7. In Dryden's *Sir Martin Mar-All*, the title character pretends to serenade his mistress, but the voice and lute playing are actually done by his man, hidden from view.

DORILANT   And to pass for a wit in town shows himself a fool every night to us, that are guilty of the plot.

HORNER   Such wits as he are, to a company of reasonable men, like rooks to the gamesters; who only fill a room at the table, but are so far from contributing to the play, that they only serve to spoil the fancy of those that do.

DORILANT   Nay, they are used like rooks too, snubbed, checked, and abused; yet the rogues will hang on.

HORNER   A pox on 'em, and all that force nature, and would be still what she forbids 'em! Affectation is her greatest monster.

HARCOURT   Most men are the contraries to that they would seem. Your bully, you see, is a coward with a long sword; the little humbly fawning physician, with his ebony cane, is he that destroys men.

DORILANT   The usurer, a poor rogue, possessed of mouldy bonds and mortgages; and we they call spendthrifts, are only wealthy, who lay out his money upon daily new purchases of pleasure.

HORNER   Ay, your arrantest cheat is your trustee or executor; your jealous man, the greatest cuckold; your churchman the greatest atheist; and your noisy pert rogue of a wit, the greatest fop, dullest ass, and worst company, as you shall see; for here he comes.

Enter Sparkish.

SPARKISH   How is't, sparks? how is't? Well, faith, Harry, I must rally thee a little, ha! ha! ha! upon the report in town of thee, ha! ha! ha! I can't hold i'faith; shall I speak?

HORNER   Yes; but you'll be so bitter then.

SPARKISH   Honest Dick and Frank here shall answer for me; I will not be extreme bitter, by the universe.

HARCOURT   We will be bound in a ten thousand pound bond, he shall not be bitter at all.

DORILANT   Nor sharp, nor sweet.

HORNER   What, not downright insipid?

SPARKISH   Nay then, since you are so brisk, and provoke me, take what follows. You must know, I was discoursing and rallying with some ladies yesterday, and they happened to talk of the fine new signs in town—

HORNER   Very fine ladies, I believe.

SPARKISH   Said I, I know where the best new sign is.—Where? says one of the ladies.—In Covent-Garden, I replied.—Said another, In what street?—In Russel-street, answered I.—Lord, says another, I'm sure there was never a fine new sign there yesterday.—Yes, but there was, said I again; and it came out of France, and has been there a fortnight.

DORILANT   A pox! I can hear no more, prithee.

HORNER   No, hear him out; let him tune his crowd a while.

HARCOURT   The worst music, the greatest preparation.

SPARKISH   Nay, faith, I'll make you laugh.—It cannot be, says a third lady.—Yes, yes, quoth I again.—Says a fourth lady—

HORNER   Look to't, we'll have no more ladies.

SPARKISH   No—then mark, mark, now. Said I to the fourth, Did you never see Mr. Horner? he lodges in Russel-street, and he's a sign of a man, you know, since he came out of France; ha! ha! ha!

HORNER   But the devil take me if thine be the sign of a jest.

SPARKISH   With that they all fell a-laughing, till they bepissed themselves. What, but it does not move you, methinks? Well, I see one had as good go to law without a witness, as break a jest without a laugher on one's side.—Come, come, sparks, but where do we dine? I have left at Whitehall an earl, to dine with you.

DORILANT   Why, I thought thou hadst loved a man with a title, better than a suit with a French trimming to't.

HARCOURT   Go to him again.

SPARKISH   No, sir, a wit to me is the greatest title in the world.

HORNER   But go dine with your earl, sir; he may be exceptious. We are your friends, and will not take it ill to be left, I do assure you.

HARCOURT   Nay, faith, he shall go to him.

SPARKISH   Nay, pray, gentlemen.

DORILANT   We'll thrust you out, if you won't; what, disappoint anybody for us?

SPARKISH   Nay, dear gentlemen, hear me.

HORNER   No, no, sir, by no means; pray go, sir.

SPARKISH   Why, dear rogues—

DORILANT   No, no.

They all thrust him out of the room.

ALL   Ha! ha! ha!

Re-enter Sparkish.

SPARKISH   But, sparks, pray hear me. What, d'ye think I'll eat then with gay shallow fops and silent coxcombs? I think wit as necessary at dinner, as a glass of good wine; and that's the reason I never have any stomach when I eat alone.—Come, but where do we dine?

HORNER   Even where you will.

SPARKISH   At Chateline's?

DORILANT   Yes, if you will.

SPARKISH   Or at the Cock?

DORILANT   Yes, if you please.

SPARKISH   Or at the Dog and Partridge?

HORNER   Ay, if you have a mind to't; for we shall dine at neither.

SPARKISH   Pshaw! with your fooling we shall lose the new play; and I would no more miss seeing a new play the first day, than I would miss sitting in the wit's row. Therefore I'll go fetch my mistress, and away.

Exit.
Enter Pinchwife.

HORNER   Who have we here? Pinchwife?

PINCHWIFE   Gentlemen, your humble servant.

HORNER   Well, Jack, by thy long absence from the town, the grumness of thy countenance, and the slovenliness of thy habit, I should give thee joy, should I not, of marriage?

PINCHWIFE (*aside*)   Death! does he know I'm married too? I thought to have concealed it from him at least.—(*Aloud.*) My long stay in the country will excuse my dress; and I have a suit of law that brings me up to town, that puts me out of humour. Besides, I must give Sparkish to-morrow five thousand pounds to lie with my sister.

HORNER   Nay, you country gentlemen, rather than not purchase, will buy anything; and he is a cracked title, if we may quibble. Well, but am I to give thee joy? I heard thou wert married.

PINCHWIFE   What then?

HORNER   Why, the next thing that is to be heard, is, thou'rt a cuckold.

PINCHWIFE (*aside*) Insupportable name!

HORNER But I did not expect marriage from such a whore-master as you; one that knew the town so much, and women so well.

PINCHWIFE Why, I have married no London wife.

HORNER Pshaw! that's all one. That grave circumspection in marrying a country wife, is like refusing a deceitful pampered Smithfield jade, to go and be cheated by a friend in the country.

PINCHWIFE (*aside*) A pox on him and his simile!—(*Aloud.*) At least we are a little surer of the breed there, know what her keeping has been, whether foiled or unsound.

HORNER Come, come, I have known a clap gotten in Wales; and there are cousins, justices' clerks, and chaplains in the country, I won't say coachmen. But she's handsome and young?

PINCHWIFE (*aside*) I'll answer as I should do.—(*Aloud.*) No, no; she has no beauty but her youth, no attraction but her modesty: wholesome, homely, and huswifely; that's all.

DORILANT He talks as like a grazier as he looks.

PINCHWIFE She's too awkward, ill-favoured, and silly to bring to town.

HARCOURT Then methinks you should bring her to be taught breeding.

PINCHWIFE To be taught! no, sir, I thank you. Good wives and private soldiers should be ignorant—I'll keep her from your instructions, I warrant you.

HARCOURT (*aside*) The rogue is as jealous as if his wife were not ignorant.

HORNER Why, if she be ill-favoured, there will be less danger here for you than by leaving her in the country. We have such variety of dainties that we are seldom hungry.

DORILANT But they have always coarse, constant, swinging stomachs in the country.

HARCOURT Foul feeders indeed!

DORILANT And your hospitality is great there.

HARCOURT Open house; every man's welcome.

PINCHWIFE So, so, gentlemen.

HORNER But prithee, why shouldst thou marry her? If she be ugly, ill-bred, and silly, she must be rich then.

PINCHWIFE As rich as if she brought me twenty thousand

pound out of this town; for she'll be as sure not to spend her moderate portion, as a London baggage would be to spend hers, let it be what it would: so 'tis all one. Then, because she's ugly, she's the likelier to be my own; and being ill-bred, she'll hate conversation; and since silly and inno-cent, will not know the difference betwixt a man of one-and-twenty and one of forty.

HORNER   Nine—to my knowledge. But if she be silly, she'll expect as much from a man of forty-nine, as from him of one-and-twenty. But methinks wit is more necessary than beauty; and I think no young woman ugly that has it, and no handsome woman agreeable without it.

PINCHWIFE   'Tis my maxim, he's a fool that marries; but he's a greater that does not marry a fool. What is wit in a wife good for, but to make a man a cuckold?

HORNER   Yes, to keep it from his knowledge.

PINCHWIFE   A fool cannot contrive to make her husband a cuckold.

HORNER   No; but she'll club with a man that can: and what is worse, if she cannot make her husband a cuckold, she'll make him jealous, and pass for one: and then 'tis all one.

PINCHWIFE   Well, well, I'll take care for one. My wife shall make me no cuckold, though she had your help, Mr. Horner. I understand the town, sir.

DORILANT (*aside*)   His help!

HARCOURT (*aside*)   He's come newly to town, it seems, and has not heard how things are with him.

HORNER   But tell me, has marriage cured thee of whoring, which it seldom does?

HARCOURT   'Tis more than age can do.

HORNER   No, the word is, I'll marry and live honest: but a marriage vow is like a penitent gamester's oath, and entering into bonds and penalties to stint himself to such a particular small sum at play for the future, which makes him but the more eager; and not being able to hold out, loses his money again, and his forfeit to boot.

DORILANT   Ay, ay, a gamester will be a gamester whilst his money lasts, and a whoremaster whilst his vigour.

HARCOURT   Nay, I have known 'em, when they are broke, and can lose no more, keep a fumbling with the box in their hands to fool with only, and hinder other gamesters.

DORILANT   That had wherewithal to make lusty stakes.

PINCHWIFE   Well, gentlemen, you may laugh at me; but you shall never lie with my wife: I know the town.

HORNER   But prithee, was not the way you were in better? is not keeping better than marriage?

PINCHWIFE   A pox on't! the jades would jilt me, I could never keep a whore to myself.

HORNER   So, then you only married to keep a whore to yourself. Well, but let me tell you, women, as you say, are like soldiers, made constant and loyal by good pay, rather than by oaths and covenants. Therefore I'd advise my friends to keep rather than marry, since too I find, by your example, it does not serve one's turn; for I saw you yesterday in the eighteenpenny place[8] with a pretty country-wench.

PINCHWIFE (*aside*)   How the devil! did he see my wife then? I sat there that she might not be seen. But she shall never go to a play again.

HORNER   What! dost thou blush, at nine-and-forty, for having been seen with a wench?

DORILANT   No, faith, I warrant 'twas his wife, which he seated there out of sight; for he's a cunning rogue, and understands the town.

HARCOURT   He blushes. Then 'twas his wife; for men are now more ashamed to be seen with them in public than with a wench.

PINCHWIFE (*aside*)   Hell and damnation! I'm undone, since Horner has seen her, and they know 'twas she.

HORNER   But prithee, was it thy wife? She was exceeding pretty: I was in love with her at that distance.

PINCHWIFE   You are like never to be nearer to her. Your servant, gentlemen. (*Offers to go.*)

HORNER   Nay, prithee stay.

PINCHWIFE   I cannot; I will not.

HORNER   Come, you shall dine with us.

PINCHWIFE   I have dined already.

HORNER   Come, I know thou hast not: I'll treat thee, dear rogue; thou sha't spend none of thy Hampshire money to-day.

8. At the theater, the middle gallery. The fashionable crowd was below, in the pit and boxes.

PINCHWIFE (*aside*) Treat me! So, he uses me already like his cuckold.

HORNER Nay, you shall not go.

PINCHWIFE I must; I have business at home. (*Exit.*)

HARCOURT To beat his wife. He's as jealous of her, as a Cheapside husband of a Covent-garden wife.

HORNER Why, 'tis as hard to find an old whoremaster without jealousy and the gout, as a young one without fear, or the pox:—

> As gout in age from pox in youth proceeds,
> So wenching past, then jealousy succeeds;
> The worst disease that love and wenching breeds.

Exeunt.

ACT TWO

A room in Pinchwife's house. Mrs. Margery Pinchwife and Alithea. Pinchwife peeping behind at the door.

MRS. PINCHWIFE Pray, sister, where are the best fields and woods to walk in, in London?

ALITHEA (*aside*) A pretty question!—(*Aloud.*) Why, sister, Mulberry-garden and St. James's-park; and, for close walks, the New Exchange.

MRS. PINCHWIFE Pray, sister, tell me why my husband looks so grum here in town, and keeps me up so close, and will not let me go a-walking, nor let me wear my best gown yesterday.

ALITHEA O, he's jealous, sister.

MRS. PINCHWIFE Jealous! what's that?

ALITHEA He's afraid you should love another man.

MRS. PINCHWIFE How should he be afraid of my loving another man, when he will not let me see any but himself?

ALITHEA Did he not carry you yesterday to a play?

MRS. PINCHWIFE Ay; but we sat amongst ugly people. He would not let me come near the gentry, who sat under us, so that I could not see 'em. He told me, none but naughty women sat there, whom they toused and moused. But I would have ventured, for all that.

ALITHEA But how did you like the play?

MRS. PINCHWIFE Indeed I was weary of the play; but I liked hugeously the actors. They are the goodliest, properest men, sister!

ALITHEA O, but you must not like the actors, sister.

MRS. PINCHWIFE Ay, how should I help it, sister? Pray, sister, when my husband comes in, will you ask leave for me to go a-walking?

ALITHEA A-walking! ha! ha! Lord, a country-gentle-woman's pleasure is the drudgery of a footpost; and she requires as much airing as her husband's horses.—(*Aside.*) But here comes your husband: I'll ask, though I'm sure he'll not grant it.

MRS. PINCHWIFE He says he won't let me go abroad for fear of catching the pox.

ALITHEA Fy! the smallpox[1] you should say.

Enter Pinchwife.

MRS. PINCHWIFE O my dear, dear bud, welcome home! Why dost thou look so fropish? who has nangered thee?

PINCHWIFE You're a fool.

Mrs. Pinchwife goes aside, and cries.

ALITHEA Faith, so she is, for crying for no fault, poor tender creature!

PINCHWIFE What, you would have her as impudent as yourself, as arrant a jilflirt, a gadder, a magpie; and to say all, a mere notorious town-woman?

ALITHEA Brother, you are my only censurer; and the honour of your family will sooner suffer in your wife there than in me, though I take the innocent liberty of the town.

PINCHWIFE Hark you, mistress, do not talk so before my wife.—The innocent liberty of the town!

ALITHEA Why, pray, who boasts of any intrigue with me? what lampoon has made my name notorious? what ill women frequent my lodgings? I keep no company with any women of scandalous reputations.

PINCHWIFE No, you keep the men of scandalous reputations company.

ALITHEA Where? would you not have me civil? answer 'em in

1. Smallpox rather than pox, since the latter is a common term for syphilis.

a box at the plays, in the drawing-room at Whitehall, in St. James'-park, Mulberry-garden, or—

PINCHWIFE   Hold, hold! Do not teach my wife where the men are to be found: I believe she's the worse for your town-documents already. I bid you keep her in ignorance, as I do.

MRS. PINCHWIFE   Indeed, be not angry with her, bud, she will tell me nothing of the town, though I ask her a thousand times a day.

PINCHWIFE   Then you are very inquisitive to know, I find?

MRS. PINCHWIFE   Not I indeed, dear; I hate London. Our place-house in the country is worth a thousand of't: would I were there again!

PINCHWIFE   So you shall, I warrant. But were you not talking of plays and players when I came in?—(*To Alithea.*) You are her encourager in such discourses.

MRS. PINCHWIFE   No, indeed, dear; she chid me just now for liking the playermen.

PINCHWIFE (*aside*)   Nay, if she be so innocent as to own to me her liking them, there is no hurt in't.—(*Aloud.*) Come, my poor rogue, but thou likest none better than me?

MRS. PINCHWIFE   Yes, indeed, but I do. The playermen are finer folks.

PINCHWIFE   But you love none better than me?

MRS. PINCHWIFE   You are my own dear bud, and I know you. I hate a stranger.

PINCHWIFE   Ay, my dear, you must love me only; and not be like the naughty town-women, who only hate their husbands, and love every man else; love plays, visits, fine coaches, fine clothes, fiddles, balls, treats, and so lead a wicked town-life.

MRS. PINCHWIFE   Nay, if to enjoy all these things be a town-life, London is not so bad a place, dear.

PINCHWIFE   How! if you love me, you must hate London.

ALITHEA (*aside*)   The fool has forbid me discovering to her the pleasures of the town, and he is now setting her agog upon them himself.

MRS. PINCHWIFE   But, husband, do the town-women love the playermen too?

PINCHWIFE   Yes, I warrant you.

MRS. PINCHWIFE   Ay, I warrant you.

PINCHWIFE   Why, you do not, I hope?

MRS. PINCHWIFE   No, no, bud. But why have we no playermen in the country?

PINCHWIFE   Ha!—Mrs. Minx, ask me no more to go to a play.

MRS. PINCHWIFE   Nay, why, love? I did not care for going: but when you forbid me, you make me, as 'twere, desire it.

ALITHEA (aside)   So 'twill be in other things, I warrant.

MRS. PINCHWIFE   Pray let me go to a play, dear.

PINCHWIFE   Hold your peace, I wo' not.

MRS. PINCHWIFE   Why, love?

PINCHWIFE   Why, I'll tell you.

ALITHEA (aside)   Nay, if he tell her, she'll give him more cause to forbid her that place.

MRS. PINCHWIFE   Pray why, dear?

PINCHWIFE   First, you like the actors; and the gallants may like you.

MRS. PINCHWIFE   What, a homely country girl! No, bud, nobody will like me.

PINCHWIFE   I tell you yes, they may.

MRS. PINCHWIFE   No, no, you jest—I won't believe you: I will go.

PINCHWIFE   I tell you then, that one of the lewdest fellows in town, who saw you there, told me he was in love with you.

MRS. PINCHWIFE   Indeed! who, who, pray who was't?

PINCHWIFE (aside)   I've gone too far, and slipped before I was aware; how overjoyed she is!

MRS. PINCHWIFE   Was it any Hampshire gallant, any of our neighbours? I promise you, I am beholden to him.

PINCHWIFE   I promise you, you lie; for he would but ruin you, as he has done hundreds. He has no other love for women but that; such as he look upon women, like basilisks, but to destroy 'em.

MRS. PINCHWIFE   Ay, but if he loves me, why should he ruin me? answer me to that. Methinks he should not, I would do him no harm.

ALITHEA   Ha! ha! ha!

PINCHWIFE   'Tis very well; but I'll keep him from doing you any harm, or me either. (Enter Sparkish and Harcourt.) But here comes company; get you in, get you in.

MRS. PINCHWIFE   But, pray, husband, is he a pretty gentleman that loves me?

PINCHWIFE   In, baggage, in.

Thrusts her in, and shuts the door.

What, all the lewd libertines of the town brought to my lodging by this easy coxcomb! 'sdeath, I'll not suffer it.

SPARKISH   Here, Harcourt, do you approve my choice?— (*To Alithea.*) Dear little rogue, I told you I'd bring you acquainted with all my friends, the wits and—

Harcourt salutes her.

PINCHWIFE   Ay, they shall know her, as well as you yourself will, I warrant you.

SPARKISH   This is one of those, my pretty rogue, that are to dance at your wedding to-morrow; and him you must bid welcome ever, to what you and I have.

PINCHWIFE (*aside*)   Monstrous!

SPARKISH   Harcourt, how dost thou like her, faith? Nay, dear, do not look down; I should hate to have a wife of mine out of countenance at anything.

PINCHWIFE (*aside*)   Wonderful!

SPARKISH   Tell me, I say, Harcourt, how dost thou like her? Thou hast stared upon her enough, to resolve me.

HARCOURT   So infinitely well, that I could wish I had a mistress too, that might differ from her in nothing but her love and engagement to you.

ALITHEA   Sir, Master Sparkish has often told me that his acquaintance were all wits and railleurs, and now I find it.

SPARKISH   No, by the universe, madam, he does not rally now; you may believe him. I do assure you, he is the honestest, worthiest, true-hearted gentleman—a man of such perfect honour, he would say nothing to a lady he does not mean.

PINCHWIFE (*aside*)   Praising another man to his mistress!

HARCOURT   Sir, you are so beyond expectation obliging, that—

SPARKISH   Nay, egad, I am sure you do admire her extremely; I see't in your eyes.—He does admire you, madam.—By the world, don't you?

HARCOURT   Yes, above the world, or the most glorious part of it, her whole sex: and till now I never thought I should have envied you, or any man about to marry, but you have the best excuse for marriage I ever knew.

ALITHEA   Nay, now, sir, I'm satisfied you are of the society of the wits and railleurs, since you cannot spare your friend, even when he is but too civil to you; but the surest sign is, since you are an enemy to marriage,—for that I hear you hate as much as business or bad wine.

HARCOURT   Truly, madam, I was never an enemy to marriage till now, because marriage was never an enemy to me before.

ALITHEA   But why, sir, is marriage an enemy to you now? because it robs you of your friend here? for you look upon a friend married, as one gone into a monastery, that is, dead to the world.

HARCOURT   'Tis indeed, because you marry him; I see, madam, you can guess my meaning. I do confess heartily and openly, I wish it were in my power to break the match; by Heavens I would.

SPARKISH   Poor Frank!

ALITHEA   Would you be so unkind to me?

HARCOURT   No, no, 'tis not because I would be unkind to you.

SPARKISH   Poor Frank! no gad, 'tis only his kindness to me.

PINCHWIFE   Great kindness to you indeed! (*Aside.*) Insensible fop, let a man make love to his wife to his face!

SPARKISH   Come, dear Frank, for all my wife there, that shall be, thou shalt enjoy me sometimes, dear rogue. By my honour, we men of wit condole for our deceased brother in marriage, as much as for one dead in earnest: I think that was prettily said of me, ha, Harcourt?—But come, Frank, be not melancholy for me.

HARCOURT   No, I assure you, I am not melancholy for you.

SPARKISH   Prithee, Frank, dost think my wife that shall be there, a fine person?

HARCOURT   I could gaze upon her till I became as blind as you are.

SPARKISH   How as I am? how?

HARCOURT   Because you are a lover, and true lovers are blind, stock blind.

SPARKISH   True, true; but by the world she has wit too, as well as beauty: go, go with her into a corner, and try if she has wit; talk to her anything, she's bashful before me.

HARCOURT   Indeed if a woman wants wit in a corner, she has it nowhere.

ALITHEA (*aside to Sparkish*) Sir, you dispose of me a little before your time—

SPARKISH Nay, nay, madam, let me have an earnest of your obedience, or—go, go, madam—

Harcourt courts Alithea aside.

PINCHWIFE How, sir! if you are not concerned for the honour of a wife, I am for that of a sister; he shall not debauch her. Be a pander to your own wife! bring men to her! let 'em make love before your face! thrust 'em into a corner together, then leave 'em in private! is this your town wit and conduct?

SPARKISH Ha! ha! ha! a silly wise rogue would make one laugh more than a stark fool, ha! ha! I shall burst. Nay, you shall not disturb 'em; I'll vex thee, by the world. (*Struggles with Pinchwife to keep him from Harcourt and Alithea.*)

ALITHEA The writings are drawn, sir, settlements made; 'tis too late, sir, and past all revocation.

HARCOURT Then so is my death.

ALITHEA I would not be unjust to him.

HARCOURT Then why to me so?

ALITHEA I have no obligation to you.

HARCOURT My love.

ALITHEA I had his before.

HARCOURT You never had it; he wants, you see, jealousy, the only infallible sign of it.

ALITHEA Love proceeds from esteem; he cannot distrust my virtue: besides, he loves me, or he would not marry me.

HARCOURT Marrying you is no more sign of his love than bribing your woman, that he may marry you, is a sign of his generosity. Marriage is rather a sign of interest than love; and he that marries a fortune covets a mistress, not loves her. But if you take marriage for a sign of love, take it from me immediately.

ALITHEA No, now you have put a scruple in my head; but in short, sir, to end our dispute, I must marry him, my reputation would suffer in the world else.

HARCOURT No; if you do marry him, with your pardon, madam, your reputation suffers in the world, and you would be thought in necessity for a cloak.

ALITHEA Nay, now you are rude, sir.—Mr. Sparkish, pray

come hither, your friend here is very troublesome, and very loving.

HARCOURT (*aside to Alithea*) Hold! hold!

PINCHWIFE D'ye hear that?

SPARKISH Why, d'ye think I'll seem to be jealous, like a country bumpkin?

PINCHWIFE No, rather be a cuckold, like a credulous cit.

HARCOURT Madam, you would not have been so little generous as to have told him.

ALITHEA Yes, since you could be so little generous as to wrong him.

HARCOURT Wrong him! no man can do't, he's beneath an injury: a bubble, a coward, a senseless idiot, a wretch so contemptible to all the world but you, that—

ALITHEA Hold, do not rail at him, for since he is like to be my husband, I am resolved to like him: nay, I think I am obliged to tell him you are not his friend.—Master Sparkish, Master Sparkish!

SPARKISH What, what?—(*To Harcourt.*) Now, dear rogue, has not she wit?

HARCOURT (*speaks surlily*) Not so much as I thought, and hoped she had.

ALITHEA Mr. Sparkish, do you bring people to rail at you?

HARCOURT Madam—

SPARKISH How! no; but if he does rail at me, 'tis but in jest, I warrant: what we wits do for one another, and never take any notice of it.

ALITHEA He spoke so scurrilously of you, I had no patience to hear him; besides, he has been making love to me.

HARCOURT (*aside*) True, damned tell-tale woman!

SPARKISH Pshaw! to show his parts—we wits rail and make love often, but to show our parts: as we have no affections, so we have no malice, we—

ALITHEA He said you were a wretch below an injury—

SPARKISH Pshaw!

HARCOURT (*aside*) Damned, senseless, impudent, virtuous jade! Well, since she won't let me have her, she'll do as good, she'll make me hate her.

ALITHEA A common bubble—

SPARKISH Pshaw!

ALITHEA A coward—

SPARKISH Pshaw, pshaw!

ALITHEA A senseless, drivelling idiot—

SPARKISH How! did he disparage my parts? Nay, then, my honour's concerned, I can't put up that, sir, by the world—brother, help me to kill him—(*Aside.*) I may draw now, since we have the odds of him:—'tis a good occasion, too, before my mistress—(*Offers to draw.*)

ALITHEA Hold, hold!

SPARKISH What, what?

ALITHEA (*aside*) I must not let 'em kill the gentleman neither, for his kindness to me: I am so far from hating him, that I wish my gallant had his person and understanding. Nay, if my honour—

SPARKISH I'll be thy death.

ALITHEA Hold, hold! Indeed, to tell the truth, the gentleman said after all, that what he spoke was but out of friendship to you.

SPARKISH How! say, I am, I am a fool, that is, no wit, out of friendship to me?

ALITHEA Yes, to try whether I was concerned enough for you; and made love to me only to be satisfied of my virtue, for your sake.

HARCOURT (*aside*) Kind, however.

SPARKISH Nay, if it were so, my dear rogue, I ask thee pardon; but why would not you tell me so, faith?

HARCOURT Because I did not think on't, faith.

SPARKISH Come, Horner does not come; Harcourt, let's be gone to the new play.—Come, madam.

ALITHEA I will not go, if you intend to leave me alone in the box, and run into the pit, as you use to do.

SPARKISH Pshaw! I'll leave Harcourt with you in the box to entertain you, and that's as good; if I sat in the box, I should be thought no judge but of trimmings.—Come away, Harcourt, lead her down.

Exeunt Sparkish, Harcourt, and Alithea.

PINCHWIFE Well, go thy ways, for the flower of the true town fops, such as spend their estates before they come to 'em, and are cuckolds before they're married. But let me go look to my own freehold.—How!

Enter Lady Fidget, Mrs. Dainty Fidget, and Mrs. Squeamish.

LADY FIDGET   Your servant, sir: where is your lady? We are come to wait upon her to the new play.

PINCHWIFE   New play!

LADY FIDGET   And my husband will wait upon you presently.

PINCHWIFE (*aside*)   Damn your civility.—(*Aloud.*) Madam, by no means; I will not see Sir Jasper here, till I have waited upon him at home; nor shall my wife see you till she has waited upon your ladyship at your lodgings.

LADY FIDGET   Now we are here, sir?

PINCHWIFE   No, madam.

MRS. DAINTY FIDGET   Pray, let us see her.

MRS. SQUEAMISH   We will not stir till we see her.

PINCHWIFE (*aside*)   A pox on you all!—(*Goes to the door, and returns.*) She has locked the door, and is gone abroad.

LADY FIDGET   No, you have locked the door, and she's within.

MRS. DAINTY FIDGET   They told us below she was here.

PINCHWIFE (*aside*)   Will nothing do?—(*Aloud.*) Well, it must out then. To tell you the truth, ladies, which I was afraid to let you know before, lest it might endanger your lives, my wife has just now the small-pox come out upon her; do not be frightened; but pray be gone, ladies; you shall not stay here in danger of your lives; pray get you gone, ladies.

LADY FIDGET   No, no, we have all had 'em.

MRS. SQUEAMISH   Alack, alack!

MRS. DAINTY FIDGET   Come, come, we must see how it goes with her. I understand the disease.

LADY FIDGET   Come!

PINCHWIFE (*aside*)   Well, there is no being too hard for women at their own weapon, lying, therefore I'll quit the field. (*Exit.*)

MRS. SQUEAMISH   Here's an example of jealousy!

LADY FIDGET   Indeed, as the world goes, I wonder there are no more jealous, since wives are so neglected.

MRS. DAINTY FIDGET   Pshaw! as the world goes, to what end should they be jealous?

LADY FIDGET   Foh! 'tis a nasty world.

MRS. SQUEAMISH   That men of parts, great acquaintance, and quality, should take up with and spend themselves and fortunes in keeping little playhouse creatures, foh!

LADY FIDGET Nay, that women of understanding, great acquaintance, and good quality, should fall a-keeping too of little creatures, foh!

MRS. SQUEAMISH Why, 'tis the men of quality's fault; they never visit women of honour and reputation as they used to do; and have not so much as common civility for ladies of our rank, but use us with the same indifferency and ill-breeding as if we were all married to 'em.

LADY FIDGET She says true; 'tis an arrant shame women of quality should be so slighted; methinks birth—birth should go for something; I have known men admired, courted, and followed for their titles only.

MRS. SQUEAMISH Ay, one would think men of honour should not love, no more than marry, out of their own rank.

MRS. DAINTY FIDGET Fy, fy, upon 'em! they are come to think cross breeding for themselves best, as well as for their dogs and horses.

LADY FIDGET They are dogs and horses for't.

MRS. SQUEAMISH One would think, if not for love, for vanity a little.

MRS. DAINTY FIDGET Nay, they do satisfy their vanity upon us sometimes; and are kind to us in their report, tell all the world they lie with us.

LADY FIDGET Damned rascals, that we should be only wronged by 'em! To report a man has had a person, when he has not had a person, is the greatest wrong in the whole world that can be done to a person.

MRS. SQUEAMISH Well, 'tis an arrant shame noble persons should be so wronged and neglected.

LADY FIDGET But still 'tis an arranter shame for a noble person to neglect her own honour, and defame her own noble person with little inconsiderable fellows, foh!

MRS. DAINTY FIDGET I suppose the crime against our honour is the same with a man of quality as with another.

LADY FIDGET How! no sure, the man of quality is likest one's husband, and therefore the fault should be the less.

MRS. DAINTY FIDGET But then the pleasure should be the less.

LADY FIDGET Fy, fy, fy, for shame, sister! whither shall we ramble? Be continent in your discourse, or I shall hate you.

MRS. DAINTY FIDGET Besides, an intrigue is so much the more notorious for the man's quality.

MRS. SQUEAMISH   'Tis true that nobody takes notice of a private man, and therefore with him 'tis more secret; and the crime's the less when 'tis not known.

LADY FIDGET   You say true; i'faith, I think you are in the right on't: 'tis not an injury to a husband, till it be an injury to our honours; so that a woman of honour loses no honour with a private person; and to say truth—

MRS. DAINTY FIDGET (*apart to Mrs. Squeamish*)   So, the little fellow is grown a private person—with her—

LADY FIDGET   But still my dear, dear honour—

Enter Sir Jasper Fidget, Horner, and Dorilant.

SIR JASPER   Ay, my dear, dear of honour, thou hast still so much honour in thy mouth—

HORNER (*aside*)   That she has none elsewhere.

LADY FIDGET   Oh, what d'ye mean to bring in these upon us?

MRS. DAINTY FIDGET   Foh! these are as bad as wits.

MRS. SQUEAMISH   Foh!

LADY FIDGET   Let us leave the room.

SIR JASPER   Stay, stay; faith, to tell you the naked truth—

LADY FIDGET   Fy, Sir Jasper! do not use that word naked.

SIR JASPER   Well, well, in short I have business at Whitehall, and cannot go to the play with you, therefore would have you go—

LADY FIDGET   With those two to a play?

SIR JASPER   No, not with t'other, but with Mr. Horner; there can be no more scandal to go with him than with Mr. Tattle, or Master Limberham.

LADY FIDGET   With that nasty fellow! no—no.

SIR JASPER   Nay, prithee, dear, hear me. (*Whispers to Lady Fidget.*)

HORNER   Ladies—

Horner and Dorilant draw near Mrs. Squeamish and Mrs. Dainty Fidget.

MRS. DAINTY FIDGET   Stand off.

MRS. SQUEAMISH   Do not approach us.

MRS. DAINTY FIDGET   You herd with the wits, you are obscenity all over.

MRS. SQUEAMISH   And I would as soon look upon a picture of

Adam and Eve, without fig-leaves, as any of you, if I could help it; therefore keep off, and do not make us sick.

DORILANT   What a devil are these?

HORNER   Why, these are pretenders to honour, as critics to wit, only by censuring others; and as every raw, peevish, out-of-humoured, affected, dull, tea-drinking, arithmetical fop, sets up for a wit by railing at men of sense, so these for honour, by railing at the court, and ladies of as great honour as quality.

SIR JASPER   Come, Mr. Horner, I must desire you to go with these ladies to the play, sir.

HORNER   I, sir?

SIR JASPER   Ay, ay, come, sir.

HORNER   I must beg your pardon, sir, and theirs; I will not be seen in women's company in public again for the world.

SIR JASPER   Ha, ha, strange aversion!

MRS. SQUEAMISH   No, he's for women's company in private.

SIR JASPER   He—poor man—he—ha! ha! ha!

MRS. DAINTY FIDGET   'Tis a greater shame amongst lewd fellows to be seen in virtuous women's company, than for the women to be seen with them.

HORNER   Indeed, madam, the time was I only hated virtuous women, but now I hate the other too; I beg your pardon, ladies.

LADY FIDGET   You are very obliging, sir, because we would not be troubled with you.

SIR JASPER   In sober sadness, he shall go.

DORILANT   Nay, if he wo' not, I am ready to wait upon the ladies, and I think I am the fitter man.

SIR JASPER   You sir! no, I thank you for that. Master Horner is a privileged man amongst the virtuous ladies, 'twill be a great while before you are so; he! he! he! he's my wife's gallant; he! he! he! No, pray withdraw, sir, for as I take it, the virtuous ladies have no business with you.

DORILANT   And I am sure he can have none with them. 'Tis strange a man can't come amongst virtuous women now, but upon the same terms as men are admitted into the Great Turk's seraglio. But heavens keep me from being an ombre player with 'em!—But where is Pinchwife? (*Exit.*)

SIR JASPER   Come, come, man; what, avoid the sweet society

of womankind? that sweet, soft, gentle, tame, noble creature, woman, made for man's companion—

HORNER   So is that soft, gentle, tame, and more noble creature a spaniel, and has all their tricks; can fawn, lie down, suffer beating, and fawn the more; barks at your friends when they come to see you, makes your bed hard, gives you fleas, and the mange sometimes. And all the difference is, the spaniel's the more faithful animal, and fawns but upon one master.

SIR JASPER   He! he! he!

MRS. SQUEAMISH   O the rude beast!

MRS. DAINTY FIDGET   Insolent brute!

LADY FIDGET   Brute! stinking, mortified, rotten French wether, to dare—

SIR JASPER   Hold, an't please your ladyship.—For shame, Master Horner! your mother was a woman—(Aside.) Now shall I never reconcile 'em.—(Aside to Lady Fidget.) Hark you, madam, take my advice in your anger. You know you often want one to make up your drolling pack of ombre players, and you may cheat him easily; for he's an ill gamester, and consequently loves play. Besides, you know you have but two old civil gentlemen (with stinking breaths too) to wait upon you abroad; take in the third into your service. The other are but crazy; and a lady should have a supernumerary gentleman-usher as a supernumerary coach-horse, lest sometimes you should be forced to stay at home.

LADY FIDGET   But are you sure he loves play, and has money?

SIR JASPER   He loves play as much as you, and has money as much as I.

LADY FIDGET   Then I am contented to make him pay for his scurrility. Money makes up in a measure all other wants in men.—(Aside.) Those whom we cannot make hold for gallants, we make fine.

SIR JASPER (aside)   So, so; now to mollify, wheedle him.—(Aside to Horner.) Master Horner, will you never keep civil company? methinks 'tis time now, since you are only fit for them. Come, come, man, you must e'en fall to visiting our wives, eating at our tables, drinking tea with our virtuous relations after dinner, dealing cards to 'em, reading plays and gazettes to 'em, picking fleas out of their smocks for 'em, collecting receipts, new songs, women, pages, and footmen for 'em.

HORNER   I hope they'll afford me better employment, sir.

SIR JASPER   He! he! he! 'tis fit you know your work before you come into your place. And since you are unprovided of a lady to flatter, and a good house to eat at, pray frequent mine, and call my wife mistress, and she shall call you gallant, according to the custom.

HORNER   Who, I?

SIR JASPER   Faith, thou sha't for my sake; come, for my sake only.

HORNER   For your sake—

SIR JASPER   Come, come, here's a gamester for you; let him be a little familiar sometimes; nay, what if a little rude? Gamesters may be rude with ladies, you know.

LADY FIDGET   Yes; losing gamesters have a privilege with women.

HORNER   I always thought the contrary, that the winning gamester had most privilege with women; for when you have lost your money to a man, you'll lose anything you have, all you have, they say, and he may use you as he pleases.

SIR JASPER   He! he! he! well, win or lose, you shall have your liberty with her.

LADY FIDGET   As he behaves himself; and for your sake I'll give him admittance and freedom.

HORNER   All sorts of freedom, madam?

SIR JASPER   Ay, ay, ay, all sorts of freedom thou canst take. And so go to her, begin thy new employment; wheedle her, jest with her, and be better acquainted one with another.

HORNER (aside)   I think I know her already; therefore may venture with her my secret for hers.

Horner and Lady Fidget whisper.

SIR JASPER   Sister cuz, I have provided an innocent playfellow for you there.

MRS. DAINTY FIDGET   Who, he?

MRS. SQUEAMISH   There's a playfellow, indeed!

SIR JASPER   Yes sure.—What, he is good enough to play at cards, blindman's-buff, or the fool with, sometimes!

MRS. SQUEAMISH   Foh! we'll have no such playfellows.

MRS. DAINTY FIDGET   No, sir; you shan't choose playfellows for us, we thank you.

SIR JASPER   Nay, pray hear me. (*Whispering to them.*)

LADY FIDGET   But, poor gentleman, could you be so generous, so truly a man of honour, as for the sakes of us women of honour, to cause yourself to be reported no man? No man! and to suffer yourself the greatest shame that could fall upon a man, that none might fall upon us women by your conversation? but, indeed, sir, as perfectly, perfectly the same man as before your going into France, sir? as perfectly, perfectly, sir?

HORNER   As perfectly, perfectly, madam. Nay, I scorn you should take my word; I desire to be tried only, madam.

LADY FIDGET   Well, that's spoken again like a man of honour: all men of honour desire to come to the test. But, indeed, generally you men report such things of yourselves, one does not know how or whom to believe; and it is come to that pass, we dare not take your words no more than your tailor's, without some staid servant of yours be bound with you. But I have so strong a faith in your honour, dear, dear, noble sir, that I'd forfeit mine for yours, at any time, dear sir.

HORNER   No, madam, you should not need to forfeit it for me; I have given you security already to save you harmless, my late reputation being so well known in the world, madam.

LADY FIDGET   But if upon any future falling-out, or upon a suspicion of my taking the trust out of your hands, to employ some other, you yourself should betray your trust, dear sir? I mean, if you'll give me leave to speak obscenely, you might tell, dear sir.

HORNER   If I did, nobody would believe me. The reputation of impotency is as hardly recovered again in the world as that of cowardice, dear madam.

LADY FIDGET   Nay, then, as one may say, you may do your worst, dear, dear sir.

SIR JASPER   Come, is your ladyship reconciled to him yet? have you agreed on matters? for I must be gone to Whitehall.

LADY FIDGET   Why, indeed, Sir Jasper, Master Horner is a thousand, thousand times a better man than I thought him. Cousin Squeamish, sister Dainty, I can name him now.

Truly, not long ago, you know, I thought his very name obscenity; and I would as soon have lain with him as have named him.

SIR JASPER   Very likely, poor madam.

MRS. DAINTY   I believe it.

MRS. SQUEAMISH   No doubt on't.

SIR JASPER   Well, well—that your ladyship is as virtuous as any she, I know, and him all the town knows—he! he! he! therefore now you like him, get you gone to your business together, go, go to your business, I say, pleasure, whilst I go to my pleasure, business.

LADY FIDGET   Come, then, dear gallant.

HORNER   Come away, my dearest mistress.

SIR JASPER   So, so; why, 'tis as I'd have it. (*Exit.*)

HORNER   And as I'd have it.

LADY FIDGET   Who for his business from his wife will run,
    Takes the best care to have her business done.

Exeunt.

ACT THREE

Scene 1

A room in Pinchwife's house.
Enter Alithea and Mrs. Pinchwife.

ALITHEA   Sister, what ails you? you are grown melancholy.

MRS. PINCHWIFE   Would it not make any one melancholy to see you go every day fluttering about abroad, whilst I must stay at home like a poor lonely sullen bird in a cage?

ALITHEA   Ay, sister; but you came young, and just from the nest to your cage: so that I thought you liked it, and could be as cheerful in't as others that took their flight themselves early, and are hopping abroad in the open air.

MRS. PINCHWIFE   Nay, I confess I was quiet enough till my husband told me what pure lives the London ladies live abroad, with their dancing, meetings, and junketings, and dressed every day in their best gowns; and I warrant you, play at nine-pins every day of the week, so they do.

Enter Pinchwife.

PINCHWIFE Come, what's here to do? you are putting the town-pleasures in her head, and setting her a-longing.

ALITHEA Yes, after nine-pins. You suffer none to give her those longings you mean but yourself.

PINCHWIFE I tell her of the vanities of the town like a confessor.

ALITHEA A confessor! just such a confessor as he that, by forbidding a silly ostler to grease the horse's teeth, taught him to do't.

PINCHWIFE Come, Mrs. Flippant, good precepts are lost when bad examples are still before us: the liberty you take abroad makes her hanker after it, and out of humour at home. Poor wretch! she desired not to come to London; I would bring her.

ALITHEA Very well.

PINCHWIFE She has been this week in town, and never desired till this afternoon to go abroad.

ALITHEA Was she not at a play yesterday?

PINCHWIFE Yes; but she ne'er asked me; I was myself the cause of her going.

ALITHEA Then if she ask you again, you are the cause of her asking, and not my example.

PINCHWIFE Well, to-morrow night I shall be rid of you; and the next day, before 'tis light, she and I'll be rid of the town, and my dreadful apprehensions.—Come, be not melancholy; for thou sha't go into the country after to-morrow, dearest.

ALITHEA Great comfort!

MRS. PINCHWIFE Pish! what d'ye tell me of the country for?

PINCHWIFE How's this! what, pish at the country?

MRS. PINCHWIFE Let me alone; I am not well.

PINCHWIFE Oh, if that be all—what ails my dearest?

MRS. PINCHWIFE Truly, I don't know: but I have not been well since you told me there was a gallant at the play in love with me.

PINCHWIFE Ha!—

ALITHEA That's by my example too!

PINCHWIFE Nay, if you are not well, but are so concerned, because a lewd fellow chanced to lie, and say he liked you, you'll make me sick too.

MRS. PINCHWIFE Of what sickness?

PINCHWIFE   O, of that which is worse than the plague, jealousy.

MRS. PINCHWIFE   Pish, you jeer! I'm sure there's no such disease in our receipt-book at home.

PINCHWIFE (*aside*)   No, thou never met'st with it, poor innocent.—Well, if thou cuckold me, 'twill be my own fault—for cuckolds and bastards are generally makers of their own fortune.

MRS. PINCHWIFE   Well, but pray, bud, let's go to a play tonight.

PINCHWIFE   'Tis just done, she comes from it. But why are you so eager to see a play?

MRS. PINCHWIFE   Faith, dear, not that I care one pin for their talk there; but I like to look upon the playermen, and would see, if I could, the gallant you say loves me: that's all, dear bud.

PINCHWIFE   Is that all, dear bud?

ALITHEA   This proceeds from my example!

MRS. PINCHWIFE   But if the play be done, let's go abroad, however, dear bud.

PINCHWIFE   Come have a little patience and thou shalt go into the country on Friday.

MRS. PINCHWIFE   Therefore I would see first some sights to tell my neighbours of. Nay, I will go abroad, that's once.

ALITHEA   I'm the cause of this desire too!

PINCHWIFE   But now I think on't, who, who was the cause of Horner's coming to my lodgings to-day? That was you.

ALITHEA   No, you, because you would not let him see your handsome wife out of your lodging.

MRS. PINCHWIFE   Why, O Lord! did the gentleman come hither to see me indeed?

PINCHWIFE   No, no.—You are not the cause of that damned question too, Mistress Alithea?—(*Aside.*) Well, she's in the right of it. He is in love with my wife—and comes after her—'tis so—but I'll nip his love in the bud; lest he should follow us into the country, and break his chariot-wheel near our house, on purpose for an excuse to come to't. But I think I know the town.

MRS. PINCHWIFE   Come, pray, bud, let's go abroad before 'tis late; for I will go, that's flat and plain.

PINCHWIFE (*aside*)   So! the obstinacy already of the town-wife;

and I must, whilst she's here, humour her like one.—(*Aloud.*)
Sister, how shall we do, that she may not be seen, or known?

ALITHEA   Let her put on her mask.

PINCHWIFE   Pshaw! a mask makes people but the more
inquisitive, and is as ridiculous a disguise as a stage-beard:
her shape, stature, habit will be known. And if we should
meet with Horner, he would be sure to take acquaintance
with us, must wish her joy, kiss her, talk to her, leer upon
her, and the devil and all. No, I'll not use her to a mask, 'tis
dangerous; for masks have made more cuckolds than the
best faces that ever were known.

ALITHEA   How will you do then?

MRS. PINCHWIFE   Nay, shall we go? The Exchange will be
shut, and I have a mind to see that.

PINCHWIFE   So—I have it—I'll dress her up in the suit we are
to carry down to her brother, little Sir James; nay, I
understand the town-tricks. Come, let's go dress her. A
mask! no—a woman masked, like a covered dish, gives a
man curiosity and appetite; when, it may be, uncovered,
'twould turn his stomach: no, no.

ALITHEA   Indeed your comparison is something a greasy one:
but I had a gentle gallant used to say, A beauty masked, like
the sun in eclipse, gathers together more gazers than if it
shined out.

Exeunt.

Scene 2

The New Exchange.
Enter Horner, Harcourt, and Dorilant.

DORILANT   Engaged to women, and not sup with us!

HORNER   Ay, a pox on 'em all!

HARCOURT   You were much a more reasonable man in the
morning, and had as noble resolutions against 'em, as a
widower of a week's liberty.

DORILANT   Did I ever think to see you keep company with
women in vain?

HORNER   In vain: no—'tis since I can't love 'em, to be
revenged on 'em.

HARCOURT   Now your sting is gone, you looked in the box amongst all those women like a drone in the hive; all upon you, shoved and ill-used by 'em all, and thrust from one side to t'other.

DORILANT   Yet he must be buzzing amongst 'em still, like other beetle-headed liquorish drones. Avoid 'em, and hate 'em, as they hate you.

HORNER   Because I do hate 'em, and would hate 'em yet more, I'll frequent 'em. You may see by marriage, nothing makes a man hate a woman more than her constant conversation. In short, I converse with 'em, as you do with rich fools, to laugh at 'em and use 'em ill.

DORILANT   But I would no more sup with women, unless I could lie with 'em, than sup with a rich coxcomb, unless I could cheat him.

HORNER   Yes, I have known thee sup with a fool for his drinking, if he could set out your hand that way only, you were satisfied, and if he were a wine-swallowing mouth, 'twas enough.

HARCOURT   Yes, a man drinks often with a fool, as he tosses with a marker, only to keep his hand in use. But do the ladies drink?

HORNER   Yes, sir; and I shall have the pleasure at least of laying 'em flat with a bottle, and bring as much scandal that way upon 'em as formerly t'other.

HARCOURT   Perhaps you may prove as weak a brother among 'em that way as t'other.

DORILANT   Foh! drinking with women is as unnatural as scolding with 'em. But 'tis a pleasure of decayed fornicators, and the basest way of quenching love.

HARCOURT   Nay, 'tis drowning love, instead of quenching it. But leave us for civil women too!

DORILANT   Ay, when he can't be the better for 'em. We hardly pardon a man that leaves his friend for a wench, and that's a pretty lawful call.

HORNER   Faith, I would not leave you for 'em, if they would not drink.

DORILANT   Who would disappoint his company at Lewis's for a gossiping?

HARCOURT   Foh! Wine and women, good apart, together are as nauseous as sack and sugar. But hark you, sir, before you go, a little of your advice; an old maimed general, when unfit for action, is fittest for counsel. I have other designs upon women than eating and drinking with them; I am in love with Sparkish's mistress, whom he is to marry to-morrow: now how shall I get her?

Enter Sparkish, looking about.

HORNER   Why, here comes one will help you to her.

HARCOURT   He! he, I tell you, is my rival, and will hinder my love.

HORNER   No; a foolish rival and a jealous husband assist their rival's designs; for they are sure to make their women hate them, which is the first step to their love for another man.

HARCOURT   But I cannot come near his mistress but in his company.

HORNER   Still the better for you; for fools are most easily cheated when they themselves are accessaries: and he is to be bubbled of his mistress as of his money, the common mistress, by keeping him company.

SPARKISH   Who is that that is to be bubbled? Faith, let me snack; I han't met with a bubble since Christmas. 'Gad, I think bubbles are like their brother woodcocks, go out with the cold weather.

HARCOURT (*apart to Horner*)   A pox! he did not hear all, I hope.

SPARKISH   Come, you bubbling rogues you, where do we sup?—Oh, Harcourt, my mistress tells me you have been making fierce love to her all the play long: ha! ha!—But I—

HARCOURT   I make love to her!

SPARKISH   Nay, I forgive thee, for I think I know thee, and I know her; but I am sure I know myself.

HARCOURT   Did she tell you so? I see all women are like these of the Exchange; who, to enhance the prize of their commodities, report to their fond customers offers which were never made 'em.

HORNER   Ay, women are apt to tell before the intrigue, as men after it, and so show themselves the vainer sex. But hast thou a mistress, Sparkish? 'Tis as hard for me to believe it, as that thou ever hadst a bubble, as you bragged just now.

SPARKISH   O, your servant, sir: are you at your raillery, sir? But we are some of us beforehand with you to-day at the play. The wits were something bold with you, sir; did you not hear us laugh?

HORNER   Yes; but I thought you had gone to plays, to laugh at the poet's wit, not at your own.

SPARKISH   Your servant, sir: no, I thank you. 'Gad I go to a play as to a country treat; I carry my own wine to one, and my own wit to t'other, or else I'm sure I should not be merry at either. And the reason why we are so often louder than the players, is, because we think we speak more wit, and so become the poet's rivals in his audience: for to tell you the truth, we hate the silly rogues; nay, so much, that we find fault even with their bawdy upon the stage, whilst we talk nothing else in the pit as loud.

HORNER   But why shouldst thou hate the silly poets? Thou hast too much wit to be one; and they, like whores, are only hated by each other: and thou dost scorn writing, I'm sure.

SPARKISH   Yes; I'd have you to know I scorn writing: but women, women, that make men do all foolish things, make 'em write songs too. Everybody does it. 'Tis even as common with lovers, as playing with fans; and you can no more help rhyming to your Phillis, than drinking to your Phillis.

HARCOURT   Nay, poetry in love is no more to be avoided than jealousy.

DORILANT   But the poets damned your songs, did they?

SPARKISH   Damn the poets! they have turned 'em into burlesque, as they call it. That burlesque is a hocus-pocus trick they have got, which, by the virtue of *Hictius doctius topsy turvy,* they make a wise and witty man in the world, a fool upon the stage you know not how: and 'tis therefore I hate 'em too, for I know not but it may be my own case; for they'll put a man into a play for looking asquint. Their predecessors were contented to make serving-men only their stage-fools: but these rogues must have gentlemen, with a pox to 'em, nay, knights; and, indeed, you shall hardly see a fool upon the stage but he's a knight. And to tell you the truth, they have kept me these six years from being a knight in earnest, for fear of being knighted in a play, and dubbed a fool.

DORILANT   Blame 'em not, they must follow their copy, the age.

HARCOURT   But why shouldst thou be afraid of being in a

play, who expose yourself every day in the play-houses, and at public places?

HORNER 'Tis but being on the stage, instead of standing on a bench in the pit.

DORILANT Don't you give money to painters to draw you like? and are you afraid of your pictures at length in a playhouse, where all your mistresses may see you?

SPARKISH A pox! painters don't draw the small-pox or pimples in one's face. Come, damn all your silly authors whatever, all books and booksellers, by the world; and all readers, courteous or uncourteous!

HARCOURT But who comes here, Sparkish?

Enter Pinchwife and Mrs. Pinchwife in man's clothes, Alithea, and Lucy.

SPARKISH Oh, hide me! There's my mistress too.

Sparkish hides himself behind Harcourt.

HARCOURT She sees you.

SPARKISH But I will not see her. 'Tis time to go to Whitehall, and I must not fail the drawing-room.

HARCOURT Pray, first carry me, and reconcile me to her.

SPARKISH Another time. Faith, the king will have supped.

HARCOURT Not with the worse stomach for thy absence. Thou art one of those fools that think their attendance at the king's meals as necessary as his physicians, when you are more troublesome to him than his doctors or his dogs.

SPARKISH Pshaw! I know my interest, sir. Prithee hide me.

HORNER Your servant, Pinchwife.—What, he knows us not!

PINCHWIFE (*to his wife aside*) Come along.

MRS. PINCHWIFE Pray, have you any ballads? give me six-penny worth.

BOOKSELLER We have no ballads.

MRS. PINCHWIFE Then give me "Covent Garden Drollery," and a play or two—Oh, here's "Tarugo's Wiles," and "The Slighted Maiden"; I'll have them.

PINCHWIFE (*apart to her*) No; plays are not for your reading. Come along; will you discover yourself?

HORNER Who is that pretty youth with him, Sparkish?

SPARKISH I believe his wife's brother, because he's something like her: but I never saw her but once.

HORNER   Extremely handsome; I have seen a face like it too. Let us follow 'em.

Exeunt Pinchwife, Mrs. Pinchwife, Alithea, and Lucy; Horner and Dorilant following them.

HARCOURT   Come, Sparkish, your mistress saw you, and will be angry you go not to her. Besides, I would fain be reconciled to her, which none but you can do, dear friend.

SPARKISH   Well, that's a better reason, dear friend. I would not go near her now for her's or my own sake; but I can deny you nothing: for though I have known thee a great while, never go, if I do not love thee as well as a new acquaintance.

HARCOURT   I am obliged to you indeed, dear friend. I would be well with her, only to be well with thee still; for these ties to wives usually dissolve all ties to friends. I would be contented she should enjoy you a-nights, but I would have you to myself a-days as I have had, dear friend.

SPARKISH   And thou shalt enjoy me a-days, dear, dear friend, never stir: and I'll be divorced from her, sooner than from thee. Come along.

HARCOURT (*aside*)   So, we are hard put to't, when we make our rival our procurer; but neither she nor her brother would let me come near her now. When all's done, a rival is the best cloak to steal to a mistress under, without suspicion; and when we have once got to her as we desire, we throw him off like other cloaks.

Exit Sparkish, Harcourt following him. Re-enter Pinchwife and Mrs. Pinchwife.

PINCHWIFE (*to Alithea*)   Sister, if you will not go, we must leave you.[1]—(*Aside.*) The fool her gallant and she will muster up all the young saunterers of this place, and they will leave their dear sempstresses to follow us. What a swarm of cuckolds and cuckold-makers are here!—Come, let's be gone, Mistress Margery.

MRS. PINCHWIFE   Don't you believe that; I han't half my bellyfull of sights yet.

PINCHWIFE   Then walk this way.

1. Directed to Alithea, who is offstage talking to Sparkish and the others.

MRS. PINCHWIFE   Lord, what a power of brave signs are here! stay—the Bull's-Head, the Ram's-Head, and the Stag's-Head, dear—

PINCHWIFE   Nay, if every husband's proper sign here were visible, they would be all alike.

MRS. PINCHWIFE   What d'ye mean by that, bud?

PINCHWIFE   'Tis no matter—no matter, bud.

MRS. PINCHWIFE   Pray tell me: nay, I will know.

PINCHWIFE   They would be all Bulls, Stags, and Ramsheads.

Exeunt Pinchwife and Mrs. Pinchwife. Re-enter Sparkish, Harcourt, Alithea, and Lucy, at the other side.

SPARKISH   Come, dear madam, for my sake you shall be reconciled to him.

ALITHEA   For your sake I hate him.

HARCOURT   That's something too cruel, madam, to hate me for his sake.

SPARKISH   Ay indeed, madam, too, too cruel to me, to hate my friend for my sake.

ALITHEA   I hate him because he is your enemy; and you ought to hate him too, for making love to me, if you love me.

SPARKISH   That's a good one! I hate a man for loving you! If he did love you, 'tis but what he can't help; and 'tis your fault, not his, if he admires you. I hate a man for being of my opinion! I'll n'er do't, by the world.

ALITHEA   Is it for your honour, or mine, to suffer a man to make love to me, who am to marry you to-morrow?

SPARKISH   Is it for your honour, or mine, to have me jealous? That he makes love to you, is a sign you are handsome; and that I am not jealous, is a sign you are virtuous. That I think is for your honour.

ALITHEA   But 'tis your honour too I am concerned for.

HARCOURT   But why, dearest madam, will you be more concerned for his honour than he is himself? Let his honour alone, for my sake and his. He! he has no honour—

SPARKISH   How's that?

HARCOURT   But what my dear friend can guard himself.

SPARKISH   O ho—that's right again.

HARCOURT   Your care of his honour argues his neglect of it, which is no honour to my dear friend here. Therefore once more, let his honour go which way it will, dear madam.

SPARKISH Ay, ay; were it for my honour to marry a woman whose virtue I suspected, and could not trust her in a friend's hands?

ALITHEA Are you not afraid to lose me?

HARCOURT He afraid to lose you, madam! No, no—you may see how the most estimable and most glorious creature in the world is valued by him. Will you not see it?

SPARKISH Right, honest Frank, I have that noble value for her that I cannot be jealous of her.

ALITHEA You mistake him. He means, you care not for me, nor who has me.

SPARKISH Lord, madam, I see you are jealous! Will you wrest a poor man's meaning from his words?

ALITHEA You astonish me, sir, with your want of jealousy.

SPARKISH And you make me giddy, madam, with your jealousy and fears, and virtue and honour. 'Gad, I see virtue makes a woman as troublesome as a little reading or learning.

ALITHEA Monstrous!

LUCY (*aside*) Well, to see what easy husbands these women of quality can meet with! a poor chambermaid can never have such ladylike luck. Besides, he's thrown away upon her. She'll make no use of her fortune, her blessing, none to a gentleman, for a pure cuckold; for it requires good breeding to be a cuckold.

ALITHEA I tell you then plainly, he pursues me to marry me.

SPARKISH Pshaw!

HARCOURT Come, madam, you see you strive in vain to make him jealous of me. My dear friend is the kindest creature in the world to me.

SPARKISH Poor fellow!

HARCOURT But his kindness only is not enough for me, without your favour, your good opinion, dear madam: 'tis that must perfect my happiness. Good gentleman, he believes all I say: would you would do so! Jealous of me! I would not wrong him nor you for the world.

SPARKISH Look you there. Hear him, hear him, and do not walk away so.

Alithea walks carelessly to and fro.

HARCOURT I love you, madam, so—

SPARKISH   How's that? Nay, now you begin to go too far indeed.

HARCOURT   So much, I confess, I say, I love you, that I would not have you miserable, and cast yourself away upon so unworthy and inconsiderable a thing as what you see here. (*Clapping his hand on his breast, points at Sparkish.*)

SPARKISH   No, faith, I believe thou wouldst not: now his meaning is plain; but I knew before thou wouldst not wrong me, nor her.

HARCOURT   No, no, Heavens forbid the glory of her sex should fall so low, as into the embraces of such a contemptible wretch, the least of mankind—my friend here—I injure him! (*Embracing Sparkish.*)

ALITHEA   Very well.

SPARKISH   No, no, dear friend, I knew it.—Madam, you see he will rather wrong himself than me, in giving himself such names.

ALITHEA   Do not you understand him yet?

SPARKISH   Yes: how modestly he speaks of himself, poor fellow!

ALITHEA   Methinks he speaks impudently of yourself, since—before yourself too; insomuch that I can no longer suffer his scurrilous abusiveness to you, no more than his love to me. (*Offers to go.*)

SPARKISH   Nay, nay, madam, pray stay—his love to you! Lord madam, has he not spoke yet plain enough?

ALITHEA   Yes, indeed, I should think so.

SPARKISH   Well then, by the world, a man can't speak civilly to a woman now, but presently she says, he makes love to her. Nay, madam, you shall stay, with your pardon, since you have not yet understood him, till he has made an éclaircissement of his love to you, that is, what kind of love it is. Answer to thy catechism, friend; do you love my mistress here?

HARCOURT   Yes, I wish she would not doubt it.

SPARKISH   But how do you love her?

HARCOURT   With all my soul.

ALITHEA   I thank him, methinks he speaks plain enough now.

SPARKISH (*to Alithea*)   You are out still.—But with what kind of love, Harcourt?

HARCOURT   With the best and the truest love in the world.

SPARKISH   Look you there then, that is with no matrimonial love, I'm sure.

ALITHEA   How's that? do you say matrimonial love is not best?

SPARKISH   'Gad, I went too far ere I was aware. But speak for thyself, Harcourt, you said you would not wrong me nor her.

HARCOURT   No, no, madam, e'en take him for Heaven's sake.

SPARKISH   Look you there, madam.

HARCOURT   Who should in all justice be yours, he that loves you most. (*Claps his hand on his breast.*)

ALITHEA   Look you there, Mr. Sparkish, who's that?

SPARKISH   Who should it be?—Go on, Harcourt.

HARCOURT   Who loves you more than women, titles, or fortune fools. (*Points at Sparkish.*)

SPARKISH   Look you there, he means me still, for he points at me.

ALITHEA   Ridiculous!

HARCOURT   Who can only match your faith and constancy in love.

SPARKISH   Ay.

HARCOURT   Who knows, if it be possible, how to value so much beauty and virtue.

SPARKISH   Ay.

HARCOURT   Whose love can no more be equalled in the world, than that heavenly form of yours.

SPARKISH   No.

HARCOURT   Who could no more suffer a rival, than your absence, and yet could no more suspect your virtue, than his own constancy in his love to you.

SPARKISH   No.

HARCOURT   Who, in fine, loves you better than his eyes, that first made him love you.

SPARKISH   Ay—Nay, madam, faith, you shan't go till—

ALITHEA   Have a care, lest you make me stay too long.

SPARKISH   But till he has saluted you; that I may be assured you are friends, after his honest advice and declaration. Come, pray, madam, be friends with him.

Re-enter Pinchwife and Mrs. Pinchwife.

ALITHEA   You must pardon me, sir, that I am not yet so
obedient to you.

PINCHWIFE   What, invite your wife to kiss men? Monstrous!
are you not ashamed? I will never forgive you.

SPARKISH   Are you not ashamed, that I should have more
confidence in the chastity of your family than you have?
You must not teach me, I am a man of honour, sir, though I
am frank and free; I am frank, sir—

PINCHWIFE   Very frank, sir, to share your wife with your
friends.

SPARKISH   He is an humble, menial friend, such as reconciles
the differences of the marriage bed; you know man and wife
do not always agree; I design him for that use, therefore
would have him well with my wife.

PINCHWIFE   A menial friend!—you will get a great many
menial friends, by showing your wife as you do.

SPARKISH   What then? It may be I have a pleasure in't, as I
have to show fine cloths at a play-house, the first day, and
count money before poor rogues.

PINCHWIFE   He that shows his wife or money, will be in
danger of having them borrowed sometimes.

SPARKISH   I love to be envied, and would not marry a wife
that I alone could love; loving alone is as dull as eating
alone. Is it not a frank age? and I am a frank person; and to
tell you the truth, it may be, I love to have rivals in a wife,
they make her seem to a man still but as a kept mistress;
and so good night, for I must to Whitehall.—Madam, I
hope you are now reconciled to my friend; and so I wish you
a good night, madam, and sleep if you can: for tomorrow
you know I must visit you early with a canonical gentleman.
Good night, dear Harcourt. (*Exit.*)

HARCOURT   Madam, I hope you will not refuse my visit
tomorrow, if it should be earlier with a canonical gentleman
than Mr. Sparkish's.

PINCHWIFE   This gentlewoman is yet under my care, therefore
you must yet forbear your freedom with her, sir. (*Coming
between Alithea and Harcourt.*)

HARCOURT   Must, sir?

PINCHWIFE   Yes, sir, she is my sister.

HARCOURT   'Tis well she is, sir—for I must be her servant,
sir.—Madam—

PINCHWIFE   Come away, sister, we had been gone, if it had not been for you, and so avoided these lewd rake-hells, who seem to haunt us.

Re-enter Horner and Dorilant.

HORNER   How now, Pinchwife!

PINCHWIFE   Your servant.

HORNER   What! I see a little time in the country makes a man turn wild and unsociable, and only fit to converse with his horses, dogs, and his herds.

PINCHWIFE   I have business, sir, and must mind it; your business is pleasure, therefore you and I must go different ways.

HORNER   Well, you may go on, but this pretty young gentle-man—

Takes hold of Mrs. Pinchwife.

HARCOURT   The lady—

DORILANT   And the maid—

HORNER   Shall stay with us; for I suppose their business is the same with ours, pleasure.

PINCHWIFE   (*aside*)   'Sdeath, he knows her, she carries it so sillily! yet if he does not, I should be more silly to discover it first.

ALITHEA   Pray, let us go, sir.

PINCHWIFE   Come, come—

HORNER   (*to Mrs. Pinchwife*)   Had you not rather stay with us?—Prithee, Pinchwife, who is this pretty young gentle-man?

PINCHWIFE   One to whom I'm a guardian.—(*Aside.*) I wish I could keep her out of your hands.

HORNER   Who is he? I never saw anything so pretty in all my life.

PINCHWIFE   Pshaw! do not look upon him so much, he's a poor bashful youth, you'll put him out of countenance.—Come away, brother. (*Offers to take her away.*)

HORNER   O, your brother!

PINCHWIFE   Yes, my wife's brother.—Come, come, she'll stay supper for us.

HORNER   I thought so, for he is very like her I saw you at the play with, whom I told you I was in love with.

MRS. PINCHWIFE (*aside*) O jeminy! is that he that was in love with me? I am glad on't, I vow, for he's a curious fine gentleman, and I love him already, too.—(*To Pinchwife.*) Is this he, bud?

PINCHWIFE (*to his wife*) Come away, come away.

HORNER Why, what haste are you in? Why won't you let me talk with him?

PINCHWIFE Because you'll debauch him; he's yet young and innocent, and I would not have him debauched for anything in the world.—(*Aside.*) How she gazes on him! the devil!

HORNER Harcourt, Dorilant, look you here, this is the likeness of that dowdy he told us of, his wife; did you ever see a lovelier creature? The rogue has reason to be jealous of his wife, since she is like him, for she would make all that see her in love with her.

HARCOURT And, as I remember now, she is as like him here as can be.

DORILANT She is indeed very pretty, if she be like him.

HORNER Very pretty? a very pretty commendation!—she is a glorious creature, beautiful beyond all things I ever beheld.

PINCHWIFE So, so.

HARCOURT More beautiful than a poet's first mistress of imagination.

HORNER Or another man's last mistress of flesh and blood.

MRS. PINCHWIFE Nay, now you jeer, sir; pray don't jeer me.

PINCHWIFE Come, come.—(*Aside.*) By Heavens, she'll discover herself!

HORNER I speak of your sister, sir.

PINCHWIFE Ay, but saying she was handsome, if like him, made him blush.—(*Aside.*) I am upon a rack!

HORNER Methinks he is so handsome he should not be a man.

PINCHWIFE (*aside*) O, there 'tis out! he has discovered her! I am not able to suffer any longer.—(*To his wife.*) Come, come away, I say.

HORNER Nay, by your leave, sir, he shall not go yet.—(*Aside to them.*) Harcourt, Dorilant, let us torment this jealous rogue a little.

HARCOURT, DORILANT How?

HORNER I'll show you.

PINCHWIFE   Come, pray let him go, I cannot stay fooling any longer; I tell you his sister stays supper for us.

HORNER   Does she? Come then, we'll all go to sup with her and thee.

PINCHWIFE   No, now I think on't, having stayed so long for us, I warrant she's gone to bed.—(*Aside.*) I wish she and I were well out of their hands.—(*To his wife.*) Come, I must rise early tomorrow, come.

HORNER   Well then, if she be gone to bed, I wish her and you a good night. But pray, young gentleman, present my humble service to her.

MRS. PINCHWIFE   Thank you heartily, sir.

PINCHWIFE (*aside*)   'Sdeath, she will discover herself yet in spite of me.—(*Aloud.*) He is something more civil to you, for your kindness to his sister, than I am, it seems.

HORNER   Tell her, dear sweet little gentleman, for all your brother there, that you have revived the love I had for her at first sight in the play-house.

MRS. PINCHWIFE   But did you love her indeed, and indeed?

PINCHWIFE (*aside*)   So, so.—(*Aloud.*) Away, I say.

HORNER   Nay, stay.—Yes, indeed, and indeed, pray do you tell her so, and give her this kiss from me. (*Kisses her.*)

PINCHWIFE (*aside*)   O Heavens! what do I suffer? Now 'tis too plain he knows her, and yet—

HORNER   And this, and this—(*Kisses her again.*)

MRS. PINCHWIFE   What do you kiss me for? I am no woman.

PINCHWIFE (*aside*)   So, there, 'tis out.—(*Aloud.*) Come, I cannot, nor will stay any longer.

HORNER   Nay, they shall send your lady a kiss too. Here, Harcourt, Dorilant, will you not? (*They kiss her.*)

PINCHWIFE (*aside*)   How! do I suffer this? Was I not accusing another just now for this rascally patience, in permitting his wife to be kissed before his face? Ten thousand ulcers gnaw away their lips.—(*Aloud.*) Come, come.

HORNER   Good night, dear little gentleman; madam, good night; farewell, Pinchwife.—(*Apart to Harcourt and Dorilant.*) Did not I tell you I would raise his jealous gall?

Exeunt Horner, Harcourt, and Dorilant.

PINCHWIFE   So, they are gone at last; stay, let me see first if the coach be at this door. (*Exit.*)

Re-enter Horner, Harcourt, and Dorilant.

HORNER   What, not gone yet? Will you be sure to do as I desired you, sweet sir?

MRS. PINCHWIFE   Sweet sir, but what will you give me then?

HORNER   Anything. Come away into the next walk. (*Exit, haling away Mrs. Pinchwife.*)

ALITHEA   Hold! hold! what d'ye do?

LUCY   Stay, stay, hold—

HARCOURT   Hold, madam, hold, let him present him—he'll come presently; nay, I will never let you go till you answer my question.

LUCY   For God's sake, sir, I must follow 'em.

Alithea and Lucy, struggling with Harcourt and Dorilant.

DORILANT   No, I have something to present you with too, you shan't follow them.

Re-enter Pinchwife.

PINCHWIFE   Where?—how—what's become of?—gone!—whither?

LUCY   He's only gone with the gentleman, who will give him something, an't please your worship.

PINCHWIFE   Something!—give him something, with a pox!—where are they?

ALITHEA   In the next walk only, brother.

PINCHWIFE   Only, only! where, where? (*Exit and returns presently, then goes out again.*)

HARCOURT   What's the matter with him? why so much concerned? But, dearest madam—

ALITHEA   Pray let me go, sir; I have said and suffered enough already.

HARCOURT   Then you will not look upon, nor pity, my sufferings?

ALITHEA   To look upon 'em, when I cannot help 'em, were cruelty, not pity; therefore, I will never see you more.

HARCOURT   Let me then, madam, have my privilege of a banished lover, complaining or railing, and giving you but a farewell reason why, if you cannot condescend to marry me, you should not take that wretch, my rival.

ALITHEA   He only, not you, since my honour is engaged so far to him, can give me a reason why I should not marry him; but if he be true, and what I think him to me, I must be so to him. Your servant, sir.

HARCOURT   Have women only constancy when 'tis a vice, and are, like Fortune, only true to fools?

DORILANT (*to Lucy, who struggles to get from him*)   Thou sha't not stir, thou robust creature; you see I can deal with you, therefore you should stay the rather, and be kind.

Re-enter Pinchwife.

PINCHWIFE   Gone, gone, not to be found! quite gone! ten thousand plagues go with 'em! Which way went they?

ALITHEA   But into t'other walk, brother.

LUCY   Their business will be done presently sure, an't please your worship; it can't be long in doing, I'm sure on't.

ALITHEA   Are they not there?

PINCHWIFE   No, you know where they are, you infamous wretch, eternal shame of your family, which you do not dishonour enough yourself you think, but you must help her to do it too, thou legion of bawds!

ALITHEA   Good brother—

PINCHWIFE   Damned, damned sister!

ALITHEA   Look you here, she's coming.

Re-enter Mrs. Pinchwife running, with her hat full of oranges and dried fruit under her arm, Horner following.

MRS. PINCHWIFE   O dear bud, look you here what I have got, see!

PINCHWIFE (*aside, rubbing his forehead*)   And what I have got here too, which you can't see.

MRS. PINCHWIFE   The fine gentleman has given me better things yet.

PINCHWIFE   Has he so?—(*Aside.*) Out of breath and coloured! —I must hold yet.

HORNER   I have only given your little brother an orange, sir.

PINCHWIFE (*to Horner*)   Thank you, sir.—(*Aside.*) You have only squeezed my orange, I suppose, and given it me again; yet I must have a city patience.—(*To his wife.*) Come, come away.

MRS. PINCHWIFE   Stay, till I have put up my fine things, bud.

Enter Sir Jasper Fidget.

SIR JASPER   O, Master Horner, come, come, the ladies stay for you; your mistress, my wife, wonders you make not more haste to her.

HORNER   I have stayed this half hour for you here, and 'tis your fault I am not now with your wife.

SIR JASPER   But, pray, don't let her know so much; the truth on't is, I was advancing a certain project to his majesty about—I'll tell you.

HORNER   No, let's go, and hear it at your house. Good night, sweet little gentleman; one kiss more, you'll remember me now, I hope.

Kisses her.

DORILANT   What, Sir Jasper, will you separate friends? He promised to sup with us, and if you take him to your house, you'll be in danger of our company too.

SIR JASPER   Alas! gentlemen, my house is not fit for you; there are none but civil women there, which are not for your turn. He, you know, can bear with the society of civil women now, ha! ha! ha! besides, he's one of my family—he's—he! he! he!

DORILANT   What is he?

SIR JASPER   Faith, my eunuch, since you'll have it; he! he! he!

Exeunt Sir Jasper Fidget and Horner.

DORILANT   I rather wish thou wert his or my cuckold. Harcourt, what a good cuckold is lost there for want of a man to make him one? Thee and I cannot have Horner's privilege, who can make use of it.

HARCOURT   Ay, to poor Horner 'tis like coming to an estate at threescore, when a man can't be the better for't.

PINCHWIFE   Come.

MRS. PINCHWIFE   Presently, bud.

DORILANT   Come, let us go too.—(*To Alithea.*) Madam, your servant.—(*To Lucy.*) Good night, strapper.

HARCOURT   Madam, though you will not let me have a good day or night, I wish you one; but dare not name the other half of my wish.

ALITHEA   Good night, sir, for ever.

MRS. PINCHWIFE I don't know where to put this here, dear bud, you shall eat it; nay, you shall have part of the fine gentleman's good things, or treat, as you call it, when we come home.

PINCHWIFE Indeed, I deserve it, since I furnished the best part of it. (*Strikes away the orange.*)

> The gallant treats presents, and gives the ball;
> But 'tis the absent cuckold pays for all.

Exeunt.

ACT FOUR

Scene 1

Pinchwife's house in the morning.
Enter Alithea dressed in new clothes, and Lucy.

LUCY Well—madam, now have I dressed you, and set you out with so many ornaments, and spent upon you ounces of essence and pulvillio; and all this for no other purpose but as people adorn and perfume a corpse for a stinking second-hand grave: such, or as bad, I think Master Sparkish's bed.

ALITHEA Hold your peace.

LUCY Nay, madam, I will ask you the reason why you would banish poor Master Harcourt for ever from your sight; how could you be so hard-hearted?

ALITHEA 'Twas because I was not hard-hearted.

LUCY No, no; 'twas stark love and kindness, I warrant.

ALITHEA It was so; I would see him no more because I love him.

LUCY Hey day, a very pretty reason!

ALITHEA You do not understand me.

LUCY I wish you may yourself.

ALITHEA I was engaged to marry, you see, another man, whom my justice will not suffer me to deceive or injure.

LUCY Can there be a greater cheat or wrong done to a man than to give him your person without your heart? I should make a conscience of it.

ALITHEA   I'll retrieve it for him after I am married a while.

LUCY   The woman that marries to love better, will be as much mistaken as the wencher that marries to live better. No, madam, marrying to increase love is like gaming to become rich; alas! you only lose what little stock you had before.

ALITHEA   I find by your rhetoric you have been bribed to betray me.

LUCY   Only by his merit, that has bribed your heart, you see, against your word and rigid honour. But what a devil is this honour! 'tis sure a disease in the head, like the megrim or falling-sickness, that always hurries people away to do themselves mischief. Men lose their lives by it; women, what's dearer to 'em, their love, the life of life.

ALITHEA   Come, pray talk you no more of honour, nor Master Harcourt; I wish the other would come to secure my fidelity to him and his right in me.

LUCY   You will marry him then?

ALITHEA   Certainly, I have given him already my word, and will my hand too, to make it good, when he comes.

LUCY   Well, I wish I may never stick pin more, if he be not an arrant natural, to t'other fine gentleman.

ALITHEA   I own he wants the wit of Harcourt, which I will dispense withal for another want he has, which is want of jealousy, which men of wit seldom want.

LUCY   Lord, madam, what should you do with a fool to your husband? You intend to be honest, don't you? then that husbandly virtue, credulity, is thrown away upon you.

ALITHEA   He only that could suspect my virtue should have cause to do it; 'tis Sparkish's confidence in my truth that obliges me to be so faithful to him.

LUCY   You are not sure his opinion may last.

ALITHEA   I am satisfied, 'tis impossible for him to be jealous after the proofs I have had of him. Jealousy in a husband—Heaven defend me from it! it begets a thousand plagues to a poor woman, the loss of her honour, her quiet, and her—

LUCY   And her pleasure.

ALITHEA   What d'ye mean, impertinent?

LUCY   Liberty is a great pleasure, madam.

ALITHEA   I say, loss of her honour, her quiet, nay, her life sometimes; and what's as bad almost, the loss of this town;

that is, she is sent into the country, which is the last ill-usage
of a husband to a wife, I think.

LUCY (*aside*) O, does the wind lie there?—(*Aloud.*) Then of
necessity, madam, you think a man must carry his wife into
the country, if he be wise. The country is as terrible, I find,
to our young English ladies, as a monastery to those abroad;
and on my virginity, I think they would rather marry a
London jailer, than a high sheriff of a county, since neither
can stir from his employment. Formerly women of wit
married fools for a great estate, a fine seat, or the like; but
now 'tis for a pretty seat only in Lincoln's-Inn-Fields, St.
James's-Fields, or the Pall-Mall.[1]

Enter Sparkish, and Harcourt, dressed like a parson.

SPARKISH   Madam, your humble servant, a happy day to you,
and to us all.

HARCOURT   Amen.

ALITHEA   Who have we here?

SPARKISH   My chaplain, faith—O madam, poor Harcourt
remembers his humble service to you; and, in obedience to
your last commands, refrains coming into your sight.

ALITHEA   Is not that he?

SPARKISH   No, fy, no; but to show that he ne'er intended to
hinder our match, has sent his brother here to join our
hands. When I get me a wife, I must get her a chaplain,
according to the custom; that is his brother, and my
chaplain.

ALITHEA   His brother!

LUCY (*aside*)   And your chaplain, to preach in your pulpit
then—

ALITHEA   His brother!

SPARKISH   Nay, I knew you would not believe it.—I told you,
sir, she would take you for your brother Frank.

ALITHEA   Believe it!

LUCY (*aside*)   His brother! ha! ha! he! he has a trick left still, it
seems.

SPARKISH   Come, my dearest, pray let us go to church before
the canonical hour is past.

ALITHEA   For shame, you are abused still.

1. A fashionable place to live in London.

SPARKISH   By the world, 'tis strange now you are so incredulous.

ALITHEA   'Tis strange you are so credulous.

SPARKISH   Dearest of my life, hear me. I tell you this is Ned Harcourt of Cambridge, by the world; you see he has a sneaking college look. 'Tis true he's something like his brother Frank; and they differ from each other no more than in their age, for they were twins.

LUCY   Ha! ha! ha!

ALITHEA   Your servant, sir; I cannot be so deceived, though you are. But come, let's hear, how do you know what you affirm so confidently?

SPARKISH   Why, I'll tell you all. Frank Harcourt coming to me this morning to wish me joy, and present his service to you, I asked him if he could help me to a parson. Whereupon he told me, he had a brother in town who was in orders; and he went straight away, and sent him, you see there, to me.

ALITHEA   Yes, Frank goes and puts on a black coat, then tells you he is Ned; that's all you have for't.

SPARKISH   Pshaw! pshaw! I tell you, by the same token, the midwife put her garter about Frank's neck, to know 'em asunder, they were so like.

ALITHEA   Frank tells you this too?

SPARKISH   Ay, and Ned there too: nay, they are both in a story.

ALITHEA   So, so; very foolish.

SPARKISH   Lord, if you won't believe one, you had best try him by your chambermaid there; for chambermaids must needs know chaplains from other men, they are so used to 'em.

LUCY   Let's see: nay, I'll be sworn he has the canonical smirk, and the filthy clammy palm of a chaplain.

ALITHEA   Well, most reverend doctor, pray let us make an end of this fooling.

HARCOURT   With all my soul, divine heavenly creature, when you please.

ALITHEA   He speaks like a chaplain indeed.

SPARKISH   Why, was there not soul, divine, heavenly, in what he said?

ALITHEA   Once more, most impertinent black coat, cease your persecution, and let us have a conclusion of this ridiculous love.

HARCOURT (*aside*) I had forgot, I must suit my style to my coat, or I wear it in vain.

ALITHEA I have no more patience left; let us make once an end of this troublesome love, I say.

HARCOURT So be it, seraphic lady, when your honour shall think it meet and convenient so to do.

SPARKISH 'Gad I'm sure none but a chaplain could speak so, I think.

ALITHEA Let me tell you, sir, this dull trick will not serve your turn; though you delay our marriage, you shall not hinder it.

HARCOURT Far be it from me, munificent patroness, to delay your marriage; I desire nothing more than to marry you presently, which I might do, if you yourself would; for my noble, good-natured, and thrice generous patron here would not hinder it.

SPARKISH No, poor man, not I, faith.

HARCOURT And now, madam, let me tell you plainly nobody else shall marry you; by Heavens! I'll die first, for I'm sure I should die after it.

LUCY How his love has made him forget his function, as I have seen it in real parsons!

ALITHEA That was spoken like a chaplain too? now you understand him, I hope.

SPARKISH Poor man, he takes it heinously to be refused; I can't blame him, 'tis putting an indignity upon him, not to be suffered; but you'll pardon me, madam, it shan't be; he shall marry us; come away, pray madam.

LUCY Ha! ha! he! more ado! 'tis late.

ALITHEA Invincible stupidity! I tell you, he would marry me as your rival, not as your chaplain.

SPARKISH Come, come, madam. (*Pulling her away.*)

LUCY I pray, madam, do not refuse this reverend divine the honour and satisfaction of marrying you; for I dare say, he has set his heart upon't, good doctor.

ALITHEA What can you hope or design by this?

HARCOURT I could answer her, a reprieve for a day only, often revokes a hasty doom. At worst, if she will not take mercy on me, and let me marry her, I have at least the lover's second pleasure, hindering my rival's enjoyment, though but for a time.

SPARKISH   Come, madam, 'tis e'en twelve o'clock, and my mother charged me never to be married out of the canonical hours. Come, come; Lord, here's such a deal of modesty, I warrant, the first day.

LUCY   Yes, an't please your worship, married women show all their modesty the first day, because married men show all their love the first day.

Exeunt.

Scene 2

A bedchamber in Pinchwife's house.
Pinchwife and Mrs. Pinchwife discovered.

PINCHWIFE   Come, tell me, I say.

MRS. PINCHWIFE   Lord! han't I told it a hundred times over?

PINCHWIFE (*aside*)   I would try, if in the repetition of the ungrateful tale, I could find her altering it in the least circumstance; for if her story be false, she is so too.—(*Aloud.*) Come, how was't, baggage?

MRS. PINCHWIFE   Lord, what pleasure you take to hear it sure!

PINCHWIFE   No, you take more in telling it I find; but speak, how was't?

MRS. PINCHWIFE   He carried me up into the house next to the Exchange.

PINCHWIFE   So, and you two were only in the room!

MRS. PINCHWIFE   Yes, for he sent away a youth that was there, for some dried fruit, and China oranges.

PINCHWIFE   Did he so? Damn him for it—and for—

MRS. PINCHWIFE   But presently came up the gentlewoman of the house.

PINCHWIFE   O, 'twas well she did; but what did he do whilst the fruit came?

MRS. PINCHWIFE   He kissed me a hundred times, and told me he fancied he kissed my fine sister, meaning me, you know, whom he said he loved with all his soul, and bid me be sure to tell her so, and to desire her to be at her window, by eleven of the clock this morning, and he would walk under it at that time.

PINCHWIFE (*aside*)   And he was as good as his word, very punctual; a pox reward him for't.

MRS. PINCHWIFE   Well, and he said if you were not within, he would come up to her, meaning me, you know, bud, still.

PINCHWIFE (*aside*)   So—he knew her certainly; but for this confession, I am obliged to her simplicity.—(*Aloud.*) But what, you stood very still when he kissed you?

MRS. PINCHWIFE   Yes, I warrant you; would you have had me discover myself?

PINCHWIFE   But you told me he did some beastliness to you, as you call it; what was't?

MRS. PINCHWIFE   Why, he put—

PINCHWIFE   What?

MRS. PINCHWIFE   Why, he put the tip of his tongue between my lips, and so mousled me—and I said, I'd bite it.

PINCHWIFE   An eternal canker seize it, for a dog!

MRS. PINCHWIFE   Nay, you need not be so angry with him neither, for to say truth, he has the sweetest breath I ever knew.

PINCHWIFE   The devil! you were satisfied with it then, and would do it again?

MRS. PINCHWIFE   Not unless he should force me.

PINCHWIFE   Force you, changeling! I tell you, no woman can be forced.

MRS. PINCHWIFE   Yes, but she may sure, by such a one as he, for he's a proper, goodly, strong man; 'tis hard, let me tell you, to resist him.

PINCHWIFE (*aside*)   So, 'tis plain she loves him, yet she has not love enough to make her conceal it from me; but the sight of him will increase her aversion for me and love for him; and that love instruct her how to deceive me and satisfy him, all idiot as she is. Love! 'twas he gave women first their craft, their art of deluding. Out of Nature's hands they came plain, open, silly, and fit for slaves, as she and Heaven intended 'em; but damned Love—well—I must strangle that little monster whilst I can deal with him.—(*Aloud.*) Go fetch pen, ink, and paper out of the next room.

MRS. PINCHWIFE   Yes, bud. (*Exit.*)

PINCHWIFE   Why should women have more invention in love

than men? It can only be, because they have more desires,
more soliciting passions, more lust, and more of the devil.
(*Re-enter Mrs. Pinchwife.*) Come, minx, sit down and write.

MRS. PINCHWIFE   Ay, dear bud, but I can't do't very well.

PINCHWIFE   I wish you could not at all.

MRS. PINCHWIFE   But what should I write for?

PINCHWIFE   I'll have you write a letter to your lover.

MRS. PINCHWIFE   O Lord, to the fine gentleman a letter!

PINCHWIFE   Yes, to the fine gentleman.

MRS. PINCHWIFE   Lord, you do but jeer: sure you jest.

PINCHWIFE   I am not so merry: come, write as I bid you.

MRS. PINCHWIFE   What, do you think I am a fool?

PINCHWIFE (*aside*)   She's afraid I would not dictate any love to
him, therefore she's unwilling.—(*Aloud.*) But you had best
begin.

MRS. PINCHWIFE   Indeed, and indeed, but I won't, so I won't.

PINCHWIFE   Why?

MRS. PINCHWIFE   Because he's in town; you may send for him
if you will.

PINCHWIFE   Very well, you would have him brought to you; is
it come to this? I say, take the pen and write, or you'll
provoke me.

MRS. PINCHWIFE   Lord, what d'ye make a fool of me for? Don't
I know that letters are never writ but from the country to
London, and from London into the country? Now he's in
town, and I am in town too; therefore I can't write to him,
you know.

PINCHWIFE (*aside*)   So, I am glad it is no worse; she is innocent
enough yet.—(*Aloud.*) Yes, you may, when your husband
bids you, write letters to people that are in town.

MRS. PINCHWIFE   O, may I so? then I'm satisfied.

PINCHWIFE   Come, begin:—"Sir"—(*Dictates.*)

MRS. PINCHWIFE   Shan't I say, "Dear Sir?"—You know one
says always something more than bare "sir."

PINCHWIFE   Write as I bid you, or I will write whore with this
penknife in your face.

MRS. PINCHWIFE   Nay, good bud—"Sir"—(*Writes.*)

PINCHWIFE   "Though I suffered last night your nauseous,
loathed kisses and embraces"—Write!

MRS. PINCHWIFE   Nay, why should I say so? You know I told
you he had a sweet breath.

PINCHWIFE   Write!

MRS. PINCHWIFE   Let me but put out "loathed."

PINCHWIFE   Write, I say!

MRS. PINCHWIFE   Well then. (*Writes.*)

PINCHWIFE   Let's see, what have you writ?—(*Takes the paper and reads.*) "Though I suffered last night your kisses and embraces"—Thou impudent creature! where is "nauseous" and "loathed"?

MRS. PINCHWIFE   I can't abide to write such filthy words.

PINCHWIFE   Once more write as I'd have you, and question it not, or I will spoil thy writing with this. I will stab out those eyes that cause my mischief. (*Holds up the penknife.*)

MRS. PINCHWIFE   O Lord! I will.

PINCHWIFE   So—so—let's see now.—(*Reads.*) "Though I suffered last night your nauseous, loathed kisses and embraces"—go on—"yet I would not have you presume that you shall ever repeat them"—so—(*She writes.*)

MRS. PINCHWIFE   I have writ it.

PINCHWIFE   On, then—"I then concealed myself from your knowledge, to avoid your insolencies."—(*She writes.*)

MRS. PINCHWIFE   So—

PINCHWIFE   "The same reason, now I am out of your hands" — (*She writes.*)

MRS. PINCHWIFE   So—

PINCHWIFE   "Makes me own to you my unfortunate, though innocent frolic, of being in man's clothes"—(*She writes.*)

MRS. PINCHWIFE   So—

PINCHWIFE   "That you may for evermore cease to pursue her, who hates and detests you"—(*She writes on.*)

MRS. PINCHWIFE   So—heigh! (*Sighs.*)

PINCHWIFE   What, do you sigh?—"detests you—as much as she loves her husband and her honour"—

MRS. PINCHWIFE   I vow, husband, he'll ne'er believe I should write such a letter.

PINCHWIFE   What, he'd expect a kinder from you? Come, now your name only.

MRS. PINCHWIFE   What, shan't I say "Your most faithful humble servant till death?"

PINCHWIFE   No, tormenting fiend!—(*Aside.*) Her style, I find, would be very soft.—(*Aloud.*) Come, wrap it up now, whilst I go fetch wax and a candle; and write on the backside, "For Mr. Horner." (*Exit.*)

MRS. PINCHWIFE "For Mr. Horner."—So, I am glad he has told me his name. Dear Mr. Horner! but why should I send thee such a letter that will vex thee, and make thee angry with me?—Well, I will not send it.—Ay, but then my husband will kill me—for I see plainly he won't let me love Mr. Horner—but what care I for my husband?—I won't, so I won't, send poor Mr. Horner such a letter—But then my husband—but oh, what if I writ at bottom my husband made me write it?—Ay, but then my husband would see't—Can one have no shift? ah, a London woman would have had a hundred presently. Stay—what if I should write a letter, and wrap it up like this, and write upon't too? Ay, but then my husband would see't—I don't know what to do.—But yet evads I'll try, so I will—for I will not send this letter to poor Mr. Horner, come what will on't.

"Dear, sweet Mr. Horner"—(*Writes and repeats what she writes.*)—so—"my husband would have me send you a base, rude, unmannerly letter; but I won't"—so—"and would have me forbid you loving me; but I won't"—so—"and would have me say to you, I hate you, poor Mr. Horner; but I won't tell a lie for him"—there—"for I'm sure if you and I were in the country at cards together"—so—"I could not help treading on your toe under the table"—so—"or rubbing knees with you, and staring in your face, till you saw me"—very well—"and then looking down, and blushing for an hour together"—so—"but I must make haste before my husband comes: and now he has taught me to write letters, you shall have longer ones from me, who am, dear, dear, poor, dear Mr. Horner, your most humble friend, and servant to command till death,—Margery Pinchwife."

Stay, I must give him a hint at bottom—so—now wrap it up just like t'other—so—now write "For Mr. Horner"—But oh now, what shall I do with it? for here comes my husband.

Re-enter Pinchwife.

PINCHWIFE (*aside*) I have been detained by a sparkish coxcomb, who pretended a visit to me; but I fear 'twas to my wife—(*Aloud.*) What, have you done?

MRS. PINCHWIFE   Ay, ay, bud, just now.

PINCHWIFE   Let's see't: what d'ye tremble for? what, you would not have it go?

MRS. PINCHWIFE   Here—(*Aside.*) No, I must not give him that: so I had been served if I had given him this.

He opens and reads the first letter.

PINCHWIFE   Come, where's the wax and seal?

MRS. PINCHWIFE (*aside*)   Lord, what shall I do now? Nay, then I have it—(*Aloud.*) Pray let me see't. Lord, you think me so arrant a fool, I cannot seal a letter; I will do't, so I will. (*Snatches the letter from him, changes it for the other, seals it, and delivers it to him.*)

PINCHWIFE   Nay, I believe you will learn that, and other things too, which I would not have you.

MRS. PINCHWIFE   So, han't I done it curiously?—(*Aside.*) I think I have; there's my letter going to Mr. Horner, since he'll needs have me send letters to folks.

PINCHWIFE   'Tis very well; but I warrant, you would not have it go now?

MRS. PINCHWIFE   Yes, indeed, but I would, bud, now.

PINCHWIFE   Well, you are a good girl then. Come, let me lock you up in your chamber, till I come back; and be sure you come not within three strides of the window when I am gone, for I have a spy in the street.—(*Exit Mrs. Pinchwife, Pinchwife locks the door.*) At least, 'tis fit she think so. If we do not cheat women, they'll cheat us, and fraud may be justly used with secret enemies, of which a wife is the most dangerous; and he that has a handsome one to keep, and a frontier town, must provide against treachery, rather than open force. Now I have secured all within, I'll deal with the foe without, with false intelligence. (*Holds up the letter. Exit.*)

Scene 3

Horner's lodging.
Enter Horner and Quack.

QUACK   Well, sir, how fadges the new design? have you not

the luck of all your brother projectors, to deceive only yourself at last?

HORNER No, good domine doctor, I deceive you, it seems, and others too; for the grave matrons, and old, rigid husbands think me as unfit for love, as they are; but their wives, sisters, and daughters know, some of 'em, better things already.

QUACK Already!

HORNER Already, I say. Last night I was drunk with half-a-dozen of your civil persons, as you call 'em, and people of honour, and so was made free of their society and dressing-rooms for ever hereafter; and am already come to the privileges of sleeping upon their pallets, warming smocks, tying shoes and garters, and the like, doctor, already, already, doctor.

QUACK You have made good use of your time, sir.

HORNER I tell thee, I am now no more interruption to 'em, when they sing, or talk bawdy, than a little squab French page who speaks no English.

QUACK But do civil persons and women of honour drink, and sing bawdy songs?

HORNER O, amongst friends, amongst friends. For your bigots in honour are just like those in religion; they fear the eye of the world more than the eye of Heaven; and think there is no virtue, but railing at vice, and no sin, but giving scandal. They rail at a poor, little, kept player, and keep themselves some young, modest pulpit comedian to be privy to their sins in their closets, not to tell 'em of them in their chapels.

QUACK Nay, the truth on't is, priests, amongst the women now, have quite got the better of us lay-confessors, physicians.

HORNER And they are rather their patients; but—

Enter Lady Fidget, looking about her.

Now we talk of women of honour, here comes one. Step behind the screen there, and but observe, if I have not particular privileges with the women of reputation already, doctor, already.

Quack retires.

LADY FIDGET   Well, Horner, am not I a woman of honour?
you see, I'm as good as my word.

HORNER   And you shall see, madam, I'll not be behindhand
with you in honour; and I'll be as good as my word too, if
you please but to withdraw into the next room.

LADY FIDGET   But first, my dear sir, you must promise to have
a care of my dear honour.

HORNER   If you talk a word more of your honour, you'll make
me incapable to wrong it. To talk of honour in the mysteries
of love, is like talking of Heaven or the Deity, in an
operation of witchcraft, just when you are employing the
devil: it makes the charm impotent.

LADY FIDGET   Nay, fy! let us not be smutty. But you talk of
mysteries and bewitching to me; I don't understand you.

HORNER   I tell you, madam, the word money in a mistress's
mouth, at such a nick of time, is not a more disheartening
sound to a younger brother, than that of honour to an eager
lover like myself.

LADY FIDGET   But you can't blame a lady of my reputation to
be chary.

HORNER   Chary! I have been chary of it already, by the report
I have caused of myself.

LADY FIDGET   Ay, but if you should ever let other women
know that dear secret, it would come out. Nay, you must
have a great care of your conduct; for my acquaintance are
so censorious, (oh, 'tis a wicked, censorious world, Mr.
Horner!) I say, are so censorious, and detracting, that
perhaps they'll talk to the prejudice of my honour, though
you should not let them know the dear secret.

HORNER   Nay, madam, rather than they shall prejudice your
honour, I'll prejudice theirs; and, to serve you, I'll lie with
'em all, make the secret their own, and then they'll keep it. I
am a Machiavel in love, madam.

LADY FIDGET   O, no sir, not that way.

HORNER   Nay, the devil take me, if censorious women are to
be silenced any other way.

LADY FIDGET   A secret is better kept, I hope, by a single
person than a multitude; therefore pray do not trust
anybody else with it, dear, dear Mr. Horner. (*Embracing
him.*)

Enter Sir Jasper Fidget.

SIR JASPER   How now!

LADY FIDGET (*aside*)   O my husband!—prevented—and what's almost as bad, found with my arms about another man— that will appear too much—what shall I say?—(*Aloud.*) Sir Jasper, come hither: I am trying if Mr. Horner were ticklish, and he's as ticklish as can be. I love to torment the confounded toad; let you and I tickle him.

SIR JASPER   No, your ladyship will tickle him better without me, I suppose. But is this your buying china? I thought you had been at the china-house.

HORNER (*aside*)   China-house! that's my cue, I must take it.—(*Aloud.*) A pox! can't you keep your impertinent wives at home? Some men are troubled with the husbands, but I with the wives; but I'd have you to know, since I cannot be your journeyman by night, I will not be your drudge by day, to squire your wife about, and be your man of straw, or scarecrow only to pies and jays, that would be nibbling at your forbidden fruit; I shall be shortly the hackney gentle-man-usher of the town.

SIR JASPER (*aside*)   He! he! he! poor fellow, he's in the right on't, faith. To squire women about for other folks is as ungrateful an employment, as to tell money for other folks.—(*Aloud.*) He! he! he! be'n't angry, Horner.

LADY FIDGET   No, 'tis I have more reason to be angry, who am left by you, to go abroad indecently alone; or, what is more indecent, to pin myself upon such ill-bred people of your acquaintance as this is.

SIR JASPER   Nay, prithee, what has he done?

LADY FIDGET   Nay, he has done nothing.

SIR JASPER   But what d'ye take ill, if he has done nothing?

LADY FIDGET   Ha! ha! ha! faith, I can't but laugh however; why, d'ye think the unmannerly toad would come down to me to the coach? I was fain to come up to fetch him, or go without him, which I was resolved not to do; for he knows china very well, and has himself very good, but will not let me see it, lest I should beg some; but I will find it out, and have what I came for yet.

HORNER (*apart to Lady Fidget, as he follows her to the door*)   Lock the door, madam.—(*Exit Lady Fidget, and locks the door.*)—

(*Aloud.*) So, she has got into my chamber and locked me out. Oh the impertinency of woman-kind! Well, Sir Jasper, plain-dealing is a jewel; if ever you suffer your wife to trouble me again here, she shall carry you home a pair of horns; by my lord mayor she shall; though I cannot furnish you myself, you are sure, yet I'll find a way.

SIR JASPER   Ha! ha! he!—(*Aside.*) At my first coming in, and finding her arms about him, tickling him it seems, I was half jealous, but now I see my folly.—(*Aloud.*) He! he! he! poor Horner.

HORNER   Nay, though you laugh now, 'twill be my turn ere long. Oh women, more impertinent, more cunning, and more mischievous than their monkeys, and to me almost as ugly!—Now is she throwing my things about and rifling all I have; but I'll get into her the back way, and so rifle her for it.

SIR JASPER   Ha! ha! ha! poor angry Horner.

HORNER   Stay here a little, I'll ferret her out to you presently, I warrant. (*Exit at the other door.*)

Sir Jasper talks through the door to his wife, she answers from within.

SIR JASPER   Wife! my Lady Fidget! wife! he is coming in to you the back way.

LADY FIDGET   Let him come, and welcome, which way he will.

SIR JASPER   He'll catch you, and use you roughly, and be too strong for you.

LADY FIDGET   Don't you trouble yourself, let him if he can.

QUACK (*aside*)   This indeed I could not have believed from him, nor any but my own eyes.

Enter Mrs. Squeamish.

MRS. SQUEAMISH   Where's this woman-hater, this toad, this ugly, greasy, dirty sloven?

SIR JASPER (*aside*)   So, the women all will have him ugly: methinks he is a comely person, but his wants make his form contemptible to 'em; and 'tis e'en as my wife said yesterday, talking of him, that a proper handsome eunuch was as ridiculous a thing as a gigantic coward.

MRS. SQUEAMISH   Sir Jasper, your servant: where is the odious beast?

SIR JASPER   He's within in his chamber, with my wife; she's playing the wag with him.

MRS. SQUEAMISH   Is she so? and he's a clownish beast, he'll give her no quarter, he'll play the wag with her again, let me tell you: come, let's go help her—What, the door's locked?

SIR JASPER   Ay, my wife locked it.

MRS. SQUEAMISH   Did she so? let's break it open then.

SIR JASPER   No, no, he'll do her no hurt.

MRS. SQUEAMISH (*aside*)   But is there no other way to get in to 'em? whither goes this? I will disturb 'em. (*Exit at another door.*)

Enter Old Lady Squeamish.

LADY SQUEAMISH   Where is this harlotry, this impudent baggage, this rambling tomrigg? [2] O Sir Jasper, I'm glad to see you here; did you not see my vile grandchild come in hither just now?

SIR JASPER   Yes.

LADY SQUEAMISH   Ay, but where is she then? where is she? Lord, Sir Jasper, I have e'en rattled myself to pieces in pursuit of her: but can you tell what she makes here? they say below, no woman lodges here.

SIR JASPER   No.

LADY SQUEAMISH   No! what does she here then? say, if it be not a woman's lodging, what makes she here? But are you sure no woman lodges here?

SIR JASPER   No, nor no man neither, this is Mr. Horner's lodging.

LADY SQUEAMISH   Is it so, are you sure?

SIR JASPER   Yes, yes.

LADY SQUEAMISH   So; then there's no hurt in't, I hope. But where is he?

SIR JASPER   He's in the next room with my wife.

LADY SQUEAMISH   Nay, if you trust him with your wife, I may with my Biddy. They say, he's a merry harmless man now, e'en as harmless a man as ever came out of Italy with a good voice, and as pretty, harmless company for a lady, as a snake without his teeth.

2. Tomboy.

SIR JASPER   Ay, ay, poor man.

Re-enter Mrs. Squeamish.

MRS. SQUEAMISH   I can't find 'em.—Oh, are you here, grand-mother? I followed, you must know, my Lady Fidget hither; 'tis the prettiest lodging, and I have been staring on the prettiest pictures—

Re-enter Lady Fidget with a piece of china in her hand, and Horner following.

LADY FIDGET   And I have been toiling and moiling for the prettiest piece of china, my dear.

HORNER   Nay, she has been too hard for me, do what I could.

MRS. SQUEAMISH   Oh, lord, I'll have some china too. Good Mr. Horner, don't think to give other people china and me none; come in with me too.

HORNER   Upon my honour, I have none left now.

MRS. SQUEAMISH   Nay, nay, I have known you deny your china before now, but you shan't put me off so. Come.

HORNER   This lady had the last there.

LADY FIDGET   Yes indeed, madam, to my certain knowledge, he has no more left.

MRS. SQUEAMISH   O, but it may be he may have some you could not find.

LADY FIDGET   What, d'ye think if he had had any left, I would not have had it too? for we women of quality never think we have china enough.

HORNER   Do not take it ill, I cannot make china for you all, but I will have a roll-waggon[3] for you too, another time.

MRS. SQUEAMISH   Thank you, dear toad.

LADY FIDGET   *(aside to Horner)*   What do you mean by that promise?

HORNER   *(aside to Lady Fidget)*   Alas, she has an innocent, literal understanding.)

LADY SQUEAMISH   Poor Mr. Horner! he has enough to do to please you all, I see.

HORNER   Ay, madam, you see how they use me.

LADY SQUEAMISH   Poor gentleman, I pity you.

HORNER   I thank you, madam: I could never find pity, but

3. A penis-shaped vase.

from such reverend ladies as you are; the young ones will never spare a man.

MRS. SQUEAMISH   Come, come, beast, and go dine with us; for we shall want a man at ombre after dinner.

HORNER   That's all their use of me, madam, you see.

MRS. SQUEAMISH   Come, sloven, I'll lead you, to be sure of you. (*Pulls him by the cravat.*)

LADY SQUEAMISH   Alas, poor man, how she tugs him! Kiss, kiss her; that's the way to make such nice women quiet.

HORNER   No, madam, that remedy is worse than the torment; they know I dare suffer anything rather than do it.

LADY SQUEAMISH   Prithee kiss her, and I'll give you her picture in little, that you admired so last night; prithee do.

HORNER   Well, nothing but that could bribe me: I love a woman only in effigy, and good painting as much as I hate them.—I'll do't, for I could adore the devil well painted. (*Kisses Mrs. Squeamish.*)

MRS. SQUEAMISH   Foh, you filthy toad! nay, now I've done jesting.

LADY SQUEAMISH   Ha! ha! ha! I told you so.

MRS. SQUEAMISH   Foh! a kiss of his—

SIR JASPER   Has no more hurt in't than one of my spaniel's.

MRS. SQUEAMISH   Nor no more good neither.

QUACK (*aside*)   I will now believe anything he tells me.

Enter Pinchwife.

LADY FIDGET   O lord, here's a man! Sir Jasper, my mask, my mask! I would not be seen here for the world.

SIR JASPER   What, not when I am with you?

LADY FIDGET   No, no, my honour—let's be gone.

MRS. SQUEAMISH   Oh grandmother, let's be gone; make haste, make haste, I know not how he may censure us.

LADY FIDGET   Be found in the lodging of anything like a man!—Away.

Exeunt Sir Jasper Fidget, Lady Fidget, Old Lady Squeamish, and Mrs. Squeamish.

QUACK   What's here? another cuckold? he looks like one, and none else sure have any business with him. (*Aside.*)

HORNER   Well, what brings my dear friend hither?

PINCHWIFE   Your impertinency.

HORNER   My impertinency!—why, you gentlemen that have got handsome wives, think you have a privilege of saying anything to your friends, and are as brutish as if you were our creditors.

PINCHWIFE   No, sir, I'll ne'er trust you any way.

HORNER   But why not, dear Jack? why diffide[4] in me thou know'st so well?

PINCHWIFE   Because I do know you so well.

HORNER   Han't I been always thy friend, honest Jack, always ready to serve thee, in love or battle, before thou wert married, and am so still?

PINCHWIFE   I believe so, you would be my second now, indeed.

HORNER   Well then, dear Jack, why so unkind, so grum, so strange to me? Come, prithee kiss me, dear rogue: gad I was always, I say, and am still as much thy servant as—

PINCHWIFE   As I am yours, sir. What, you would send a kiss to my wife, is that it?

HORNER   So, there 'tis—a man can't show his friendship to a married man, but presently he talks of his wife to you. Prithee, let thy wife alone, and let thee and I be all one, as we were wont. What, thou art as shy of my kindness, as a Lombard-street alderman of a courtier's civility at Locket's!

PINCHWIFE   But you are over-kind to me, as kind as if I were your cuckold already; yet I must confess you ought to be kind and civil to me, since I am so kind, so civil to you, as to bring you this: look you there, sir. (*Delivers him a letter.*)

HORNER   What is't?

PINCHWIFE   Only a love-letter, sir.

HORNER   From whom?—how! this is from your wife—hum—and hum—(*Reads.*)

PINCHWIFE   Even from my wife, sir: am I not wondrous kind and civil to you now too?—(*Aside.*) But you'll not think her so.

HORNER (*aside*)   Ha! is this a trick of his or hers?

PINCHWIFE   The gentleman's surprised I find.—What, you expected a kinder letter?

HORNER   No faith, not I, how could I?

PINCHWIFE   Yes, yes, I'm sure you did. A man so well made as

4. Distrust.

you are, must needs be disappointed, if the women declare not their passion at first sight or opportunity.

HORNER (*aside*) But what should this mean? Stay, the post-script—(*Reads aside.*) "Be sure you love me, whatsoever my husband says to the contrary, and let him not see this, lest he should come home and pinch me, or kill my squirrel."— It seems he knows not what the letter contains.

PINCHWIFE Come, ne'er wonder at it so much.

HORNER Faith, I can't help it.

PINCHWIFE Now, I think I have deserved your infinite friendship and kindness, and have showed myself sufficiently an obliging kind friend and husband; am I not so, to bring a letter from my wife to her gallant?

HORNER Ay, the devil take me, art thou, the most obliging, kind friend and husband in the world, ha! ha!

PINCHWIFE Well, you may be merry, sir; but in short I must tell you, sir, my honour will suffer no jesting.

HORNER What dost thou mean?

PINCHWIFE Does the letter want a comment? Then, know, sir, though I have been so civil a husband, as to bring you a letter from my wife, to let you kiss and court her to my face, I will not be a cuckold, sir, I will not.

HORNER Thou art mad with jealousy. I never saw thy wife in my life but at the play yesterday, and I know not if it were she or no. I court her, kiss her!

PINCHWIFE I will not be a cuckold, I say; there will be danger in making me a cuckold.

HORNER Why, wert thou not well cured of thy last clap?

PINCHWIFE I wear a sword.

HORNER It should be taken from thee, lest thou shouldst do thyself a mischief with it; thou art mad, man.

PINCHWIFE As mad as I am, and as merry as you are, I must have more reason from you ere we part. I say again, though you kissed and courted last night my wife in man's clothes, as she confesses in her letter—

HORNER (*aside*) Ha!

PINCHWIFE Both she and I say, you must not design it again, for you have mistaken your woman, as you have done your man.

HORNER (*aside*) O—I understand something now—(*Aloud.*) Was that thy wife! Why wouldst thou not tell me 'twas she?

Faith, my freedom with her was your fault, not mine.

PINCHWIFE (*aside*)   Faith, so 'twas.

HORNER   Fy! I'd never do't to a woman before her husband's face, sure.

PINCHWIFE   But I had rather you should do't to my wife before my face, than behind my back; and that you shall never do.

HORNER   No—you will hinder me.

PINCHWIFE   If I would not hinder you, you see by her letter she would.

HORNER   Well, I must e'en acquiesce then, and be contented with what she writes.

PINCHWIFE   I'll assure you 'twas voluntarily writ; I had no hand in't you may believe me.

HORNER   I do believe thee, faith.

PINCHWIFE   And believe her too, for she's an innocent creature, has no dissembling in her: and so fare you well, sir.

HORNER   Pray, however, present my humble service to her, and tell her, I will obey her letter to a tittle, and fulfil her desires, be what they will, or with what difficulty soever I do't; and you shall be no more jealous of me, I warrant her, and you.

PINCHWIFE   Well then, fare you well; and play with any man's honour but mine, kiss any man's wife but mine, and welcome. (*Exit.*)

HORNER   Ha! ha! ha! doctor.

QUACK   It seems, he has not heard the report of you, or does not believe it.

HORNER   Ha! ha!—now, doctor, what think you?

QUACK   Pray let's see the letter—hum—"for—dear—love you—" (*Reads the letter.*)

HORNER   I wonder how she could contrive it! What say'st thou to't? 'tis an original.

QUACK   So are your cuckolds too originals: for they are like no other common cuckolds, and I will henceforth believe it not impossible for you to cuckold the Grand Signior amidst his guards of eunuchs, that I say.

HORNER   And I say for the letter, 'tis the first love-letter that ever was without flames, darts, fates, destinies, lying and dissembling in't.

Enter Sparkish pulling in Pinchwife.

SPARKISH   Come back, you are a pretty brother-in-law, neither go to church nor to dinner with your sister bride!

PINCHWIFE   My sister denies her marriage, and you see is gone away from you dissatisfied.

SPARKISH   Pshaw! upon a foolish scruple, that our parson was not in lawful orders, and did not say all the common-prayer; but 'tis her modesty only I believe. But let all women be never so modest the first day, they'll be sure to come to themselves by night, and I shall have enough of her then. In the meantime, Harry Horner, you must dine with me: I keep my wedding at my aunt's in the Piazza.

HORNER   Thy wedding! what stale maid has lived to despair of a husband, or what young one of a gallant?

SPARKISH   O, your servant, sir—this gentleman's sister then,—no stale maid.

HORNER   I'm sorry for't.

PINCHWIFE (*aside*)   How comes he so concerned for her?

SPARKISH   You sorry for't? why, do you know any ill by her?

HORNER   No, I know none but by thee; 'tis for her sake, not yours, and another man's sake that might have hoped, I thought.

SPARKISH   Another man! another man! what is his name?

HORNER   Nay, since 'tis past, he shall be nameless.—(*Aside.*) Poor Harcourt! I am sorry thou hast missed her.

PINCHWIFE (*aside*)   He seems to be much troubled at the match.

SPARKISH   Prithee, tell me—Nay, you shan't go, brother.

PINCHWIFE   I must of necessity, but I'll come to you to dinner. (*Exit.*)

SPARKISH   But, Harry, what, have I a rival in my wife already? But with all my heart, for he may be of use to me hereafter; for though my hunger is now my sauce, and I can fall on heartily without, the time will come, when a rival will be as good sauce for a married man to a wife, as an orange to veal.

HORNER   O thou damned rogue! thou hast set my teeth on edge with thy orange.

SPARKISH   Then let's to dinner—there I was with you again. Come.

HORNER   But who dines with thee?

SPARKISH My friends and relations, my brother Pinchwife, you see, of your acquaintance.

HORNER And his wife?

SPARKISH No, 'gad, he'll ne'er let her come amongst us good fellows; your stingy country coxcomb keeps his wife from his friends, as he does his little firkin of ale, for his own drinking, and a gentleman can't get a smack on't; but his servants, when his back is turned, broach it at their pleasures, and dust it away, ha! ha! ha!—'Gad, I am witty, I think, considering I was married today, by the world; but come—

HORNER No, I will not dine with you, unless you can fetch her too.

SPARKISH Pshaw! what pleasure canst thou have with women now, Harry?

HORNER My eyes are not gone; I love a good prospect yet, and will not dine with you unless she does too; go fetch her, therefore, but do not tell her husband 'tis for my sake.

SPARKISH Well, I'll go try what I can do; in the meantime, come away to my aunt's lodging, 'tis in the way to Pinchwife's.

HORNER The poor woman has called for aid, and stretched forth her hand, doctor; I cannot but help her over the pale out of the briars.

Exeunt.

Scene 4

A room in Pinchwife's house. Mrs. Pinchwife alone, leaning on her elbow.—A table, pen, ink and paper.

MRS. PINCHWIFE Well, 'tis e'en so, I have got the London disease they call love; I am sick of my husband, and for my gallant. I have heard this distemper called a fever, but methinks 'tis like an ague; for when I think of my husband, I tremble, and am in a cold sweat, and have inclinations to vomit; but when I think of my gallant, dear Mr. Horner, my hot fit comes, and I am all in a fever indeed; and, as in other fevers, my own chamber is tedious to me, and I would fain be removed to his, and then methinks I should be well. Ah, poor Mr. Horner! Well, I cannot, will not stay here; therefore I'll make an end of my letter to him, which shall be a finer letter than my last, because I have studied it like anything. Oh sick, sick! (*Takes the pen and writes.*)

Enter Pinchwife, who seeing her writing, steals softly behind her and looking over her shoulder, snatches the paper from her.

PINCHWIFE   What, writing more letters?

MRS. PINCHWIFE   O Lord, bud, why d'ye fright me so?

She offers to run out; he stops her, and reads.

PINCHWIFE   How's this? nay, you shall not stir, madam:—"Dear, dear, dear Mr. Horner"—very well—I have taught you to write letters to good purpose—but let us see't. "First, I am to beg your pardon for my boldness in writing to you, which I'd have you to know I would not have done, had not you said first you loved me so extremely, which if you do, you will never suffer me to lie in the arms of another man whom I loathe, nauseate, and detest."—Now you can write these filthy words. But what follows?—"Therefore, I hope you will speedily find some way to free me from this unfortunate match, which was never, I assure you, of my choice, but I'm afraid 'tis already too far gone; however, if you love me, as I do you, you will try what you can do; but you must help me away before tomorrow, or else, alas! I shall be for ever out of your reach, for I can defer no longer our—our—" what is to follow "our"?—speak, what—our journey into the country I suppose—Oh woman, damned woman! and Love, damned Love, their old tempter! for this is one of his miracles; in a moment he can make those blind that could see, and those see that were blind, those dumb that could speak, and those prattle who were dumb before; nay, what is more than all, make these dough-baked, senseless, indocile animals, women, too hard for us their politic lords and rulers, in a moment. But make an end of your letter, and then I'll make an end of you thus, and all my plagues together. (*Draws his sword.*)

MRS. PINCHWIFE   O Lord, O Lord, you are such a passionate man, bud!

Enter Sparkish.

SPARKISH　How now, what's here to do?

PINCHWIFE　This fool here now!

SPARKISH　What! drawn upon your wife? You should never do that, but at night in the dark, when you can't hurt her. This is my sister-in-law, is it not? ay, faith, e'en our country Margery; (*pulls aside her handkerchief*) one may know her. Come, she and you must go dine with me; dinner's ready, come. But where's my wife? is she not come home yet? where is she?

PINCHWIFE　Making you a cuckold; 'tis that they all do, as soon as they can.

SPARKISH　What, the wedding-day? no, a wife that designs to make a cully of her husband will be sure to let him win the first stake of love, by the world. But come, they stay dinner for us: come, I'll lead down our Margery.

PINCHWIFE　No—sir, go, we'll follow you.

SPARKISH　I will not wag without you.

PINCHWIFE　(*aside*)　This coxcomb is a sensible torment to me amidst the greatest in the world.

SPARKISH　Come, come, Madam Margery.

PINCHWIFE　No; I'll lead her my way: what, would you treat your friends with mine, for want of your own wife?—(*Leads her to the other door, and locks her in and returns.—Aside*) I am contented my rage should take breath—

SPARKISH　I told Horner this.

PINCHWIFE　Come now.

SPARKISH　Lord, how shy you are of your wife! but let me tell you, brother, we men of wit have amongst us a saying, that cuckolding, like the small-pox, comes with a fear; and you may keep your wife as much as you will out of danger of infection, but if her constitution incline her to't, she'll have it sooner or later, by the world, say they.

PINCHWIFE　(*aside*)　What a thing is a cuckold, that every fool can make him ridiculous!—(*Aloud.*) Well, sir—but let me advise you, now you are come to be concerned, because you suspect the danger, not to neglect the means to prevent it, especially when the greatest share of the malady will light upon your own head, for

Hows'e'er the kind wife's belly comes to swell,
The husband breeds for her, and first is ill.

Exeunt.

ACT FIVE

Scene 1

Pinchwife's house.
Enter Pinchwife and Mrs. Pinchwife. A table and candle.

PINCHWIFE   Come, take the pen and make an end of the letter, just as you intended; if you are false in a tittle, I shall soon perceive it, and punish you as you deserve.—(*Lays his hand on his sword.*) Write what was to follow—let's see—"You must make haste, and help me away before to-morrow, or else I shall be for ever out of your reach, for I can defer no longer our"—What follows "our"?

MRS. PINCHWIFE   Must all out, then, bud?—Look you there, then.

Mrs. Pinchwife takes the pen and writes.

PINCHWIFE   Let's see—"For I can defer no longer our—wedding—Your slighted Alithea."—What's the meaning of this? my sister's name to't? speak, unriddle.

MRS. PINCHWIFE   Yes, indeed, bud.

PINCHWIFE   But why her name to't? speak—speak, I say.

MRS. PINCHWIFE   Ay, but you'll tell her then again. If you would not tell her again—

PINCHWIFE   I will not:—I am stunned, my head turns round.—Speak.

MRS. PINCHWIFE   Won't you tell her, indeed, and indeed?

PINCHWIFE   No; speak, I say.

MRS. PINCHWIFE   She'll be angry with me; but I had rather she should be angry with me than you, bud; And, to tell you the truth, 'twas she made me write the letter, and taught me what I should write.

PINCHWIFE (*aside*)   Ha!—I thought the style was somewhat better than her own.—(*Aloud.*) Could she come to you to teach you, since I had locked you up alone?

MRS. PINCHWIFE   O, through the key-hole, bud.

PINCHWIFE   But why should she make you write a letter for her to him, since she can write herself?

MRS. PINCHWIFE   Why, she said because—for I was unwilling to do it—

PINCHWIFE   Because what—because?

MRS. PINCHWIFE   Because, lest Mr. Horner should be cruel, and refuse her; or be vain afterwards, and show the letter, she might disown it, the hand not being hers.

PINCHWIFE (*aside*)   How's this? Ha!—then I think I shall come to myself again.—This changeling could not invent this lie: but if she could, why should she? she might think I should soon discover it.—Stay—now I think on't too, Horner said he was sorry she had married Sparkish; and her disowning her marriage to me makes me think she has evaded it for Horner's sake: yet why should she take this course? But men in love are fools; women may well be so—(*Aloud.*) But hark you, madam, your sister went out in the morning, and I have not seen her within since.

MRS. PINCHWIFE   Alack-a-day, she has been crying all day above, it seems, in a corner.

PINCHWIFE   Where is she? let me speak with her.

MRS. PINCHWIFE (*aside*)   O Lord, then she'll discover all!—(*Aloud.*) Pray hold, bud; what, d'ye mean to discover me? she'll know I have told you then. Pray, bud, let me talk with her first.

PINCHWIFE   I must speak with her, to know whether Horner ever made her any promise, and whether she be married to Sparkish or no.

MRS. PINCHWIFE   Pray, dear bud, don't, till I have spoken with her, and told her that I have told you all; for she'll kill me else.

PINCHWIFE   Go then, and bid her come out to me.

MRS. PINCHWIFE   Yes, yes, bud.

PINCHWIFE   Let me see—(*Pausing.*)

MRS. PINCHWIFE (*aside*)   I'll go, but she is not within to come to him: I have just got time to know of Lucy her maid, who first set me on work, what lie I shall tell next; for I am e'en at my wit's end. (*Exit.*)

PINCHWIFE   Well, I resolve it, Horner shall have her: I'd rather give him my sister than lend him my wife; and such

an alliance will prevent his pretensions to my wife, sure. I'll
make him of kin to her, and then he won't care for her.

Re-enter Mrs. Pinchwife.

MRS. PINCHWIFE   O Lord, bud! I told you what anger you
would make me with my sister.

PINCHWIFE   Won't she come hither?

MRS. PINCHWIFE   No, no. Lack-a-day, she's ashamed to look
you in the face: and she says, if you go in to her, she'll run
away down stairs, and shamefully go herself to Mr. Horner,
who has promised her marriage, she says; and she will have
no other, so she won't.

PINCHWIFE   Did he so?—promise her marriage!—then she
shall have no other. Go tell her so; and if she will come and
discourse with me a little concerning the means, I will about
it immediately. Go.—(*Exit Mrs. Pinchwife.*) His estate is
equal to Sparkish's, and his extraction is much better than
his, as his parts are; but my chief reason is, I'd rather be
akin to him by the name of brother-in-law than that of
cuckold. (*Re-enter Mrs. Pinchwife.*) Well, what says she now?

MRS. PINCHWIFE   Why, she says, she would only have you lead
her to Horner's lodging; with whom she first will discourse
the matter before she talks with you, which yet she cannot
do; for alack, poor creature, she says she can't so much as
look you in the face, therefore she'll come to you in a mask.
And you must excuse her, if she make you no answer to any
question of yours, till you have brought her to Mr. Horner;
and if you will not chide her, nor question her, she'll come
out to you immediately.

PINCHWIFE   Let her come: I will not speak a word to her, nor
require a word from her.

MRS. PINCHWIFE   Oh, I forgot: besides she says, she cannot
look you in the face, though through a mask; therefore
would desire you to put out the candle.

PINCHWIFE   I agree to all. Let her make haste.—There, 'tis
out—(*Puts out the candle. Exit Mrs. Pinchwife.*) My case is
something better: I'd rather fight with Horner for not lying
with my sister, than for lying with my wife; and of the two, I
had rather find my sister too forward than my wife. I
expected no other from her free education, as she calls it,
and her passion for the town. Well, wife and sister are

names which make us expect love and duty, pleasure and comfort; but we find 'em plagues and torments, and are equally, though differently, troublesome to their keeper; for we have as much ado to get people to lie with our sisters as to keep 'em from lying with our wives.

Re-enter Mrs. Pinchwife masked, and in hoods and scarfs, and a night-gown and petticoat of Alithea's.

What, are you come, sister? let us go then.—But first, let me lock up my wife. Mrs. Margery, where are you?

MRS. PINCHWIFE   Here, bud.

PINCHWIFE   Come hither, that I may lock you up: get you in.—(*Locks the door.*) Come, sister, where are you now?

Mrs. Pinchwife gives him her hand; but when he lets her go, she steals softly on to the other side of him, and is led away by him for his sister, Alithea.

Scene 2

Horner's lodging.
Horner and Quack.

QUACK   What, all alone? not so much as one of your cuckolds here, nor one of their wives! They use to take their turns with you, as if they were to watch you.

HORNER   Yes, it often happens that a cuckold is but his wife's spy, and is more upon family duty when he is with her gallant abroad, hindering his pleasure, than when he is at home with her playing the gallant. But the hardest duty a married woman imposes upon a lover is keeping her husband company always.

QUACK   And his fondness wearies you almost as soon as hers.

HORNER   A pox! keeping a cuckold company, after you have had his wife, is as tiresome as the company of a country squire to a witty fellow of the town, when he has got all his money.

QUACK   And as at first a man makes a friend of the husband to get the wife, so at last you are fain to fall out with the wife to be rid of the husband.

HORNER Ay, most cuckold-makers are true courtiers; when once a poor man has cracked his credit for 'em, they can't abide to come near him.

QUACK But at first, to draw him in, are so sweet, so kind, so dear! just as you are to Pinchwife. But what becomes of that intrigue with his wife?

HORNER A pox! he's as surly as an alderman that has been bit; and since he's so coy, his wife's kindness is in vain, for she's a silly innocent.

QUACK Did she not send you a letter by him?

HORNER Yes; but that's a riddle I have not yet solved. Allow the poor creature to be willing, she is silly too, and he keeps her up so close—

QUACK Yes, so close, that he makes her but the more willing, and adds but revenge to her love; which two, when met, seldom fail of satisfying each other one way or other.

HORNER What! here's the man we are talking of, I think.

Enter Pinchwife, leading in his wife masked, muffled, and in her sister's gown.

Pshaw!

QUACK Bringing his wife to you is the next thing to bringing a love-letter from her.

HORNER What means this?

PINCHWIFE The last time, you know, sir, I brought you a love-letter; now, you see, a mistress; I think you'll say I am a civil man to you.

HORNER Ay, the devil take me, will I say thou art the civilest man I ever met with; and I have known some. I fancy I understand thee now better than I did the letter. But, hark thee, in thy ear—

PINCHWIFE What?

HORNER Nothing but the usual question, man: is she sound, on thy word?

PINCHWIFE What, you take her for a wench, and me for a pimp?

HORNER Pshaw! wench and pimp, paw[1] words; I know thou art an honest fellow, and hast a great acquaintance among the ladies, and perhaps hast made love for me, rather than let me make love to thy wife.

1. Naughty.

PINCHWIFE   Come, sir, in short, I am for no fooling.

HORNER   Nor I neither: therefore prithee, let's see her face presently. Make her show, man: art thou sure I don't know her?

PINCHWIFE   I am sure you do know her.

HORNER   A pox! why dost thou bring her to me then?

PINCHWIFE   Because she's a relation of mine—

HORNER   Is she, faith, man? then thou art still more civil and obliging, dear rogue.

PINCHWIFE   Who desired me to bring her to you.

HORNER   Then she is obliging, dear rogue.

PINCHWIFE   You'll make her welcome for my sake, I hope.

HORNER   I hope she is handsome enough to make herself welcome. Prithee let her unmask.

PINCHWIFE   Do you speak to her; she would never be ruled by me.

HORNER   Madam—(*Mrs. Pinchwife whispers to Horner.*) She says she must speak with me in private. Withdraw, prithee.

PINCHWIFE   (*aside*) She's unwilling, it seems, I should know all her indecent conduct in this business—(*Aloud.*) Well then, I'll leave you together, and hope when I am gone, you'll agree; if not, you and I shan't agree, sir.

HORNER   What means the fool? if she and I agree 'tis no matter what you and I do. (*Whispers to Mrs. Pinchwife, who makes signs with her hand for him to be gone.*)

PINCHWIFE   In the meantime I'll fetch a parson, and find out Sparkish, and disabuse him. You would have me fetch a parson, would you not? Well then—now I think I am rid of her, and shall have no more trouble with her—our sisters and daughters, like usurers' money, are safest when put out; but our wives, like their writings, never safe, but in our closets under lock and key. (*Exit.*)

Enter Boy.

BOY   Sir Jasper Fidget, sir, is coming up. (*Exit.*)

HORNER   Here's the trouble of a cuckold now we are talking of. A pox on him! has he not enough to do to hinder his wife's sport, but he must other women's too?—Step in here, madam.

Exit Mrs. Pinchwife. Enter Sir Jasper Fidget.

SIR JASPER My best and dearest friend.

HORNER (*aside to Quack*) The old style, doctor.—(*Aloud.*) Well, be short, for I am busy. What would your impertinent wife have now?

SIR JASPER Well guessed, i'faith; for I do come from her.

HORNER To invite me to supper! Tell her, I can't come: go.

SIR JASPER Nay, now you are out, faith; for my lady, and the whole knot of the virtuous gang, as they call themselves, are resolved upon a frolic of coming to you to-night in masquerade, and are all dressed already.

HORNER I shan't be at home.

SIR JASPER (*aside*) Lord, how churlish he is to women!— (*Aloud.*) Nay, prithee don't disappoint 'em; they'll think 'tis my fault: prithee don't. I'll send in the banquet and the fiddles. But make no noise on't; for the poor virtuous rogues would not have it known, for the world, that they go a-masquerading; and they would come to no man's ball but yours.

HORNER Well, well—get you gone; and tell 'em, if they come, 'twill be at the peril of their honour and yours.

SIR JASPER He! he! he!—we'll trust you for that: farewell. (*Exit.*)

HORNER Doctor, anon you too shall be my guest,
But now I'm going to a private feast.

Exeunt.

Scene 3

The Piazza of Covent Garden.
Enter Sparkish with a letter in his hand, Pinchwife following.

SPARKISH But who would have thought a woman could have been false to me? By the world, I could not have thought it.

PINCHWIFE You were for giving and taking liberty: she has taken it only, sir, now you find in that letter. You are a frank person, and so is she, you see there.

SPARKISH Nay, if this be her hand—for I never saw it.

PINCHWIFE 'Tis no matter whether that be her hand or no; I am sure this hand, at her desire, led her to Mr. Horner, with whom I left her just now, to go fetch a parson to 'em at their desire too, to deprive you of her for ever; for it seems yours was but a mock marriage.

SPARKISH Indeed, she would needs have it that 'twas Harcourt himself, in a parson's habit, that married us; but I'm sure he told me 'twas his brother Ned.

PINCHWIFE O, there 'tis out; and you were deceived, not she: for you are such a frank person. But I must be gone.—You'll find her at Mr. Horner's. Go, and believe your eyes. (*Exit.*)

SPARKISH Nay, I'll to her, and call her as many crocodiles, sirens, harpies, and other heathenish names, as a poet would do a mistress who had refused to hear his suit, nay more, his verses on her.—But stay, is not that she following a torch at t'other end of the Piazza? and from Horner's certainly—'tis so.

Enter Alithea following a torch, and Lucy behind.

You are well met, madam, though you don't think so. What, you have made a short visit to Mr. Horner? but I suppose you'll return to him presently, by that time the parson can be with him.

ALITHEA Mr. Horner and the parson, sir!

SPARKISH Come, madam, no more dissembling, no more jilting; for I am no more a frank person.

ALITHEA How's this?

LUCY (*aside*) So, 'twill work, I see.

SPARKISH Could you find out no easy country fool to abuse? none but me, a gentleman of wit and pleasure about the town? But it was your pride to be too hard for a man of parts, unworthy false woman! false as a friend that lends a man money to lose; false as dice, who undo those that trust all they have to 'em.

LUCY (*aside*) He has been a great bubble, by his similes, as they say.

ALITHEA You have been too merry, sir, at your wedding-dinner, sure.

SPARKISH What, d'ye mock me too?

ALITHEA Or you have been deluded.

SPARKISH By you.

ALITHEA Let me understand you.

SPARKISH Have you the confidence, (I should call it something else, since you know your guilt), to stand my just reproaches? you did not write an impudent letter to Mr. Horner? who I find now has clubbed with you in deluding me with his aversion for women, that I might not, forsooth, suspect him for my rival.

LUCY (*aside*) D'ye think the gentleman can be jealous now, madam?

ALITHEA I write a letter to Mr. Horner!

SPARKISH Nay, madam, do not deny it. Your brother showed it me just now; and told me likewise, he left you at Horner's lodging to fetch a parson to marry you to him: and I wish you joy, madam, joy, joy; and to him too, much joy; and to myself more joy, for not marrying you.

ALITHEA (*aside*) So, I find my brother would break off the match; and I can consent to't, since I see this gentleman can be made jealous.—(*Aloud.*) O Lucy, by his rude usage and jealousy, he makes me almost afraid I am married to him. Art thou sure 'twas Harcourt himself, and no parson, that married us?

SPARKISH No, madam, I thank you. I suppose, that was a contrivance too of Mr. Horner's and yours, to make Harcourt play the parson; but I would as little as you have him one now, no, not for the world. For, shall I tell you another truth? I never had any passion for you till now, for now I hate you. 'Tis true, I might have married your portion, as other men of parts of the town do sometimes; and so, your servant. And to show my unconcernedness, I'll come to your wedding, and resign you with as much joy, as I would a stale wench to a new cully; nay, with as much joy as I would after the first night, if I had been married to you. There's for you; and so your servant, servant. (*Exit.*)

ALITHEA How was I deceived in a man!

LUCY You'll believe then a fool may be made jealous now? for that easiness in him that suffers him to be led by a wife, will likewise permit him to be persuaded against her by others.

ALITHEA But marry Mr. Horner! my brother does not intend it, sure: if I thought he did, I would take thy advice, and Mr. Harcourt for my husband. And now I wish, that if there be any overwise woman of the town, who, like me, would marry a fool for fortune, liberty, or title, first, that her husband may love play, and be a cully to all the town but her, and suffer none but Fortune to be mistress of his purse; then, if for liberty, that he may send her into the country, under the conduct of some huswifely mother-in-law; and if for title, may the world give 'em none but that of cuckold.

LUCY   And for her greater curse, madam, may he not deserve it.

ALITHEA   Away, impertinent! Is not this my old Lady Lanterlu's?

LUCY   Yes, madam.—(*Aside.*) And here I hope we shall find Mr. Harcourt.

Exeunt.

Scene 4

Horner's lodging. A table, banquet, and bottles. Enter Horner, Lady Fidget, Mrs. Dainty Fidget, and Mrs. Squeamish.

HORNER (*aside*)   A pox! they are come too soon—before I have sent back my new mistress. All that I have now to do is to lock her in, that they may not see her.

LADY FIDGET   That we may be sure of our welcome, we have brought our entertainment with us, and are resolved to treat thee, dear toad.

MRS. DAINTY FIDGET   And that we may be merry to purpose, have left Sir Jasper and my old Lady Squeamish, quarrelling at home at backgammon.

MRS. SQUEAMISH   Therefore let us make use of our time, lest they should chance to interrupt us.

LADY FIDGET   Let us sit then.

HORNER   First, that you may be private, let me lock this door and that, and I'll wait upon you presently.

LADY FIDGET   No, sir, shut 'em only, and your lips for ever; for we must trust you as much as our women.

HORNER   You know all vanity's killed in me; I have no occasion for talking.

LADY FIDGET   Now, ladies, supposing we had drank each of us our two bottles, let us speak the truth of our hearts.

MRS. DAINTY FIDGET *and* MRS. SQUEAMISH   Agreed.

LADY FIDGET   By this brimmer, for truth is nowhere else to be found—(*Aside to Horner.*) not in thy heart, false man!

HORNER (*aside to Lady Fidget*)   You have found me a true man, I'm sure.

LADY FIDGET (*aside to Horner*)   Not every way.—But let us sit and be merry. (*Sings.*)

Why should our damned tyrants oblige us to live
On the pittance of pleasure which they only give?
    We must not rejoice
    With wine and with noise:
In vain we must wake in a dull bed alone,
Whilst to our warm rival the bottle they're gone.
    Then lay aside charms,
    And take up these arms.

'Tis wine only gives 'em their courage and wit:
Because we live sober, to men we submit.
    If for beauties you'd pass,
    Take a lick of the glass,
'Twill mend your complexions, and when they are gone,
    The best red we have is the red of the grape:
Then, sisters, lay't on,
    And damn a good shape.

MRS. DAINTY FIDGET   Dear brimmer! Well, in token of our openness and plain-dealing, let us throw our masks over our heads.

HORNER (*aside*)   So, 'twill come to the glasses anon.

MRS. SQUEAMISH   Lovely brimmer! let me enjoy him first.

LADY FIDGET   No, I never part with a gallant till I've tried him. Dear brimmer! that makest our husbands short-sighted.

MRS. DAINTY FIDGET   And our bashful gallants bold.

MRS. SQUEAMISH   And, for want of a gallant, the butler lovely in our eyes.—Drink, eunuch.

LADY FIDGET   Drink, thou representative of a husband.— Damn a husband!

MRS. DAINTY FIDGET   And, as it were a husband, an old keeper.

MRS. SQUEAMISH   And an old grandmother.

HORNER   And an English bawd, and a French surgeon.

LADY FIDGET   Ay, we have all reason to curse 'em.

HORNER   For my sake, ladies?

LADY FIDGET   No, for our own; for the first spoils all young gallants' industry.

MRS. DAINTY FIDGET   And the other's art makes 'em bold only with common women.

MRS. SQUEAMISH   And rather run the hazard of the vile distemper amongst them, than of a denial amongst us.

MRS. DAINTY FIDGET   The filthy toads choose mistresses now as they do stuffs, for having been fancied and worn by others.

MRS. SQUEAMISH   For being common and cheap.

LADY FIDGET   Whilst women of quality, like the richest stuffs, lie untumbled, and unasked for.

HORNER   Ay, neat, and cheap, and new, often they think best.

MRS. DAINTY FIDGET   No, sir, the beasts will be known by a mistress longer than by a suit.

MRS. SQUEAMISH   And 'tis not for cheapness neither.

LADY FIDGET   No; for the vain fops will take up druggets, and embroider 'em. But I wonder at the depraved appetites of witty men; they use to be out of the common road, and hate imitation. Pray tell me, beast, when you were a man, why you rather chose to club with a multitude in a common house for an entertainment, than to be the only guest at a good table.

HORNER   Why, faith, ceremony and expectation are unsufferable to those that are sharp bent. People always eat with the best stomach at an ordinary, where every man is snatching for the best bit.

LADY FIDGET   Though he get a cut over the fingers.—But I have heard, that people eat most heartily of another man's meat, that is, what they do not pay for.

HORNER   When they are sure of their welcome and freedom; for ceremony in love and eating is as ridiculous as in fighting: falling on briskly is all should be done on those occasions.

LADY FIDGET   Well then, let me tell you, sir, there is no where more freedom than in our houses; and we take freedom from a young person as a sign of good breeding; and a person may be as free as he pleases with us, as frolic, as gamesome, as wild as he will.

HORNER   Han't I heard you all declaim against wild men?

LADY FIDGET   Yes; but for all that, we think wildness in a man as desirable a quality as in a duck or rabbit: a tame man! foh!

HORNER   I know not, but your reputations frightened me as much as your faces invited me.

LADY FIDGET   Our reputation! Lord, why should you not think that we women make use of our reputation, as you men of yours, only to deceive the world with less suspicion? Our virtue is like the statesman's religion, the quaker's word, the gamester's oath, and the great man's honour; but to cheat those that trust us.

MRS. SQUEAMISH   And that demureness, coyness, and modesty, that you see in our faces in the boxes at plays, is as much a sign of a kind woman, as a vizard-mask in the pit.

MRS. DAINTY FIDGET   For, I assure you, women are least masked when they have the velvet vizard on.

LADY FIDGET   You would have found us modest women in our denials only.

MRS. SQUEAMISH   Our bashfulness is only the reflection of the men's.

MRS. DAINTY FIDGET   We blush when they are shamefaced.

HORNER   I beg your pardon, ladies, I was deceived in you devilishly. But why that mighty pretence to honour?

LADY FIDGET   We have told you; but sometimes 'twas for the same reason you men pretend business often, to avoid ill company, to enjoy the better and more privately those you love.

HORNER   But why would you ne'er give a friend a wink then?

LADY FIDGET   Faith, your reputation frightened us, as much as ours did you, you were so notoriously lewd.

HORNER   And you so seemingly honest.

LADY FIDGET   Was that all that deterred you?

HORNER   And so expensive—you allow freedom, you say.

LADY FIDGET   Ay, ay.

HORNER   That I was afraid of losing my little money, as well as my little time, both which my other pleasures required.

LADY FIDGET   Money! foh! you talk like a little fellow now: do such as we expect money?

HORNER   I beg your pardon, madam, I must confess, I have heard that great ladies, like great merchants, set but the higher prices upon what they have, because they are not in necessity of taking the first offer.

MRS. DAINTY FIDGET   Such as we make sale of our hearts?

MRS. SQUEAMISH   We bribed for our love? foh!

HORNER   With your pardon ladies, I know, like great men in offices, you seem to exact flattery and attendance only from your followers; but you have receivers about you, and such fees to pay, a man is afraid to pass your grants. Besides, we must let you win at cards, or we lose your hearts; and if you make an assignation, 'tis at a goldsmith's, jeweller's, or china-house; where for your honour you deposit to him, he must pawn his to the punctual cit, and so paying for what you take up, pays for what he takes up.

MRS. DAINTY FIDGET   Would you not have us assured of our gallants' love?

MRS. SQUEAMISH   For love is better known by liberality than by jealousy.

LADY FIDGET   For one may be dissembled, the other not.— (*Aside.*) But my jealousy can be no longer dissembled, and they are telling ripe.—(*Aloud.*)—Come, here's to our gallants in waiting, whom we must name, and I'll begin. This is my false rogue. (*Claps him on the back.*)

MRS. SQUEAMISH   How!

HORNER (*aside*)   So, all will out now.

MRS. SQUEAMISH (*aside to Horner*)   Did you not tell me, 'twas for my sake only you reported yourself no man?

MRS. DAINTY FIDGET (*aside to Horner*)   Oh, wretch! did you not swear to me, 'twas for my love and honour you passed for that thing you do?

HORNER   So, so.

LADY FIDGET   Come, speak, ladies: this is my false villain.

MRS. SQUEAMISH   And mine too.

MRS. DAINTY FIDGET   And mine.

HORNER   Well then, you are all three my false rogues too, and there's an end on't.

LADY FIDGET   Well then, there's no remedy; sister sharers, let us not fall out, but have a care of our honour. Though we get no presents, no jewels of him, we are savers of our honour, the jewel of most value and use, which shines yet to the world unsuspected, though it be counterfeit.

HORNER   Nay, and is e'en as good as if it were true, provided the world think so; for honour, like beauty now, only depends on the opinion of others.

LADY FIDGET   Well, Harry Common, I hope you can be true to three. Swear; but 'tis to no purpose to require your oath, for you are as often forsworn as you swear to new women.

HORNER   Come, faith, madam, let us e'en pardon one another; for all the difference I find betwixt we men and you women, we forswear ourselves at the beginning of an amour, you as long as it lasts.

Enter Sir Jasper Fidget and Old Lady Squeamish.

SIR JASPER   Oh, my Lady Fidget, was this your cunning, to come to Mr. Horner without me? but you have been nowhere else, I hope.

LADY FIDGET   No, Sir Jasper.

LADY SQUEAMISH   And you came straight hither, Biddy?

MRS. SQUEAMISH   Yes, indeed, lady grandmother.

SIR JASPER   'Tis well, 'tis well; I knew when once they were thoroughly acquainted with poor Horner, they'd ne'er be from him: you may let her masquerade it with my wife and Horner, and I warrant her reputation safe.

Enter Boy.

BOY   O, sir, here's the gentleman come, whom you bid me not suffer to come up, without giving you notice, with a lady too, and other gentlemen.

HORNER   Do you all go in there, whilst I send 'em away; and, boy, do you desire 'em to stay below till I come, which shall be immediately.

Exeunt Sir Jasper Fidget, Lady Fidget, Old Lady Squeamish, Mrs. Squeamish, and Mrs. Dainty Fidget.

BOY   Yes, sir. (*Exit.*)

Exit Horner at the other door, and returns with Mrs. Pinchwife.

HORNER   You would not take my advice, to be gone home before your husband came back, he'll now discover all; yet pray, my dearest, be persuaded to go home, and leave the rest to my management; I'll let you down the back way.

MRS. PINCHWIFE   I don't know the way home, so I don't.

HORNER My man shall wait upon you.

MRS. PINCHWIFE No, don't you believe that I'll go at all; what, are you weary of me already?

HORNER No, my life, 'tis that I may love you long, 'tis to secure my love, and your reputation with your husband; he'll never receive you again else.

MRS. PINCHWIFE What care I? d'ye think to frighten me with that? I don't intend to go to him again; you shall be my husband now.

HORNER I cannot be your husband, dearest, since you are married to him.

MRS. PINCHWIFE O, would you make me believe that? Don't I see every day at London here, women leave their first husbands, and go and live with other men as their wives? pish, pshaw! you'd make me angry, but that I love you so mainly.

HORNER So, they are coming up—In again, in, I hear 'em.—(*Exit Mrs. Pinchwife.*) Well, a silly mistress is like a weak place, soon got, soon lost, a man has scarce time for plunder; she betrays her husband first to her gallant, and then her gallant to her husband.

Enter Pinchwife, Alithea, Harcourt, Sparkish, Lucy, and a Parson.

PINCHWIFE Come, madam, 'tis not the sudden change of your dress, the confidence of your asseverations, and your false witness there, shall persuade me I did not bring you hither just now; here's my witness, who cannot deny it, since you must be confronted.—Mr. Horner, did not I bring this lady to you just now?

HORNER (*aside*) Now must I wrong one woman for another's sake,—but that's no new thing with me, for in these cases I am still on the criminal's side against the innocent.

ALITHEA Pray speak, sir.

HORNER (*aside*) It must be so. I must be impudent, and try my luck; impudence used to be too hard for truth.

PINCHWIFE What, you are studying an evasion or excuse for her! Speak, sir.

HORNER No, faith, I am something backward only to speak in women's affairs or disputes.

PINCHWIFE She bids you speak.

ALITHEA Ay, pray, sir, do, pray satisfy him.

HORNER   Then truly, you did bring that lady to me just now.

PINCHWIFE   O ho!

ALITHEA   How, sir?

HARCOURT   How, Horner?

ALITHEA   What mean you, sir? I always took you for a man of honour.

HORNER (*aside*)   Ay, so much a man of honour, that I must save my mistress, I thank you, come what will on't.

SPARKISH   So, if I had had her, she'd have made me believe the moon had been made of a Christmas pie.

LUCY (*aside*)   Now could I speak, if I durst, and solve the riddle, who am the author of it.

ALITHEA   O unfortunate woman! A combination against my honour! which most concerns me now, because you share in my disgrace, sir, and it is your censure, which I must now suffer, that troubles me, not theirs.

HARCOURT   Madam, then have no trouble, you shall now see 'tis possible for me to love too, without being jealous; I will not only believe your innocence myself, but make all the world believe it.—(*Aside to Horner.*) Horner, I must now be concerned for this lady's honour.

HORNER   And I must be concerned for a lady's honour too.

HARCOURT   This lady has her honour, and I will protect it.

HORNER   My lady has not her honour, but has given it me to keep, and I will preserve it.

HARCOURT   I understand you not.

HORNER   I would not have you.

MRS. PINCHWIFE   What's the matter with 'em all? (*Peeping in behind.*)

PINCHWIFE   Come, come, Mr. Horner, no more disputing; here's the parson, I brought him not in vain.

HARCOURT   No, sir, I'll employ him, if this lady please.

PINCHWIFE   How! what d'ye mean?

SPARKISH   Ay, what does he mean?

HORNER   Why, I have resigned your sister to him, he has my consent.

PINCHWIFE   But he has not mine, sir; a woman's injured honour, no more than a man's, can be repaired or satisfied by any but him that first wronged it; and you shall marry her presently, or—(*Lays his hand on his sword.*)

Re-enter Mrs. Pinchwife.

MRS. PINCHWIFE   O Lord, they'll kill poor Mr. Horner! besides, he shan't marry her whilst I stand by, and look on; I'll not lose my second husband so.

PINCHWIFE   What do I see?

ALITHEA   My sister in my clothes!

SPARKISH   Ha!

MRS. PINCHWIFE (*to Pinchwife*)   Nay, pray now don't quarrel about finding work for the parson, he shall marry me to Mr. Horner; or now, I believe, you have enough of me.

HORNER (*aside*)   Damned, damned loving changeling!

MRS. PINCHWIFE   Pray, sister, pardon me for telling so many lies of you.

HORNER   I suppose the riddle is plain now.

LUCY   No, that must be my work.—Good sir, hear me. (*Kneels to Pinchwife, who stands doggedly with his hat over his eyes.*)

PINCHWIFE   I will never hear woman again, but make 'em all silent thus—(*Offers to draw upon his wife.*)

HORNER   No, that must not be.

PINCHWIFE   You then shall go first, 'tis all one to me. (*Offers to draw on Horner, but is stopped by Harcourt.*)

HARCOURT   Hold!

Re-enter Sir Jasper Fidget, Lady Fidget, Old Lady Squeamish, Mrs. Dainty Fidget, and Mrs. Squeamish.

SIR JASPER   What's the matter? what's the matter? pray, what's the matter, sir? I beseech you communicate, sir.

PINCHWIFE   Why, my wife has communicated, sir, as your wife may have done too, sir, if she knows him, sir.

SIR JASPER   Pshaw, with him! ha! ha! he!

PINCHWIFE   D'ye mock me, sir? a cuckold is a kind of a wild beast; have a care, sir.

SIR JASPER   No, sure, you mock me, sir. He cuckold you! it can't be, ha! ha! he! why, I'll tell you, sir—(*Offers to whisper.*)

PINCHWIFE   I tell you again, he has whored my wife, and yours too, if he knows her, and all the women he comes near; 'tis not his dissembling, his hypocrisy, can wheedle me.

SIR JASPER   How! does he dissemble? is he a hypocrite? Nay, then—how—wife—sister, is he a hypocrite?

LADY SQUEAMISH A hypocrite! a dissembler! Speak, young harlotry, speak, how?

SIR JASPER Nay, then—O my head too!—O thou libidinous lady!

LADY SQUEAMISH O thou harloting harlotry! hast thou done't then?

SIR JASPER Speak, good Horner, art thou a dissembler, a rogue? hast thou—

HORNER So!

LUCY (*apart to Horner*) I'll fetch you off, and her too, if she will but hold her tongue.

HORNER (*apart to Lucy*) Canst thou? I'll give thee—

LUCY (*to Pinchwife*) Pray have but patience to hear me, sir, who am the unfortunate cause of all this confusion. Your wife is innocent, I only culpable; for I put her upon telling you all these lies concerning my mistress, in order to the breaking off the match between Mr. Sparkish and her, to make way for Mr. Harcourt.

SPARKISH Did you so, eternal rotten tooth? Then, it seems, my mistress was not false to me, I was only deceived by you. Brother, that should have been, now man of conduct, who is a frank person now, to bring your wife to her lover, ha?

LUCY I assure you, sir, she came not to Mr. Horner out of love, for she loves him no more—

MRS. PINCHWIFE Hold, I told lies for you, but you shall tell none for me, for I do love Mr. Horner with all my soul, and nobody shall say me nay; pray, don't you go to make poor Mr. Horner believe to the contrary; 'tis spitefully done of you, I'm sure.

HORNER (*aside to Mrs. Pinchwife*) Peace, dear idiot.

MRS. PINCHWIFE Nay, I will not peace.

PINCHWIFE Not till I make you.

Enter Dorilant and Quack.

DORILANT Horner, your servant; I am the doctor's guest, he must excuse our intrusion.

QUACK But what's the matter, gentlemen? for Heaven's sake, what's the matter?

HORNER Oh, 'tis well you are come. 'Tis a censorious world we live in; you may have brought me a reprieve, or else I had died for a crime I never committed, and these innocent ladies had suffered with me; therefore, pray satisfy these worthy, honourable, jealous gentlemen—that—(*Whispers*.)

QUACK   O, I understand you, is that all?—Sir Jasper, by Heavens, and upon the word of a physician, sir—(*Whispers to Sir Jasper*.)

SIR JASPER   Nay, I do believe you truly.—Pardon me, my virtuous lady, and dear of honour.

LADY SQUEAMISH   What, then all's right again?

SIR JASPER   Ay, ay, and now let us satisfy him too.

They whisper with Pinchwife.

PINCHWIFE   An eunuch! Pray, no fooling with me.

QUACK   I'll bring half the chirurgeons in town to swear it.

PINCHWIFE   They!—they'll swear a man that bled to death through his wounds, died of an apoplexy.

QUACK   Pray, hear me, sir—why, all the town has heard the report of him.

PINCHWIFE   But does all the town believe it?

QUACK   Pray, inquire a little, and first of all these.

PINCHWIFE   I'm sure when I left the town, he was the lewdest fellow in't.

QUACK   I tell you, sir, he has been in France since; pray, ask but these ladies and gentlemen, your friend Mr. Dorilant. Gentlemen and ladies, han't you all heard the late sad report of poor Mr. Horner?

ALL THE LADIES   Ay, ay, ay.

DORILANT   Why, thou jealous fool, dost thou doubt it? he's an arrant French capon.

MRS. PINCHWIFE   'Tis false, sir, you shall not disparage poor Mr. Horner, for to my certain knowledge—

LUCY   O, hold!

MRS. SQUEAMISH (*aside to Lucy*)   Stop her mouth!

LADY FIDGET (*to Pinchwife*)   Upon my honour, sir, 'tis as true—

MRS. DAINTY FIDGET   D'ye think we would have been seen in his company?

MRS. SQUEAMISH   Trust our unspotted reputations with him?

LADY FIDGET (*aside to Horner*)   This you get, and we too, by trusting your secret to a fool.

HORNER   Peace, madam.—(*Aside to Quack*.) Well, doctor, is not this a good design, that carries a man on unsuspected, and brings him off safe?

PINCHWIFE (*aside*) Well, if this were true—but my wife—

Dorilant whispers with Mrs. Pinchwife.

ALITHEA Come, brother, your wife is yet innocent, you see; but have a care of too strong an imagination, lest, like an overconcerned timorous gamester, by fancying an unlucky cast, it should come. Women and fortune are truest still to those that trust 'em.

LUCY And any wild thing grows but the more fierce and hungry for being kept up, and more dangerous to the keeper.

ALITHEA There's doctrine for all husbands, Mr. Harcourt.

HARCOURT I edify, madam, so much, that I am impatient till I am one.

DORILANT And I edify so much by example, I will never be one.

SPARKISH And because I will not disparage my parts, I'll ne'er be one.

HORNER And I, alas! can't be one.

PINCHWIFE But I must be one—against my will to a country wife, with a country murrain[2] to me!

MRS. PINCHWIFE (*aside*) And I must be a country wife still too, I find; for I can't, like a city one, be rid of my musty husband, and do what I list.

HORNER Now, sir, I must pronounce your wife innocent, though I blush whilst I do it; and I am the only man by her now exposed to shame, which I will straight drown in wine, as you shall your suspicion; and the ladies' troubles we'll divert with a ballad.—Doctor, where are your maskers?

LUCY Indeed, she's innocent, sir, I am her witness; and her end of coming out was but to see her sister's wedding; and what she has said to your face of her love to Mr. Horner, was but the usual innocent revenge on a husband's jealousy; —was it not, madam, speak?

MRS. PINCHWIFE (*aside to Lucy and Horner*) Since you'll have me tell more lies—(*Aloud.*) Yes, indeed, bud.

PINCHWIFE

For my own sake fain I would all believe;
Cuckolds, like lovers, should themselves deceive.

2. Plague, pestilence.

But—(*Sighs.*)
His honour is least safe (too late I find)
Who trusts it with a foolish wife or friend.

A dance of cuckolds.

HORNER

Vain fops but court and dress, and keep a pother,
To pass for women's men with one another;
But he who aims by women to be prized,
First by the men, you see, must be despised.

Exeunt.

EPILOGUE

Spoken by Mrs. Knep[1]

Now you the vigorous, who daily here
O'er vizard-mask in public domineer,
And what you'd do to her, if in place where;
Nay, have the confidence to cry, "Come out!"
Yet when she says, "Lead on!" you are not stout;
But to your well-dressed brother straight turn round,
And cry "Pox on her, Ned, she can't be sound!"
Then slink away, a fresh one to engage,
With so much seeming heat and loving rage,
You'd frighten listening actress on the stage;
Till she at last has seen you huffing come,
And talk of keeping in the tiring-room,
Yet cannot be provoked to lead her home.
Next, you Falstaffs of fifty, who beset
Your buckram maidenheads, which your friends get;
And whilst to them you of achievements boast,
They share the booty, and laugh at your cost.
In fine, you essenced boys, both old and young,
Who would be thought so eager, brisk, and strong,
Yet do the ladies, not their husbands wrong;
Whose purses for your manhood make excuse,

---

1. The actress playing Lady Fidget.

And keep your Flanders mares for show not use;
Encouraged by our woman's man to-day,
A Horner's part may vainly think to play;
And may intrigues so bashfully disown,
That they may doubted be by few or none;
May kiss the cards at picquet, ombre, loo,
And so be taught to kiss the lady too;
But, gallants, have a care, faith, what you do.
The world, which to no man his due will give,
You by experience know you can deceive,
And men may still believe you vigorous,
But then we women—there's no cozening us.